"It's amazing how many toys are based upon physics and chemistry principles. Learning science concepts with toys is an exciting adventure for children. Their natural interest and curiosity in science combined with their desire to 'play' with toys provides great motivation to learn."

Jeannie Tuschl—Tulip Grove School, Nashville, Tennessee

"I really learned that there are many toys that can be used to teach science. I hope to expand the use of the TOYS concept in my classroom."

Elizabeth Henline—Mount Orab Middle School, Mount Orab, Ohio

"The toys, experiments, and activities are classroom-friendly to students of all ages."

Mary Hurst—McKinley Elementary School, Middletown, Ohio

"TOYS is a great program, with lots and lots of new and exciting ideas to use in the classroom."

JoAnne Lewis—Stanberry Elementary, King City, Missouri

"I would highly recommend TOYS for all science teachers."

Sarah Birdwell—Butterfield Junior High, Van Buren, Arkansas

D1361010

"With TOYS, science really becomes part of everyday experiences and materials."

Mary White—Monmouth High School, Monmouth, Illinois

"Teaching Science with TOYS is a wonderful way to motivate children. It's a super program!"

Cindy Waltershausen—Western Illinois University, Monmouth, Illinois

"I received so many new ideas to try out in my classroom that my students will be enjoying learning science without even realizing it!"

Regina Bonamico—Chauncy Rose Middle School, Terre Haute, Indiana

"TOYS activities will enable me to help develop a love for science, genuine inquiry, and higher-level thinking skills with my students. TOYS provides a wealth of ideas to introduce hands-on learning."

Rita Glavan—St. Pius X, Pickerington, Ohio

Teaching Science with TOYS Program Staff

K–3 Team

Mickey Sarquis
Assistant Professor of Chemistry
Miami University Middletown
Middletown, Ohio

Dwight Portman
Physics Teacher
Winton Woods High School
Cincinnati, Ohio

Mark Beck
Science Specialist
Indian Meadows Primary School
Ft. Wayne, Indiana

4–6 Team

John Williams
Associate Professor of Chemistry
Miami University Hamilton
Hamilton, Ohio

Beverley Taylor
Associate Professor of Physics
Miami University Hamilton
Hamilton, Ohio

Cheryl Vajda
Teacher
Stewart Elementary
Oxford, Ohio

7–9 Team

Jerry Sarquis
Professor of Chemistry
Miami University
Oxford, Ohio

Jim Poth
Professor of Physics
Miami University
Oxford, Ohio

Gary Lovely
Physics Teacher
Edgewood Middle School
Hamilton, Ohio

Tom Runyan
Science Teacher
Garfield Alternative School
Middletown, Ohio

Other Staff

Lynn Hogue
TOYS Program Manager
Miami University Middletown
Middletown, Ohio

Susan Gertz
Document Production Manager
Miami University Middletown
Middletown, Ohio

Teaching Chemistry with TOYS

Activities for Grades K–9

Jerry L. Sarquis

Mickey Sarquis

John P. Williams

Terrific Science Press
Miami University Middletown
Middletown, Ohio

LEARNING TRIANGLE PRESS

▲

Connecting kids, parents, and teachers through learning

An imprint of McGraw-Hill

McGraw-Hill
A Division of The McGraw·Hill Companies

Terrific Science Press
Miami University Middletown
4200 East University Blvd.
Middletown, Ohio 45042
513/424-4444

pbk   8 9 10 11 MAL/MAL 4 3 2 1

This material is based upon work supported by the National Science Foundation under Grant Number TPE-9055448. This project was supported, in part, by the National Science Foundation. Any opinions, findings, and conclusions or recommendations expressed in this material are those of the authors and do not necessarily reflect the views of the National Science Foundation.

Library of Congress Cataloging-in-Publication Data

Teaching chemistry with toys : activities for grades K–9 / by Terrific
  Science Press, Jerry L. Sarquis, Mickey Sarquis, and John P. Williams
      p. cm.
    Includes index.
    ISBN 0-07-064722-4 (paper)
    1. Chemistry—Study and teaching (Elementary) 2. Chemistry—Study
  and teaching—Activity programs. I. Terrific Science Press.
  QD40.T42 1995
  372.3'5—dc20   95-2028
                                                          CIP

Acquisitions editor: Kimberly Tabor

Contents

Activities for Grades K–3 9

Activities for Grades 4–6 105

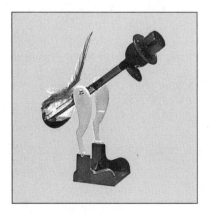

Acknowledgments

The authors wish to thank the following individuals who have contributed to the success of the Teaching Science with TOYS program and to the development of the activities in this book.

Activity Developers/Peer Writers:

Mark Beck	Indian Meadows Primary School	Ft. Wayne, IN
Alison Dowd	Talawanda Middle School	Oxford, OH
Sally Drabenstott	Sacred Heart School	Fairfield, OH
Lynn Hogue	Terrific Science Programs	Middletown, OH
Anita Kroger	Hamilton County Office of Education	Cincinnati, OH
Jo Parkey	Smith Middle School	Vandalia, OH

Teacher Mentors:

Mark Beck	Indian Meadows Primary School	Ft. Wayne, IN
Gary Lovely	Edgewood Middle School	Hamilton, OH
Tom Runyan	Garfield Alternative School	Middletown, OH
Cheryl Vajda	Stewart Elementary School	Oxford, OH
Sue Walpole	FERMCO	Cincinnati, OH

Terrific Science Press Design and Production Team:

Susan Gertz, Amy Stander, Lisa Taylor, Thomas Nackid, Stephen Gentle, Anne Munson

Reviewers:

George Kaufmann	California State University	Fresno, CA
Mamie Moy	University of Houston	Houston, TX
Ron Perkins	Greenwich High School	Greenwich, CT
Joseph Schmuckler	Temple University	Philadelphia, PA
Marie Sherman	St. Ursuline Academy (retired)	St. Louis, MO
Linda Woodward	University of Southwestern Louisiana	Lafayette, LA

University and District Affiliates:

Matt Arthur	Ashland University	Ashland, OH
Zexia Barnes	Morehead State University	Morehead, KY
Sue Anne Berger	Colorado School of Mines	Golden, CO
J. Hoyt Bowers	Wayland Baptist University	Plainview, TX
Joanne Bowers	Plainview High School	Plainview, TX
Herb Bryce	Seattle Central Community College	Seattle, WA
David Christensen	The University of Northern Iowa	Cedar Falls, IA
Laura Daly	Texas Christian University	Fort Worth, TX
Mary Beth Dove	Butler Elementary School	Butler, OH
Dianne Epp	East High School	Lincoln, NE
Babu George	Sacred Heart University	Fairfield, CT
James Golen	University of Massachusetts	North Dartmouth, MA
Richard Hansgen	Bluffton College	Bluffton, OH
Cindy Johnston	Lebanon Valley College of Pennsylvania	Annville, PA
Karen Levitt	University of Pittsburgh	Pittsburgh, PA
Donald Murad	University of Toledo	Perrysburg, OH
Hasker Nelson	African-American Math Science Coalition	Cincinnati, OH
Judy Ng	James Madison High School	Vienna, VA
Larry Peck	Texas A & M University	College Station, TX
Carol Stearns	Princeton University	Princeton, NJ
Doris Warren	Houston Baptist University	Houston, TX
Richard Willis	Kennebunk High School	Kennebunk, ME
Steven Wright	University of Wisconsin–Stevens Point	Stevens Point, WI

Foreword

As a child or as an adult, most of us find it difficult to walk past a colorful display of toys without pausing, smiling, and taking a closer look. The urge to roll the truck down the hill, bounce the Silly Putty™, or wind up the walking dinosaur is nearly irresistible. We typically associate toys with fun, discovery, and creativity. In contrast, if presented with a display of chemistry and physics experiments, "fun, discovery, and creativity" unfortunately would not be the words that come to most peoples' minds.

In 1986, a group of colleagues at Miami University wanted to give teachers (and through teachers, students) the opportunity to find out that "fun, discovery, and creativity" are words that very much describe the exploration of physics and chemistry principles. Our idea was to teach basic chemistry and physics principles using toys, thus capitalizing on the natural attractiveness of toys and also showing that physical science is an integral part of our everyday experiences.

We were fortunate to obtain funding from the Ohio Board of Regents to offer the first Teaching Science with TOYS course for teachers here at Miami University. During that year we worked with a tremendous group of teachers who took the toy-based physical science they learned back to their classrooms with wonderful results. Through funding from the National Science Foundation, we have been able to continue the TOYS program here at Miami University and around the country through our University and District Affiliates. Over the past eight years, we have met and worked with over 700 educators from across the United States and around the world. During these years we have continued to develop and test new toy-based science activities in our courses. This book is a product of those years of development.

The teachers we have worked with in the TOYS program are as different from each other as any group of people can be. They come from urban areas, rural settings, and everywhere in between. Some had lots of science background; others had none. Their students reflect the diversity of our nation's schools. But despite their differences, these teachers have had at least one thing in common—the desire to give each of their students the chance to enjoy learning about physical science. Through their feedback in the laboratory and via classroom testing, each of these dedicated professionals has contributed to this book. We thank them.

From TOYS participants and from our follow-up evaluations, we know that toy-based science is making a difference in classrooms, schools, and entire districts. We believe that the best way to learn to teach discovery-based science is to experience it yourself with support from experienced colleagues, just like the best way for your students to learn science is to do discovery-based science with your support and guidance. However, we realize that all teachers do not have the opportunity to attend professional development courses such as the one we offer. Thus, we are delighted to be able to offer many of the activities from our program in book form. We welcome you to join TOYS teachers around the country through your use of the activities in this book and wish you all the best in your teaching.

Teaching Science with TOYS Staff

Introduction

Science is asking questions about the world we live in and trying to find the answers. Students of science should do more than memorize definitions and parrot facts; to make sense of science, students must be given opportunities to make connections between scientific phenomena and their own world.

With this book, you and your students will delve into the mysteries of such fun toys as Silly Putty™ and Shrinky Dinks®. You will learn why "Gro Beasts" expand and study the principles behind Drinking Birds and Density Batons. Your students will experience the minds-on, hands-on learning that will improve their problem-solving skills while also improving their science content knowledge.

Teaching Science with TOYS

The National Science Foundation-funded Teaching Science with TOYS project is located at Miami University in Ohio. The goal of the project is to enhance teachers' knowledge of physics and chemistry and to encourage activity-based, discovery-oriented science instruction. The TOYS project promotes toys as an ideal mechanism for science instruction because they are an everyday part of the students' world and carry a user-friendly message. Through TOYS and its affiliated programs, thousands of teachers nationwide have brought activity-based science into their classrooms, using teacher-tested TOYS activities. Through written materials such as this book, many more teachers and students can share in the fun and learning of the TOYS project.

Becoming Involved with the TOYS Project

By using the activities in this book, you are joining a national network of teachers and other science educators who are committed to integrating toy-based science into their curricula. If you have a TOYS Affiliate (a college or university science educator who conducts local TOYS programs) in your area, you may want to get involved in local TOYS programming.

Another way to extend your TOYS involvement is by attending a Teaching Science with TOYS graduate-credit course for teachers of grades K–12 at Miami University in Ohio. The program uses a workshop-style format in which participating teachers receive instruction in small, grade-level-specific groups. Teachers do not need a special science background to participate in the program; the program faculty review relevant science principles as they are applied to the toy-based activities being featured. Participants spend much of their time exploring hands-on, toy-based science activities.

TOYS is open to all science educators of grades K–12. Applicants should be actively teaching or assigned to a science support position. For more information or an application, write Teaching Science with TOYS, Miami University Middletown, 4200 East University Blvd., Middletown, Ohio 45042; call 513/424-4444 x421; or e-mail *hoguelm@muohio.edu.*

Using this Book

Teaching Chemistry with TOYS—Activities for Grades K–9 is a collection of some of the chemistry activities used in the Teaching Science with TOYS professional development program for teachers at Miami University. The TOYS activities have been compiled into this and the companion *Teaching Physics with TOYS—Activities for Grades K–9* as a resource for teachers who want to use toy-based physical science activities in the classroom, but who may not be able to attend a TOYS workshop at the Miami site or one of the Affiliate sites nationwide. The activities do not assume any particular prior knowledge of physical science, and complete activity explanations are included.

Organization of the Book

This book consists of three main sections: the introductory material, the toy-based chemistry activities, and the appendixes (an index by key process skills, an index by topics, and an alphabetical listing of activities).

The TOYS activities in this book are divided into three grade-level groupings: K–3, 4–6, and 7–9. Each activity provides complete instructions for use in your classroom. These activities have been classroom-tested by teachers like yourself and have been demonstrated to be practical, safe, and effective in the targeted grade-level range. Each activity includes a photograph of the toy or activity setup and the following sections:

- Grade Levels:
  Although the activities are specifically written for a particular grade level, many activities can be used successfully by teachers of younger or older students. Suggested grade levels for the science activity and cross-curricular integration are listed.

- Key Science Topics:
  Key science topics are listed for all activities.

- Student Background:
  If appropriate, background knowledge or experience is suggested that would be valuable for students prior to doing the activity.

- Key Process Skills:
  These process skills assist teachers whose lesson planning includes a process focus. See Appendix A for an index of key process skills for all activities.

- Time Required:
  An estimated time for doing the Procedure is listed. The time does not include Extensions or Variations. This estimate is based on feedback from classroom testing, but your time may vary depending on your classroom and teaching style.

- Materials:
  Materials are listed for the Procedure and for any Extensions or Variations. Materials are divided into amounts per class, per group, and per student. Most materials can be purchased from grocery, discount department, or hardware stores. Quantities or sizes may be listed in English measure, metric measure, or both, depending on what is clear and appropriate in each case.

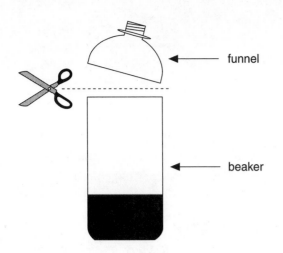

funnel

beaker

Measuring containers for liquids can be made by pouring a measured amount of a liquid into a disposable cup and marking the height of the liquid with a permanent marker. Beakers and funnels can be made from empty 1-liter or 2-liter plastic soft-drink bottles as shown to the left. Sources are listed for unusual items.

- **Safety and Disposal:** Special safety and/or disposal procedures are listed if required. See pages 7–8 for a more detailed discussion of safety and disposal issues.

- **Getting Ready:** Information is provided in Getting Ready when preparation is needed before beginning the activity with the students.

- **Procedure:** The steps in the Procedure are directed toward you, the teacher, and include cautions and suggestions where appropriate. Quantities or sizes may be listed in English measure, metric measure, or both, depending on what is clear and appropriate in each case.

- **Variations and Extensions:** Variations are alternative methods for doing the Procedure. Extensions are methods for furthering student understanding of topics.

- **Explanation:** The Explanation is written to you, the teacher, and is intended to be modified for students.

- **Cross-Curricular Integration:** Cross-Curricular Integration offers ideas for integrating the science activity with other areas of the curriculum.

- **Further Reading:** Further Reading provides suggested readings for teachers and students to extend their knowledge of the topic.

- **Contributors:** Individuals, including Teaching Science with TOYS graduates, who contributed significantly to the development of the activity are listed.

- **Handout Master:** Masters for handouts are provided for some activities. These may include data, assessment, and/or observation sheets as well as other types. Permission is granted to copy these for classroom use.

Notes and safety cautions are included in activities as needed and are indicated by the following icons and type style:

Notes are preceded by an arrow and appear in italics.

Cautions are preceded by an exclamation point and appear in italics.

Pedagogical Strategies

TOYS program staff members recognize that no single instructional strategy best meets the needs of all students at all times. Howard Gardner, author of *The Unschooled Mind*, views each learner as possessing a distinctive profile of "intelligences" or ways of learning, remembering, performing, and understanding. These differences are thought to dramatically affect what instructional approach is most likely to be effective for a given student. For example, kinesthetic demonstrations, which involve students in role-playing and dramatic simulations, can be useful in providing an understanding of the particle nature of matter and other relatively abstract science concepts.

With this in mind, a variety of instructional approaches can be effectively used to present the toy-based science activities in this book. We have included some suggestions for incorporating guided and open-ended inquiry, process skills and cross-curricular integration of science, learning cycles, and cooperative learning. These pedagogical strategies are based on modern methods of science education that originated with theories of cognitive functioning introduced by Jean Piaget (Piaget, 1958); these theories can be summarized by the following statements:

- If students are to give up misconceptions about science, they must have an opportunity to actively reconstruct their world view based on exploration, interpretation, and organization of new ideas (Bybee, 1990).
- Exploration, interpretation, and organization of new ideas are most effective in a curriculum where hands-on, inquiry-based activities are integrated into learning-cycle units (Renner, 1988).
- Hands-on, inquiry-based activities that involve conceptual change, problem-solving, divergent thinking, and creativity are particularly effective in cooperative learning situations (Johnson, 1990).

The general suggestions in this pedagogical strategies section are provided by teachers who have used TOYS activities in a variety of ways. Some teachers have used a selected series of activities from this book as the basis of a special classroom unit on toys in science which lasted for several weeks. Other teachers have used individual activities throughout the school year in conjunction with the topics ordinarily taught. This section is intended to provide you with some ideas for integrating the TOYS activities into your own curriculum. These TOYS activities are not intended to comprise a stand-alone curriculum; rather, the activities are intended to complement and enrich your own curriculum. We encourage you to consider how these activities can meet the needs of your students and fit your own teaching style.

The Particle Nature of Matter

To be able to explain the nature and interactions of matter, it is necessary to know about the nature of the particles that make it up. As adults, you have probably heard and used the terms atoms, molecules, and ions. Remember, however, that young children do not have the conceptual background to correctly distinguish between these three terms. In the elementary grades, we strongly recommend that you use the general term "particles" with students to prevent creating misconceptions that will later be difficult—if not impossible—to correct. Additionally, with elementary students, limit your discussion to the general idea that all matter is made up of particles that are too small to be seen by the human eye and that, in spite of our inability to see these particles, their existence accounts for matter as we know it. The discussion of the various types of particles (atoms, molecules, ions) should be held to later years in the curriculum when the students are conceptually ready for this level of detail. Our recommendations are consistent with those of the American Association for the Advancement of Science *Benchmarks for Science Literacy* and the National Science Foundation-funded S_2C_2 (School Science Curriculum Conference) report, a joint report of the American Chemical Society and the American Association of Physics Teachers.

Webbing and Charting

In introducing any new unit, you may wish to begin by stating the general topic and asking the students to help you identify some more specific subtopics. With the general topics and subtopics identified, students are then ready to consider three important questions: What do we already know about this topic? What do we want to find out about this topic? How can we find out?

Questions should be considered in this order, with students being encouraged to provide many answers to each. Record the responses on a large easel-sized chart so that the responses can remain on the class bulletin board throughout the unit for continual reference. We recommend that you have your students address one question at a time and that you allow sufficient time for discussion and response before the next question is addressed. Be sure that students think of an answer to "How can we find out?" for each item listed in "What do we want to find out?" In addition to acting as facilitator of this lesson, you may wish to act as recorder and list the student responses on the charts. By first jotting down cryptic notes from the students' responses and subsequently recopying the notes into neat handwriting and complete sentences, the teacher can model an important part of the writing process often not shown to students.

Process Skills and Cross-Curricular Integration

The skills of science and other subjects such as language arts and math are remarkably similar. Process skills such as sequencing, recording information, communicating, and classifying span many disciplines. Primary students can become motivated readers and writers through science activities. Older students develop their abilities to identify and control variables, make meaningful conclusions, and communicate ideas clearly. Most of the activities in this book have specific suggestions for cross-curricular integration. Appendix A lists the principal science process skills that are employed in each of the activities.

As the teacher, it is important that you avoid the common trap of being a forecaster of what to wait for or what will happen. Rather, enable your students to be involved in the process of science and to construct their own understanding. Challenge them to make predictions. Help them record their predictions, do the experiment, record their observations, and reflect on how their observations and predictions varied or were the same. By using constructivist methods, you can help your students develop the skills necessary to eventually take responsibility for their own learning. Provide your students with multiple examples of a given concept to help them develop a foundation necessary for reliable predictions. Encourage them to become involved in the activity.

Challenge your students to be good predictors and good communicators. Young students whose writing skills are limited can still predict and communicate through speaking and drawing. Science affords opportunities to expand students' vocabulary. It affords opportunities for recording procedures so that the activity can be repeated at home. It affords the students a common ground for success with immediate reinforcement of accomplishing a task at hand. Science provides motivation to take on difficult challenges while helping younger children develop the concentration skills necessary to complete multiple-step activities.

Learning Cycles

You can select groups of activities from this book to create a variety of learning-cycle units. A learning cycle consists of a three-phase approach to actively involve students in investigative science experiences. Each phase plays a distinct role in enabling students to challenge their old views about the unit's topic so they can successfully reconstruct and internalize new science concepts. The three phases of the learning cycle each have specific objectives and are presented in order. Different authors may have different names for the phases, but the phases always play the same basic roles. Here, we call them exploration, concept introduction, and concept extension. An awareness activity can precede the exploration phase, but is not absolutely necessary. However, omitting any of the three phases or presenting the phases out of order reduces the effectiveness of the learning cycle.

- The awareness activity uses a thought-provoking or discrepant event to help students realize that they may have preconceived ideas about a particular science topic. Students will be more receptive learners if they become aware of their own preconceptions.
- The exploration phase challenges students' preconceptions through a hands-on activity in which they are told how to make observations and collect data but are not given any new vocabulary or explanations about what to expect. The teacher assumes the role of facilitator, posing questions and assisting students as they work.
- The concept introduction phase asks students to form new ideas based on their observations. The teacher helps students see how patterns in data reveal the concepts being defined in the lesson. The teacher may further develop concepts using textbooks, audiovisual aids, and other materials.
- The concept extension phase allows students to extend their understanding of the topic by using what they know to solve a new problem or conduct an experiment.

Cooperative Learning

For late primary or intermediate students and older, you may wish to use some formal cooperative strategies while doing these activities. Some activities already contain specific cooperative-learning suggestions. Cooperative learning has been well documented as enhancing student achievement. Several popular models for cooperative groups have been described by D.W. and R.T. Johnson, Robert Slavin, Spencer Kajan, Eliot Aronsen, and others. Although these models vary, they typically include elements of group goals or positive interdependence and individual accountability. Often, cooperative models suggest specific roles for each student. If students have not been using cooperative learning routinely, time must be spent at the beginning of the assignment explaining individual accountability and group interdependence and reviewing social skills needed for cooperative group work. Students should understand that their grades are dependent upon each person carrying out the assigned task. The teacher should observe the groups at work and assist them with social and academic skills when necessary.

Safety

Hands-on activities and demonstrations add fun and excitement to science education at any level. However, even the simplest activity can become dangerous when the proper safety precautions are ignored, when done incorrectly, or when performed by students without proper supervision. The activities in this book have been extensively reviewed by hundreds of classroom teachers of grades K–12 and by university scientists. We have done all we can to assure the safety of the activities. It is up to you to assure their safe execution!

Be Careful—and Have Fun!

- Never attempt an activity if you are unfamiliar or uncomfortable with the procedures or materials involved. Consult a high school or college science teacher for advice or ask them to perform the activity for your class. They are often delighted to help.

- Activities should be undertaken only at the recommended grade levels and only with adult supervision.

- Always practice activities yourself before performing them with your class. This is the only way to become thoroughly familiar with an activity, and familiarity will help prevent potentially hazardous (or merely embarrassing) mishaps. In addition, you may find variations that will make the activity more meaningful to your students.

- Read each activity carefully and observe all safety precautions and disposal procedures.

- You, your assistants, and any students observing at close range must wear safety goggles if indicated in the activity and at any other time you deem necessary.

- Special safety instructions are not given for everyday classroom materials being used in a typical manner. Use common sense when working with hot, sharp, or breakable objects, such as flames, scissors, or glassware. Keep tables or desks covered to avoid stains. Keep spills cleaned up to avoid falls.

- Recycling/reuse instructions are not given for everyday materials. We encourage you to reuse and recycle the materials according to local recycling procedures.

- In some activities, potentially hazardous items such as power tools are to be used by the teacher only to make a toy or set up the activity. These items appear under the heading "For Getting Ready Only."

- Read and follow the American Chemical Society Minimum Safety Guidelines for Chemical Demonstrations on the next page. Remember that you are a role model for your students— your attention to safety will help them develop good safety habits while assuring that everyone has fun with these activities.

- Collect and read the Materials Safety Data Sheets (MSDS) for all of the chemicals used in your experiments. MSDS's provide physical property data, toxicity information, and handling and disposal specifications for chemicals. They can be obtained upon request from manufacturers and distributors of these chemicals. In fact, MSDS's are often shipped with the chemicals when they are ordered. These should be collected and made available to students, faculty, or parents should anyone want MSDS information about specific chemicals in these activities.

ACS Minimum Safety Guidelines for Chemical Demonstrations

This section outlines safety procedures that must be followed at all times.

Chemical Demonstrators Must:

1. know the properties of the chemicals and the chemical reactions involved in all demonstrations presented.

2. comply with all local rules and regulations.

3. wear appropriate eye protection for all chemical demonstrations.

4. warn the members of the audience to cover their ears whenever a loud noise is anticipated.

5. plan the demonstration so that harmful quantities of noxious gases (e.g., NO_2, SO_2, H_2S) do not enter the local air supply.

6. provide safety shield protection wherever there is the slightest possibility that a container, its fragments or its contents could be propelled with sufficient force to cause personal injury.

7. arrange to have a fire extinguisher at hand whenever the slightest possibility for fire exists.

8. not taste or encourage spectators to taste any non-food substance.

9. not use demonstrations in which parts of the human body are placed in danger (such as placing dry ice in the mouth or dipping hands into liquid nitrogen).

10. not use "open" containers of volatile, toxic substances (e.g., benzene, CCl_4, CS_2, formaldehyde) without adequate ventilation as provided by fume hoods.

11. provide written procedure, hazard, and disposal information for each demonstration whenever the audience is encouraged to repeat the demonstration.

12. arrange for appropriate waste containers for and subsequent disposal of materials harmful to the environment.

Activities for Grades K–3

Unfixed and Fixed Shapes

Crystal Pictures

Crayon Prints from a Change of State

Smell-Good Diffusion Ornaments

Smelly Balloons

The Scratch-and-Sniff Challenge

Density Batons

Clay Boats

Are Mittens Warm?

Magic Worms

Fortune-Telling Fish

Paint with Water Books

Weather Bunnies

Twirly Whirly Milk

UNFIXED AND FIXED SHAPES

Students predict and observe the shapes of liquids and solids under various conditions.

Jars containing fixed and unfixed shapes

GRADE LEVELS

Science activity appropriate for grades K–6
Cross-Curricular Integration intended for grades K–3

KEY SCIENCE TOPICS

- attractive forces
- density
- fluidity versus rigidity
- properties of liquids and solids

KEY PROCESS SKILLS

- observing — Students observe differences in the liquid and solid states using water and ice as examples.

- predicting — Students predict the positions of liquids and solids in a jar as the jar is moved.

TIME REQUIRED

Setup	5–10	minutes
Performance	15–30	minutes
Cleanup	5	minutes

Materials

For "Getting Ready"
Per class
- food color
- water
- small ice cubes, ice chips, or snow
- transparent tape
- access to a freezer
- 3 clear jars with lids, such as peanut butter jars

 Plastic is preferable for use with younger students since glass can break more easily and is more hazardous. Also, plastic jars are less likely to break when frozen.

For "Introducing the Activity"
Per class
- pencil
- water

- tall, thin container
- large, flat dish

For the "Procedure"
Per class
- jars prepared in "Getting Ready"
- (optional) additional small jars or clear plastic vials with caps
- (optional) colored chalk
- (optional) tape

For "Variations and Extensions"

❶ Per class
- jar of colored water from the "Procedure"
- a little boat

❷ Per class
- molds of various sizes and shapes
- Kool-Aid®
- water

Safety and Disposal

If using glass containers, caution students to handle them carefully. Advise students not to put the ice cubes in their mouths.

No special disposal procedures are required.

Getting Ready

1. Half-fill a jar with water, add a few drops of food color, and put the lid on.

2. If using glass, tape the glass to keep it from shattering if it breaks.

3. If glass jars are to be used, wrap the outside of a second jar with transparent tape in a crisscross pattern in case the glass should crack during the subsequent freezing. Half-fill this jar with colored water and freeze it with the lid off. Replace the lid before using the jar in the classroom.

4. Prepare several small ice cubes, some ice chips, or snow (colored with food color for visibility if desired). Half-fill a third jar with the cubes, chips, or snow.

Introducing the Activity

Pour some water into a tall, thin container. Then, pour the same water into a large, flat dish. Ask the students to describe what happened to the shape of the water. Next, put a pencil in the tall, thin container and then in the flat dish. Ask the students to describe what happened to the shape of the pencil. Use the different behavior of the pencil and the water to distinguish between a solid and a liquid. (Solids have a definite shape, while liquids do not.)

Procedure

Part A: Liquid Water

1. Show students the jar of liquid colored water. Have students describe what they see.

2. Set the jar of water on the table and draw a picture of the jar and its contents on the blackboard. Label the water and the air. (See Figure 1.)

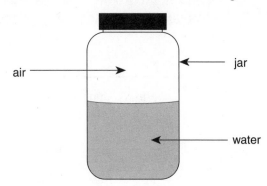

air ← → jar

→ water

Figure 1: Draw a picture of the jar and its contents on the board.

3. On the blackboard, sketch the empty jars in the four different positions shown on the "Where Does the Water Go?" Data Sheet (provided).

4. Without picking up the jar, ask students to imagine the jar of water in each position on their Data Sheet. Challenge them to predict and draw the position of the water line of the jar in these different positions.

 Students can check their own pictures during Step 5 or you may want to collect drawings at this point to check for understanding.

5. After students complete their drawings, hold the jar of colored water next to each picture on the board to demonstrate the location of the water. Then sketch the water line in each jar using colored chalk if available.

6. (optional) If enough jars are available, give each student a jar or vial of water and allow students to manipulate the jars to check their findings. Encourage them to test different jar positions.

Part B: Solid Water

1. Show students the jar containing ice cubes, ice chips, or snow. Have students describe what they see and describe all the ways this jar differs from the water jar.

2. Repeat Part A, Steps 2–6, using the jar of ice cubes, ice chips, or snow.

3. Bring out the jar of frozen water as prepared in "Getting Ready," Step 2. Explain to the students how the jar of water was prepared.

 Use the frozen water as soon as possible after removing from the freezer. If the ice begins to melt, the solid block of ice may slide down when the jar is inverted in Step 4.

4. Repeat Part A, Steps 2–6, using the jar of frozen water. Challenge students to form a hypothesis that explains the differences observed in the three jars.

5. (optional) With the jar inverted, allow the ice to begin melting and observe as the ice block falls to the "bottom" of the jar.

Variations and Extensions

1. Ask the students what they think will happen to the water in Part A if the jar is put on its side and rolled. Float a little boat on the water in the jar before rolling the jar.

2. Make Kool-Aid® according to the directions. Pour it into molds of different sizes and shapes. Freeze the Kool-Aid®. Remove the Kool-Aid® cubes from their molds. (Note that a solid has a definite shape.) Have the students use the sense of taste to enjoy Kool-Aid® ice cubes.

Explanation

 The following explanation is intended for the teacher's information. Modify the explanation for students as required.

Liquids take the shape of the container they are in and, due to gravity, fill the bottom of a container before the upper levels can be filled. In Part A, when the jar is in its original position (with the base of the jar on the table) the water conforms to the bottom half of the jar and its surface is level and horizontal to the ground across most of its surface. You might observe the slight upward curve of the water at the sides of the jar, which is a result of the attraction of water to glass. (A similar but less pronounced observation can be noted in plastic containers.) As you tilt the jar, the liquid water shifts to remain on the new "bottom" of the jar and conforms to its shape. In liquid water, the water particles have enough energy to slip and slide past each other. This allows liquid water to flow to conform to the shape of the container. (See Figure 2.)

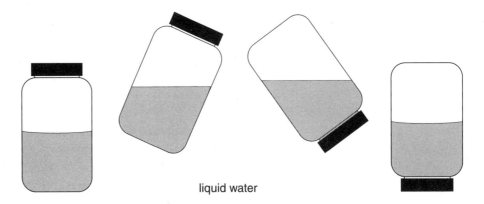

liquid water

Figure 2: Liquids take the shape of the container they are in and fill the bottom of a container before the upper levels can be filled.

Unlike liquids, solids have their own characteristic shapes and do not take the shape of the container they are in. This is readily apparent if ice cubes are used in Part B. As long as they remain frozen, the individual ice cubes retain their shape. When you rotate the jar, the ice cubes fall to the new "bottom." (See Figure 3.) However, unlike liquid water, the ice cubes do not flow to conform to the jar's shape nor do they have a horizontal water line. If you use ice chips or snow, the individual shapes of the solids are more difficult to see because they are so small. Still, the small pieces do have their own shapes. The water particles that make up the ice or snow are fixed in a given position within the crystals. These particles do not have enough energy to move past one another (they cannot flow), so a solid has a fixed shape.

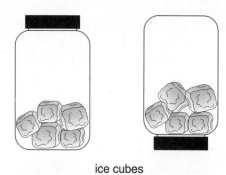

ice cubes

Figure 3: Solids have their own characteristic shapes
and do not take the shape of the container they are in.

When the activity is repeated with the water that was frozen directly in the jar, the ice does not shift as the container moves. In fact, unless the ice has begun to melt around the walls of the jar, it will stay in the same location, seeming to defy density and gravity when the jar is inverted. (See Figure 4.) This observation may at first be surprising until you consider what happens when you make ice cubes at home (assuming you have ice cube trays and not an automatic ice maker). When water freezes, it expands. This causes ice cubes to stick to the tray even when inverted; often the tray must be struck or twisted to dislodge the ice cubes. The same is true for the ice that was frozen in the jar. As water freezes, it expands to a greater volume than liquid water. This is because ice is less dense than liquid water. (This fact is easily observed by placing ice into a glass of water. The ice floats.) This expansion often lodges the ice firmly into the original position, holding the ice in place; however, once the ice begins to melt, the liquid at the edges runs down and the piece of ice slides down the walls.

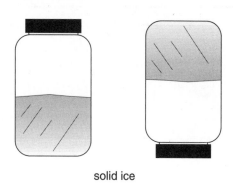

solid ice

Figure 4: Ice that is frozen directly in the
jar does not shift as the container moves.

This activity can be used to discuss the properties of liquids and solids or used to challenge students to form a hypothesis for a surprising event.

Assessment

Options:

• Construct a large chart for the class with separate columns for "fixed" and "unfixed" shapes. Have students bring in or cut out pictures from magazines that show examples of each. Let students classify all the pictures and place them in their proper columns on the chart.

- Divide the class into cooperative learning teams. Give each student a different-colored pen. Give each team a tray with a variety of liquids and solids on it and several empty cups so the students can test how the various objects pour and transfer. On a sheet of paper, have each team member record a prediction and observation for each object on the tray using his or her own pen color. Have the students sign their names at the bottom of the paper using their colored pens.

Cross-Curricular Integration

Art:
- Ask students to draw pictures to answer the following question: "If someone sent you a jar full of something, what would you like it to be?"

Language arts:
- Have students make a list of root words and other words these root words can be used to make. For example, the word "fix" can be used to make the words "fixed" and "unfixed."

Contributors

Teressa Jacobs, Mt. Airy School, Cincinnati, OH; Teaching Science with TOYS, 1993–94.

Mary Jane Kendall, Sherwood Elementary School, Cincinnati, OH; Teaching Science with TOYS, 1989–90.

Ann Veith, Rosedale Elementary School, Middletown, OH; Teaching Science with TOYS, 1991–92.

Handout Master

A master for the following handout is provided:
- Where Does the Water Go?—Data Sheet

Copy as needed for classroom use.

UNFIXED AND FIXED SHAPES

Where Does the Water Go?—Data Sheet

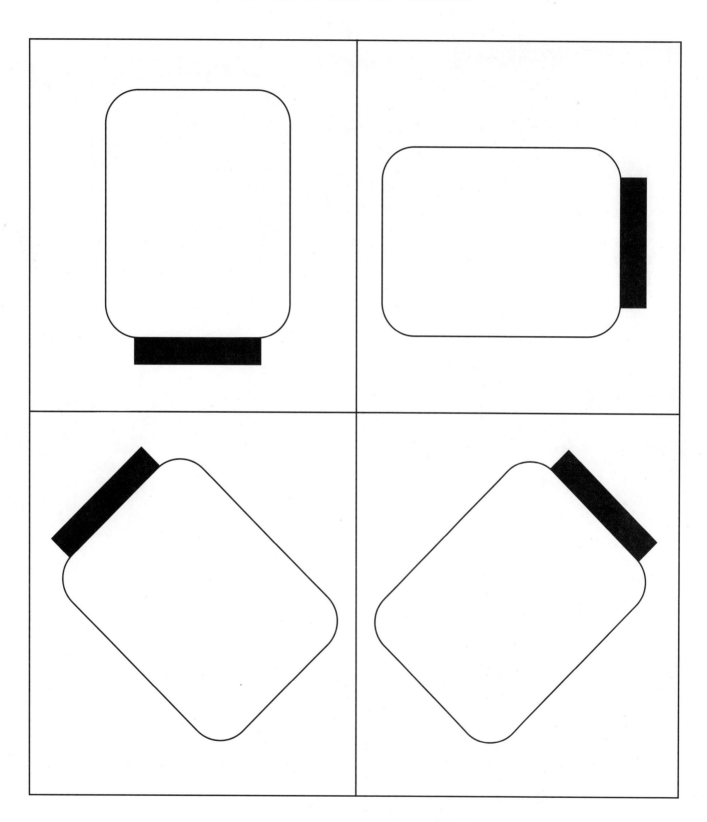

CRYSTAL PICTURES

*Students observe crystal formation on various types of papers
while drawing pictures or writing secret messages.*

A crystal picture

GRADE LEVELS

Science activity appropriate for grades K–6
Cross-Curricular Integration intended for grades K–3

KEY SCIENCE TOPICS

- crystals, crystallization
- evaporation
- solids

KEY PROCESS SKILLS

• observing	Students prepare and observe crystal patterns.
• comparing/contrasting	Students compare and contrast the macroscopic geometric crystal patterns of various crystalline solids.

TIME REQUIRED

Setup	10–15	minutes
Performance	30	minutes
Cleanup	10	minutes

Materials

For the "Procedure"
Per class or group
- 1 container for each solution made
- 1 plastic spoon for each solution made
- 1 or more of the following solutions made in the proportions noted:
  - 1 spoonful Epsom salt ($MgSO_4 \cdot 7H_2O$) in 2 spoonsful water
  - 1 spoonful Morton Lite Salt® (potassium chloride, KCl) in 3 spoonsful water
  - 1 spoonful alum ($KAl(SO_4)_2 \cdot 12H_2O$) in 2 spoonsful water
  - 1 spoonful table sugar (sucrose, $C_{12}H_{22}O_{11}$) in 2 spoonsful water
  - 1 spoonful kosher, pickling, or table salt (NaCl) in 3 spoonsful water

➤ *Since additives in table salt cloud the solution, kosher or pickling salt is preferable.*

- labels and marking pen
- 1 paintbrush or cotton-tipped swab for each solution

- magnifying lens
- (optional) geode or piece of jewelry (such as a pin, pendant, or ring) made of a crystalline material

Per student or group of students
- 1 piece of black or dark-colored construction paper
- 1 piece of white or light-colored construction paper
- 1 piece of glossy paper such as notebook paper
- (optional) wide-tipped marking pen

For "Variations and Extensions"

❶ All materials listed for the "Procedure" except
- substitute different concentrations of some solutions

❷ All materials listed for the "Procedure" plus the following:
- crayons
- wax and/or a candle

❺ Per class
- black construction paper
- magnifying lenses

❻ Per class
All the materials listed for the "Procedure" plus the following:
- 1 spoonful monosodium glutamate (MSG) in 2 spoonful water

Safety and Disposal

While the crystalline materials used in this activity are common household items, do not allow students to taste or ingest them. All solutions can be disposed of down the drain, but it is recommended that solutions be allowed to evaporate (See Extension 3) and solids saved for future use.

Getting Ready

1. Use the proportions noted in the "Materials" list to prepare solutions. Use heaping spoonful for the solids and hot tap water if available. Stir to mix—it may take 5–10 minutes for the solids to dissolve. Residual solid in the bottom of the cup will not interfere with the activity. Amounts given are enough for about 10 trials, depending on volume of spoons used. Clearly label solutions with numbers. (Alternatively, students could prepare their own solutions.)

2. (optional) Stations can be set up with a different solution, a paintbrush or cotton swab, and (optional) a magnifying lens at each station. Groups of students move from one station to another station in repeating Step 3 of the "Procedure."

3. For younger children the teacher may wish to rule off the paper and label the sections as described in Step 1 of the "Procedure."

Have students begin the activity by starting a journal about crystals. Each time their knowledge changes or increases, have them add to their journals. Explain that crystals are common solids with beautiful and regular shapes. Every single snowflake that falls is made of six-sided ice crystals. Grains of salt are crystals and so are grains of sugar. If possible, display a geode (which includes numerous crystals) or a piece of jewelry made of a single crystal. (See Figure 1.) The activity can be introduced with the following challenges: "Which solution makes the best crystals on the white paper?" "How about on the black or glossy paper?"

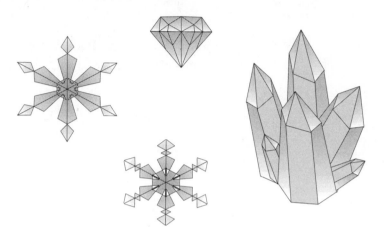

Figure 1: Crystals come in many shapes and sizes.

Procedure

1. Give each student or group of students a sheet of black or dark-colored construction paper, white or light-colored construction paper, and white glossy paper. Have them divide each page into quarters using a pencil and ruler or by folding the paper in half lengthwise and then in half widthwise.

   If students test more than four solutions, they'll need more than one sheet of each kind of paper.

2. Have students write the number of each of the solutions they will test on a different quarter of the paper.

3. For each solution, have students use a different brush or cotton swab to write a message or draw a picture within the appropriate quarter of the paper. Keep a brush with each solution to avoid contamination.

4. Let the papers dry. This usually takes 10–30 minutes.

5. After papers are dry, have students observe the crystal pictures and compare them. If desired, have them use magnifying lenses to get a close-up look.

6. (optional) Using a pencil or wide-tipped marking pen, gently rub the pencil lead or water-soluble ink over about half of the crystal patterns on the white construction paper and glossy paper. Compare the results.

    Rub carefully to avoid dislodging too many crystals.

Variations and Extensions

1. Use solutions of different concentrations (that is, different ratios of solid to water), and observe differences in the amounts of crystals formed.

2. Have students draw on the paper with a crayon, wax, or candle, then brush on the solution. Observe the effect where crayon or wax has been applied.

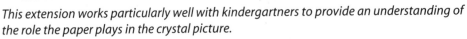 *This extension works particularly well with kindergartners to provide an understanding of the role the paper plays in the crystal picture.*

3. Allow the solutions to evaporate in their containers and observe the resulting crystals. Compare these crystals to the ones on the crystal pictures.

4. On a snowy day, take sheets of black construction paper outside and wait for the paper to become cold. Have students catch snowflakes on the papers and study them with a magnifying lens. Have them count the six sides.

5. Use MSG in water instead of the other solutions. (MSG produces shiny, glass-like streaks, not distinct crystals like the solids used in the "Procedure.")

Explanation

The following explanation is intended for the teacher's information. Modify the explanation for students as required.

Crystals are regularly shaped solids. The shapes of the crystals are due to a specific, regular pattern of the particles that make up the crystals. There are many different shapes of crystals: cubic, hexagonal, pyramidal, and so on.

In this activity, the paper provides a surface on which the crystallization can occur. The crystals form more quickly on the construction paper. This is because the construction paper soaks up or absorbs the water, spreading the solution over a larger area. When the water is spread over a larger area, the rate of evaporation is faster. As the water evaporates from the paper, the solid crystals form. The crystals form more slowly on the glossy paper because it is the least water-absorbent, so the water evaporates from a smaller area.

The message or picture that is drawn on the light-colored paper can be made more visible if it is gently rubbed with a marker or the lead of a pencil. If the crystals are closely packed together, they tend not to pick up the lead or marker, but the uncoated paper does. This allows the message to be read as a color reverse.

Assessment

Have students complete the "My Crystal Picture" Assessment Sheet (provided).

Cross-Curricular Integration

Art:
- After testing the various solutions and papers, students can create artwork using their favorite combinations.
- If the lesson is done in the winter, have the students cut snowflakes from folded paper and decorate with glitter. Hang the snowflakes in a window.

Language arts:
- Have students write poems or stories about the crystal pictures.
- Write a class story entitled, "The Search for the Missing Crystal."
- Have students think of adjectives to describe crystals.
- Read aloud or suggest that students read the following book:
  - *Two Bad Ants,* by Chris Van Allsburg (Houghton Mifflin, ISBN 0-395-4866-88)
    Two ants get into trouble after discovering a bowl of sugar crystals.

Math:
- Study geometric shapes.

Social studies:
- Invite a jeweler to speak to the class on crystals and precious stones (how gems are cut from minerals, etc.).
- Use a world map to identify locations where various minerals are found. (For example, amethyst and topaz come from Brazil; diamonds from Africa; emeralds from Colombia; sapphires from Kashmir; and rubies from Burma.)

Reference

"Growing Crystals," "Crystal Gardens;" *Fun with Chemistry: A Guidebook of K–12 Activities;* Sarquis, M., Sarquis, J., Eds; Institute for Chemical Education: Madison, WI, 1993; Vol. 2, pp 271–280.

Contributors

Nancy Mitchell, Cincinnati Public Schools, Cincinnati, OH; Teaching Science with TOYS, 1991–92.
Barbara Toman, Fairfield City Schools, Hamilton, OH; Teaching Science with TOYS, 1990–91.
Ann Veith, Rosedale Elementary School, Middletown, OH; Teaching Science with TOYS, 1991–92.

Handout Master

A master for the following handout is provided:
- My Crystal Picture—Assessment Sheet

Copy as needed for classroom use.

Name _____   Date _____

CRYSTAL PICTURES

My Crystal Picture—Assessment Sheet

1. Describe your crystal picture. Use as many adjectives as you can think of.

   _____

   _____

   _____

   _____

   _____

   _____

2. Finish this sentence. Crystal pictures are _____

   _____

3. Does your crystal picture remind you of anything else you have ever seen? Explain.

   _____

   _____

   _____

   _____

4. Write three sentences telling what you learned in today's lesson.

   _____

   _____

   _____

   _____

   _____

CRAYON PRINTS FROM A CHANGE OF STATE

*Two different procedures allow students to apply
the concept of changes of state of matter to produce works of art.*

A crayon print message

KEY SCIENCE TOPICS

- freezing and melting
- liquid and solid
- physical changes

KEY PROCESS SKILLS

• observing	Students observe changes of state as a wax crayon is heated and cooled.
• predicting	Students predict the state of matter of wax at various temperatures.

TIME REQUIRED

	Part A	Part B
Setup	10 minutes	15 minutes
Performance	5 minutes/print	5 minutes
Cleanup	5 minutes	5 minutes

Materials

For the "Procedure"
Part A, per class
- aluminum foil
- electric food-warming tray
- crayons
- oven mitts
- various kinds of paper (copy, construction, white, colored)

Part B, per class
- crayons
- an iron
- waxed paper
- crayon sharpener
- (optional) scissors
- (optional) string and hanger

For the "Variation"
All materials listed for Part A plus:
Per class
- materials to mount prints or to make greeting cards

Safety and Disposal

Adult supervision is necessary. The students should be told to exercise care near the warming tray because the surface of the tray is very warm. Students should wear oven mitts for Part A. In Part B, the teacher should be the only one to use the iron, and the students should be cautioned that a hot iron could cause serious burns if touched. No special disposal procedures are required.

Getting Ready

For Part A, cover the surface of the food-warming tray with aluminum foil and turn on the food-warming tray. For Part B, remove the paper wrapping from several crayons and preheat the iron.

Introducing the Activity

Ask the students, "What happens to an ice cube that is warmed?" *It melts to form liquid water.* "What happens when the liquid water is cooled?" *It freezes if it is cooled enough.* Tell them the activity will involve heating crayons and observing changes of state. Discuss the safety procedures that will be necessary.

Procedure

Part A: A Picture

Be careful to keep the oven mitt away from the part of the crayon that is melting.

1. With an oven mitt on, have the student draw with the crayon on the heated aluminum foil on the food-warming tray. The crayon will melt as the student draws. (See Figure 1.)

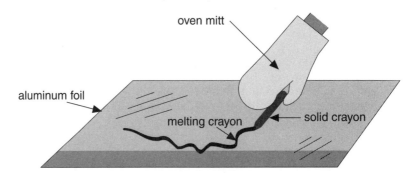

Figure 1: Draw on the aluminum-foil-covered warming tray.

2. Ask students, "What evidence do you have that the crayon has melted?" *It changes into a liquid.* "Which of our senses tell us that the crayon is melting?" *Sight, smell.*

3. Have students repeat the process using different-colored crayons until the desired combination of liquid crayon color is created. Colors may be swirled together.

4. With the oven mitt on, have a student lay a piece of plain white paper over the melted crayons, pressing and smoothing down the entire sheet of paper. Remove the sheet from the tray and observe the print.

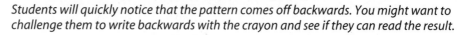

Students will quickly notice that the pattern comes off backwards. You might want to challenge them to write backwards with the crayon and see if they can read the result.

5. Ask the students, "What happened to the liquid crayon when it cooled?" *(It solidified.)*

6. Remove the foil-covering and allow the excess liquid crayon to cool (and solidify) on the foil to create a second picture.

7. Have another student repeat the procedure.

You may wish to re-cover the warming tray with a new piece of foil when the melted crayon residue begins to build up.

Part B: A Window Sun Catcher

1. Have students make crayon shavings using a crayon sharpener.

2. Fold a piece of waxed paper in half, unfold, and sprinkle crayon shavings on one half of the paper.

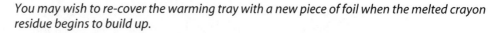

Don't use too many crayon shavings—it will look too cluttered.

3. Fold the other half of the waxed paper over the shavings so the shavings are "sandwiched" inside. (See Figure 2.)

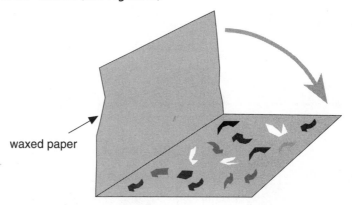

waxed paper

Figure 2: Sandwich crayon shavings in a sheet of waxed paper.

You should be the only one to use the hot iron.
4. Move the hot iron over the top layer of waxed paper until the crayon shavings melt, then remove it.

5. Once the wax paper is cool, return it to the students for examination.

6. If desired, cut the wax paper into pieces and give each student a piece to take home or hang in the window as a sun catcher.

Variation

Colored picture prints can be mounted on colored construction paper or used to make greeting cards.

Explanation

The following explanation is intended for the teacher's information. Modify the explanation for students as required.

In this activity, solid crayons are melted to form a liquid and allowed to cool to form a solid. In the solid state, the particles that make up the crayons are held in place by the attractive forces between the particles. While the particles in the solid state are able to vibrate and rotate in place, they do not have enough energy to move from one place to another. This causes solids to have specific shapes.

In the activity, heat is added to the crayon to melt it. Melting is the process of changing from the solid state to the liquid state. The energy added to the particles allows them to overcome some of the attractive forces that were previously responsible for holding them in place. In the liquid state, the particles are still touching each other but are able to slip and slide past each other.

When the liquid crayon is allowed to cool, it solidifies once again. This process is called freezing. (Many students have the misconception that freezing occurs only in freezers. For crayons, the freezing temperature is above room temperature.) The energy loss (in this case to the paper and air) allows the attractive forces to again hold the particles rigidly in place, removing their ability to move from one place to another.

Both melting and freezing are examples of physical changes. The particles that make up the crayons are the same composition regardless of the state they are in; what is different is the amount of energy that the particles possess.

Assessment

Options:

*   Have students complete the "Heat or Cool?" Assessment Sheet (provided).

*   Have students make two signs, one showing a solid crayon, which they label "solid," and the other a melted crayon, which they label "liquid." (See Figure 3.) Students can use these signs in a game of classification in which you hold up pictures or actual items and the students classify them. Alternatively, you can present various scenarios about different phase changes and have students use their signs to show the final results. For example: Julie buys a chocolate ice-cream cone from the ice-cream truck. It is a very hot day and the sun is shining on her ice cream. If Julie does not quickly finish her ice cream, what will it become, liquid or solid?

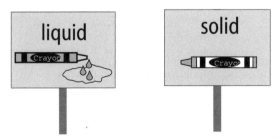

Figure 3: Students make two signs, one showing
a solid crayon and the other a liquid crayon.

Art:
*   With additional melted crayons, have the students use a paintbrush and paper to create a wax painting of something your class is currently studying. After the picture is complete, have the students compose acrostics (acronyms) about their paintings. For example, if the picture was a landscape of Mount Rainier in Washington, the following would be an appropriate acrostic:

> **M**ajestic mountain
> **O**utstanding view
> **U**nbelievably beautiful
> **N**ature's high-rise
> **T**remendous
>
> **R**ugged Terrain
> **A** gigantic vanilla ice-cream cone
> **I**cing on top
> **N**orthwest institution
> **I**ncredible sunset
> **E**verlasting impression
> **R**ainier

Language arts:
*   Have students do word-search puzzle on crayons.
*   Have students write their own directions describing how they made their prints.
*   Write to a crayon company and request information on the history of crayons.
*   Read aloud or suggest that students read one or more of the following books:
    *   *How Is a Crayon Made?,* by Oz Charles (Scholastic, ISBN 0-590-45997-X)
    Describes, in text and step-by-step photographs, the manufacture of a crayon from wax to finished product.

Social studies:
*   Study how crayons are made in a factory. Discuss what it would be like having a job in a factory. What other things might be made in a factory?

Reference

Watson, P. *Liquid Magic;* Lothrop, Lee & Shepard: New York, 1982.

Contributors

Mary Haggard, Goldwood Primary School, Rocky River, OH; Teaching Science with TOYS, 1991–92.
Lynn Hogue, Winton Woods High School, Cincinnati, OH; Teaching Science with TOYS staff member.
Gina Marchesini, Syre Elementary School, Seattle, WA; Teaching Science with TOYS, 1992.
Julie Thompson, Syre Elementary School, Seattle, WA; Teaching Science with TOYS, 1992.
Ann Veith, Rosedale Elementary School, Middletown, OH; Teaching Science with TOYS, 1991–92.

Handout Master

A master for the following handout is provided:
*   "Heat or Cool?"—Assessment Sheet
Copy as needed for classroom use.

CRAYON PRINTS FROM A CHANGE OF STATE

Heat or Cool?—Assessment Sheet

Write "heat" or "cool" in each blank.

 + _____ =

 + _____ =

 + _____ =

 + _____ =

 + _____ =

 + _____ =

SMELL-GOOD DIFFUSION ORNAMENTS

Students prepare a mixture and use the sense of smell to characterize different components of it.

Smell-Good Diffusion Ornaments with spices

Materials

For the "Procedure"
Per class (makes about 100 ¾-inch x ¾-inch ornaments)
- ½ cup applesauce
- 8 tablespoons cinnamon
- 1½ tablespoons ground cloves
- 1½ tablespoons nutmeg
- 1-cup measure
- 3 small, zipper-type plastic bags
- bowl
- aluminum foil
- rolling pin
- mixing spoon

- spatula
- paper towels
- knife to cut dough
- (optional) pencil
- (optional) wax paper
- (optional) ribbons for hanging the ornaments
- (optional) wooden circles or other shapes
- (optional) potpourri pot
- (optional) glue

For "Variations and Extensions"

❷ Per class
- 7 cups flour
- 3½ cups salt
- 3½ cups water
- acrylic paint
- piece of Smell-Good Ornament dough (made in the "Procedure")
- (optional) cookie cutters in various shapes
- yarn or lace

❸ Per class
- glue
- water
- newspaper
- hole puncher
- (optional) tempera paint

❹ Per student
- small piece of soft Smell-Good Ornament dough (made in the "Procedure")
- various containers such as zipper-type plastic bags, paper bags, waxed paper, aluminum foil, cardboard boxes

❺ All materials listed for Variation 4, except
- substitute dried Smell-Good Ornament dough for the soft dough

❼ All materials listed for the "Procedure" plus the following:
- access to an oven

Safety and Disposal

No special safety or disposal procedures are required.

Getting Ready

Measure each of the ingredients into an appropriate container (for example, applesauce in a 1-cup measure; dry spices in separate zipper-type plastic bags). Label each appropriately.

Introducing the Activity

If possible, plug in a potpourri pot and have a nice smell in the air when the students enter the room in the morning. As students enter the room and notice the smell, tell them "Today we will be doing a project involving our sense of smell." Ask the students, "How do you know when someone is baking cookies even if you are not in the kitchen?" Ask them to name other things that smell good to them and that they recognize by smell. Be sure the students understand that this is an exercise in smell, not taste. (optional) On a chart, record and graph the numbers of students that like particular smells. You might want to include the spices to be used in the activity in the chart.

Procedure

1. Gather the ingredients in front of the students. Let them smell each and describe their observations.

2. Ask the students to predict what will happen when these are mixed. Will all the individual odors be observable? Will one predominate? What consistency will the mixture have?

3. Mix all of the spices and the applesauce together in a bowl and stir well. Let the students observe and smell the mixture. Discuss their predictions.

The mixture should resemble soft dough. If the mixture is too wet, add more cinnamon until the consistency is correct.

4. Tell the students you'd like to use the mixture to make ornaments. Ask them to suggest ways to do this.

5. Spread the mixture onto a sheet of aluminum foil. Cover with an additional sheet of foil or wax paper. Using the rolling pin, roll the mixture into a sheet approximately ¼ inch thick. Remove the top sheet of foil.

6. Cut the dough into about ¾-inch x ¾-inch square ornaments. If desired, have students make holes in the middle of the ornaments using a pencil. Ribbons can be strung through the holes so the ornaments can be hung. With a spatula, remove each ornament from the rest of the sheet and place it on a paper towel to dry. Remind the students to put their names on the paper towels.

7. Allow the squares to air-dry for several days. Have the students observe and smell their ornaments daily. The squares also need to be turned over daily with a spatula.

8. After several days, ask the students if they think the ornaments are dried out enough to hang on a ribbon. Have them explain their reasons. Discuss the drying process and where the water goes when it leaves the ornaments.

9. Continue to let the ornaments dry if needed.

When the ornaments are dry they are easily broken. To help protect them from breaking, you can glue the ornaments onto a wooden circle or other shape.

10. (optional) Once the ornaments are dry and hard, thread a ribbon through the hole and tie it.

1. Have the students work in cooperative groups. Each student can have a specific job.

2. Have the students make "Secret Scent Necklaces" out of dough as follows: Mix 7 cups of flour, 3½ cups of salt, and 3½ cups of water. Knead the dough. Chill. Knead again. Divide the dough into four pieces. Roll it out and use a cookie cutter to make your shape (such as a pumpkin or gingerbread girl or boy). Make a small hole near the top of each ornament and bake at 300°F for about an hour, until the pieces are lightly browned. Allow the pieces to cool, then have the students paint them with acrylic paints. Have them thread a long string or ribbon through the hole and tie it above the hole, leaving an equal amount of string on each side. Have the students thread colorful beads onto the strings and tie the strings at the ends to form necklaces. Have the students glue a small piece of dried Smell-Good Ornament dough to the backs of their necklaces. Encourage the students to ask others to guess the secret of their necklaces and name the sense they used to find out.

3. Have the students make papier-mâché Secret Scent Necklaces as follows: Choose a shape for the necklace ornaments and cut 15 identical copies of this shape from newspaper. Have the students paint each piece with watered-down glue and stack them one on top of the other. Punch a hole through the stack for the string. Allow the necklaces to dry overnight. Once dry, have students paint the necklaces if desired. Glue a smelly dough piece to the back. Lace yarn or plastic lacing through the hole to complete the necklace.

4. Once the ornaments are formed in shapes, place them in different containers (such as zipper-type plastic bags, paper bags, waxed paper, aluminum foil, cardboard boxes, etc.). Compare how long it takes them to dry.

5. Place the dried ornaments in different containers to see how long each will maintain its characteristic odor.

6. Use the following modified recipes so three teams add only one of each of the dry spices and a fourth team uses the original proportions. (See Table 1.)

Table 1: Scent Recipes	
Team	Recipe
A	2 tablespoons applesauce 3 tablespoons nutmeg
B	2 tablespoons applesauce 3 tablespoons cloves
C	2 tablespoons applesauce 3 tablespoons cinnamon
D	2 tablespoons applesauce 2 tablespoons cinnamon 1½ teaspoons cloves 1½ teaspoons nutmeg

7. Have the students place ornaments at various distances from their noses and determine the maximum distance at which the scent can be detected.

8. Try drying the ornaments in an oven at low temperature (about 200–250°F). See if this affects the odor.

Explanation

The following explanation is intended for the teacher's information. Modify the explanation for students as required.

All matter is made up of tiny particles. They are so small that under normal conditions you can't see them, but in some cases you can detect their presence by your sense of smell. The spices used in this activity contain particles that have certain characteristic odors. When these smelly particles reach special receptors on the inside of our noses, a series of complex chemical reactions begins that ultimately results in the perception that you smell a particular substance.

But how do these "smelly" particles in the solid spices or ornaments reach our noses? The particles are volatile, which means they easily change to a gas. As gaseous particles, they mix readily with the air and quickly diffuse (or spread out) until some reach our noses.

Assessment

In cooperative groups, have the students design and carry out an experiment to determine which two of four possible spices are present in an unknown spice mixture. Give each group a small sample (about ½ teaspoon) of the unknown spice mixture in a zipper-type plastic bag. Provide each group with a small amount (about ½ teaspoon) of each of the four possible spices (in its own labeled bag), a magnifying lens (optional), and a sheet of white paper to use as a work surface. (A white background makes it easy to see the small particles of spices.) Possible spices include cinnamon, allspice, nutmeg, ginger, basil, and oregano.

Cross-Curricular Integration

Language arts:
* Have the students write stories about a smell that makes them remember something that has happened to them.
* What odors do students associate with special holidays?
* Have the students complete a science acrostic (acronym): Write the words "smell" and "good" on the board. Instruct the students to choose one of these words and write it vertically on a piece of lined paper, with one letter to a line. Instruct the students to write one word, phrase, or sentence that begins with each letter of their word. An example follows:

> **G**ingerbread is delicious
> **O**dors spread out through the air
> **O**rnaments can be made from applesauce
> **D**iffuse means "spread out"

* Read aloud or suggest that students read one or more of the following books:
  ○ *Gingerbread Man* (any version)
  ○ *Smelling,* by Richard Allington (Raintree, ISBN 0817212930)
    This book describes 14 categories of aromas, including those associated with holidays, cleanliness, and illness.

- ○ *Smelling: A Troll Question Book,* by Kathie Smith and Victoria Crenson (Troll, ISBN 0816710104)

  This question and answer format explains how the nose smells, explains the relationship between smell and taste, and provides other olfactory information.
- ○ *A Sniff in Time,* by Susan Saunders (Atheneum, ISBN 0689308906)

  A hungry wizard leaves James with the ability to smell into the future.
- ○ *Turtle Tale,* by Frank Asch (Dial, ISBN 0803787855)

  This is a story about a turtle who decides to keep his head inside his shell. He can't see where he is going, but he can smell his way to the river.
- ○ *What Your Nose Knows,* by Jane Belk Moncure (Children's Press, ISBN 0516032550)

  This book describes the many things your nose can identify by their smells.

Life science:
- Discuss how smell is used by animals to find food, mark territory, and alert them to danger. Note that not all animals smell with a nose (for example, snakes and insects).

Math:
- Have students measure the ingredients.
- Ask students to name their favorite smells and record the first 10 answers along the bottom of the graph on the attached worksheet. Have each student choose which of these 10 smells he or she likes the best. Graph the results.
- Have older students construct gingerbread houses using various geometric shapes.

Social studies:
- Visit a nursing home. Sing songs about friendship and leave ornaments for the residents to keep in their rooms.
- The ornaments could be used as a culminating activity for a study of international Christmas, focusing on the customs of many different countries and cultures. The children will especially enjoy the study of Germany if you bring in (or make as a class) gingerbread.

Reference

Sue McCabe, Mary Esther Elementary School, Mary Esther, FL, personal communication.

Contributors

Lynn Hogue (activity developer), Winton Woods High School, Cincinnati, OH; Teaching Science with TOYS staff member.

Kim Kline, Central Elementary School, Lawrenceburg, IN; Teaching Science with TOYS, 1992–93.

Karen Mitchell, Sherman Elementary School, Toledo, OH; Teaching Science with TOYS, 1992–93.

Ann Veith, Rosedale Elementary, Middletown, OH; Teaching Science with TOYS, 1991–92.

SMELLY BALLOONS

Can different smells travel through the wall of a balloon?

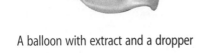

A balloon with extract and a dropper

GRADE LEVELS

Science activity appropriate for grades K–12
Cross-Curricular Integration intended for grades K–5

KEY SCIENCE TOPICS

- diffusion
- particulate nature of matter
- volatility

KEY PROCESS SKILLS

• observing	Students use their sense of smell to observe the movement of an odor through the wall of a balloon.
• collecting data	Students collect data using different extracts.

TIME REQUIRED

Setup	5–15	minutes
Performance	15–25	minutes
Cleanup	5	minutes

Materials

For the "Procedure"
Per group
- dropper
- marking pen
- rubber balloon
- several different flavoring extracts such as vanilla, peppermint, orange, etc.

Each group should use a different extract and a different-colored balloon.

- (optional) glue
- (optional) balloon pump

For "Variations and Extensions"
❶ Per class
- natural and artificial flavorings

❷ Per class
  • assorted solid materials with strong odors such as cloves, nutmeg, garlic, or onions
  • rubber balloon for each material
  • marking pen

❸ All materials listed for the "Procedure" plus the following:
  • Mylar, other metallized, or plastic-treated balloons

❹ All materials listed for the "Procedure" except
  • substitute zipper-type plastic bags for balloons

Safety and Disposal

You should blow up the balloon for very young students. There is a danger that they might inhale instead of blow and get the balloon stuck in the windpipe. No special disposal procedures are required.

Getting Ready

For younger students, you may wish to do Steps 1–3 of the "Procedure" in advance.

Introducing the Activity

Options:

• You may wish to introduce the activity with a discussion about using our sense of smell to make observations. When introducing any activity that involves the smelling of potentially unknown odors, instruct the students about protecting themselves. Show the students how to use the wafting procedure and remind them to avoid prolonged inhalation of objectionable odors. (See Figure 1.) Such odors are typically not good for us. Tell students that they will be asked to identify the contents of a balloon by smell alone. Emphasize that in spite of the fact that you have selected safe materials for the activity, they should use the wafting procedure as a first line of detection, smelling the balloon more closely only after they have established it is not an offensive odor.

Use your free hand to gently fan the vapors from the object towards your nose.

Figure 1: Show your students how to use the wafting procedure to smell unknown odors.

• The week before you do this activity, you may wish to feature a different smell each day (such as peanut butter, lemon, roses, popcorn, and coffee). Have the room smell like these substances when the students enter in the morning. Discuss the odors smelled, and talk about how those odors reach our noses and are detected. Responses to this topic can lead into a discussion on air. Blow up a balloon and seal it. Discuss that the balloon is filled with air. Leave the balloon for a week and have the students observe that it decreases in size. Ask them what happened and how the air got out of the balloon. Have the students put part of their shirts over their mouths and blow through them. Although the students can't see the pores in the material, they should observe that air passes through it. Relate this to the deflating balloon. Even though the students can't see the pores in the balloon, they should understand that the pores are there.

- For the upper grades, you may wish to discuss how the particles responsible for odors travel based upon particle theory.

Procedure

1. Give each group a rubber balloon, a dropper, and a flavoring extract.

2. Have the students color the balloons on the "What's the Scent?" Data Sheet (provided) to correspond with the balloons to be used. (Alternatively, assign each group a number and have them write the group number on the balloon. Then have students write the numbers on the Data Sheet.)

3. Instruct each group to put one or two drops of the extract into their balloon by inserting a dropper as far as possible into the balloon. This way the extract does not get on the neck of the balloon.

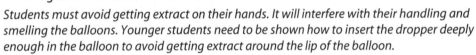 *Students must avoid getting extract on their hands. It will interfere with their handling and smelling the balloons. Younger students need to be shown how to insert the dropper deeply enough in the balloon to avoid getting extract around the lip of the balloon.*

4. Have each group blow up the balloon, tie it off, and shake it a few times.

5. Have groups pass the balloons around. Smell them, first using the wafting procedure and then smelling more closely. Record the odors they think they can detect.

6. (optional) Have the students indicate their predictions by cutting out the "Scent Circles" Template (provided) and gluing them to the Data Sheet.

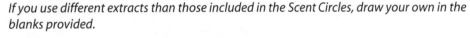 *If you use different extracts than those included in the Scent Circles, draw your own in the blanks provided.*

7. After all the groups are finished making observations, make a list of the odors students identified for each balloon, count the number of different answers, and then have each "home group" tell what was actually used in their balloon.

Variations and Extensions

1. Compare artificial and natural extracts (for example, artificial vanilla versus natural vanilla). Can students detect a difference?

2. Compare extracts to odiferous spices or vegetables (such as nutmeg, cloves, or chopped garlic or onion). Place dry spices in balloons to determine if their odor permeates through the balloon wall.

3. Place extract in a balloon as described in the "Procedure" and find out how long your students can detect the odor. Have them smell the balloon every hour or so and record observations. Repeat this variation using a Mylar, other metallized, or plastic-treated balloon. Compare the permeability of the different balloon materials.

4. Substitute zipper-type plastic bags in place of balloons. Have students compare the time it takes to smell extracts through balloons (fast), room-temperature plastic bags (slow), and plastic bags from the freezer (very slow).

5. Make up pairs of balloons with the same extract and challenge the students to use their sense of smell to find both balloons of each pair.

Explanation

 The following explanation is intended for the teacher's information. Modify the explanation for students as required.

All matter is made up of tiny particles. They are so small that under normal conditions you can't see them, but in some cases you can detect their presence by smelling them. Each of the extracts and other smelly substances used in this activity contain particles that have certain characteristic odors. When these smelly particles reach special receptors inside our noses, a series of complex chemical reactions begins that ultimately result in the perception that you smell a particular substance.

This activity shows that the gaseous particles responsible for certain odors can pass through the wall of a common latex rubber balloon. Leading students to this conclusion should be the goal of this activity for teachers of lower grades. The following discussion is provided for teachers and/or for students in the upper grades.

To explain this phenomenon, we need to consider three important factors: the volatility of the particles responsible for odors, the permeability of balloons to gaseous particles, and the solubility of one chemical in another.

Flavoring extracts are usually a mixture of several components that have been extracted from the seed, flower, or plant using alcohol or water. The molecules that are responsible for the characteristic odor of the extract are usually fairly volatile, which means they easily vaporize from the liquid to the gaseous state.

If you have ever observed an air- or helium-filled latex balloon over a period of days, you have seen the balloon shrink as the gaseous molecules inside moved to the outside through the microscopic pores in the balloon. The speed at which a gas diffuses is related to its molecular mass. The larger the molecular mass, the slower it diffuses. That's why helium-filled balloons shrink faster than air-filled balloons. (Helium atoms have less mass than the nitrogen and oxygen molecules found in air.)

While it is possible that some molecules of the odiferous extract pass through the pores in the balloon, it is important to note that these molecules of extract are considerably larger and more massive than molecules of water or alcohol that are typically the solvents for the extracts. Vanillin, for example, is the molecule in vanilla that gives it its characteristic odor. Vanillin has the chemical formula $C_8H_8O_3$. On a per molecule basis, vanillin is about 38 times more massive than helium, 18 times more massive than water, and about five times more massive than nitrogen or oxygen gas. Because the odor of vanillin is detected outside the balloon very quickly, this would lead us to conclude that another factor must be involved in the movement of the odor molecules through the balloon walls.

What then, could this other factor be? It is proposed that the molecules of extract actually interact with and perhaps even dissolve in the latex layer of the balloon. On a molecular level, the latex layer is actually relatively thick, containing several layers of long latex molecules interwoven through each other. Molecules of extract gradually could dissolve in the strands of latex as they moved through the latex to the outside. When the extract reaches the outside of the balloon it moves through the air to our noses.

Assessment

The ability of gas to pass through porous materials can be demonstrated through a whole group exercise. The goal of this exercise is to enable students to experience the activity and be able to state what is happening in their own words.

1. Take the class to a large area such as a gymnasium to complete the following whole-group assessment activity.

2. Instruct a majority of the class to form a circle, holding hands, legs spread apart so their feet are touching. Share with the class that these students represent the balloon. Place a few students in the middle of the circle to represent the particles responsible for the gaseous scent. (See Figure 2.)

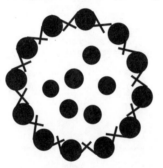

Figure 2: Students form a circular "balloon" with "scent" particles in the middle.

3. The students in the middle will then be directed to demonstrate how, as scent molecules, they might get through a porous material like the balloon. Students will then generate ideas about being able to slowly crawl or step through openings between arms and legs of the people in the circle, or loosen and move through the linked hands and legs. Discussion could take place about how the students should leave the middle of the circle. Was the odor detected immediately? Did the odor all leave at once, or did some continue to stay in the balloon?

4. Next ask the students what they could do to become a nonporous material. The class could then provide ideas about dropping their arms, bringing their legs together, and standing shoulder to shoulder. The circle is obviously smaller, but it becomes quite evident that the students that represent the molecules responsible for the scent now do not have an easy way out of the "container" unless it is broken.

5. The final step is to return to the classroom, and you have the option of providing an assessment activity to determine individual accountability. Students can describe in writing or draw a picture of what took place in the gym and/or what they believed happened with the molecules responsible for the scent inside of the balloon.

Cross-Curricular Integration

Art:
- Have students make craft items that have a smell, such as potpourri.

Language arts:
Have students do the following:
- Write stories using a starter list of words from the activity.
- Write stories from the point of view of a snake—snakes use their tongues to smell their surroundings.
- Write questions relating to the activity for their classmates. The questions should concentrate on "who," "what," "why," "where," "when," and "how."
- Write an "Interview with a Nose" as a summary for the activity. This interview could draw its questions from the activity, and the nose's answers could be creative or scientific.

Life science:
- Have students study the following:
  - How do the human senses work?
  - How do animals use pheromones to communicate?
  - What kinds of animals (for example, some types of nocturnal animals) use smell as their predominant sense?

Social studies:
- Have students cook and smell foods from different countries (for example, curry/India, chili/Mexico, or French bread/France).

Reference

Mebane, R.C.; Rybolt, T.R. *Adventures with Atoms and Molecules;* Enslow: Hillside, NJ, 1985; pp 8–9.

Contributors

Susan Brutsche, Bellevue City Schools, Bellevue, OH; Teaching Science with TOYS, 1991–92.
Donna Essman, Stanton Primary School, New Boston, OH; Teaching Science with TOYS, 1991–92.
Marilyn Hayes, John XXIII Elementary School, Middletown, OH; Teaching Science with TOYS, 1990–91.
Bonnie Marx, Miami East Junior High School, Piqua, OH; Teaching Science with TOYS, 1991–92.
Jill Swango, Brownsburg Junior High School, Brownsburg, IN; Teaching Science with TOYS, 1992–93.
James Warren, New Boston Elementary School, New Boston, OH; Teaching Science with TOYS, 1991–92.

Handout Masters

Masters for the following handouts are provided:
- What's the Scent?—Data Sheet
- Scent Circles—Template

Copy as needed for classroom use.

Name _____   Date _____

SMELLY BALLOONS

What's the Scent?—Data Sheet

(Write the balloon colors and color the balloons in the boxes below.)

Color of Balloon	Guesses	Actual Scent

SMELLY BALLOONS

Scent Circles—Template

banana · banana · strawberry · strawberry

  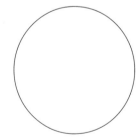 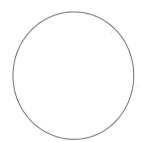

cherry · cherry · peppermint · peppermint

chocolate · chocolate · orange · orange

lemon · lemon

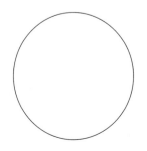 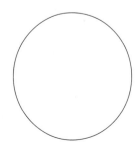 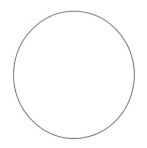 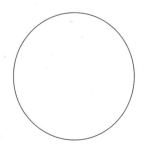

THE SCRATCH-AND-SNIFF CHALLENGE

Students identify substances by smell and investigate how microencapsulation works.

Scratch-and-sniff stickers

GRADE LEVELS

Science activity appropriate for grades K–6
Cross-Curricular Integration intended for grades K–5

KEY SCIENCE TOPICS

- diffusion
- evaporation
- microencapsulation
- senses and odors

KEY PROCESS SKILLS

- observing — Students use their sense of smell to detect various odors.

- making models — Plastic bubble wrap is used to model microencapsulation used in scratch-and-sniff stickers.

TIME REQUIRED

Setup	10–20	minutes
Performance	30–40	minutes
Cleanup	5	minutes

Materials

For "Getting Ready"
- a permanent marker

For "Introducing the Activity"
Per class
- several scratch-and-sniff stickers

For the "Procedure"
Part A, per group
- 1 smelly bag made from the following:
  - 1 cotton ball, cotton makeup removal pad, or small piece of felt or sponge
  - 1 small zipper-type plastic bag (such as a sandwich bag)

- 1 of the following "smelly" substances:

vanilla	almond	smoke (liquid)
coconut	peanut butter	banana
mint	grape	pineapple
lemon	strawberry	Vick's® vapor rub
orange	chocolate	Kool-Aid®
cinnamon	pine (cleaner)	Jell-O®

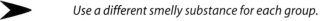 *Use a different smelly substance for each group.*

Part B, per group
- 1 scratch-and-sniff sticker

For "Variations and Extensions"

❶ Per class
- all of the smelly bags used in Part A

Per student
- (optional) 1 scratch-and-sniff sticker

❷ Per class
- sheet of large bubble wrap
- syringe with small needle
- transparent tape or hot-melt glue stick (can be melted with either a hot glue gun or candle and matches)

Safety and Disposal

If Variation 2 is done, inject flavored extracts into the bubble wrap ahead of time. Be careful not to stick yourself with the needle. Keep the needle covered with the plastic tip except when filling the needle or injecting the extracts. Students should NEVER have access to the syringe. Store the syringe safely for future use.

Getting Ready

1. If non-liquid smelly substances are used, dissolve them in small amounts of water to make concentrated solutions.

2. Prepare each smelly bag by moistening a cotton ball, pad, or piece of felt with two or three drops of a different smelly solution and placing it into a small zipper-type plastic bag. Using a permanent marker, number each bag. Record the number and contents for your reference. You need only prepare one bag of each smell to be tested. Before using with the class, blow a little air into each bag to simulate an inflated capsule.

Introducing the Activity

Show the students the scratch-and-sniff stickers. If they are not already familiar with these stickers, pass one or two around the class and allow the students to scratch, sniff, and identify the odor. Challenge the class to suggest how the scratch-and-sniff sticker is made, why it must be scratched to let the smell out, and how the smell gets from the sticker to a person's nose. Let them brainstorm ideas in groups and document their ideas in pictures or notes.

When introducing any activity that involves the smelling of potentially unknown odors, instruct the students about protecting themselves. Show the students how to use the wafting procedure and remind them to avoid prolonged inhalation of objectionable odors. (See Figure 1.) Such odors are typically not good for us.

Use your free hand to gently fan the vapors from the object towards your nose.

Figure 1: Show your students how to use the wafting procedure to smell unknown odors.

Procedure

Part A: The Smelly Bags

1. Distribute one smelly bag and a "Guess that Smell!" Observation Sheet (provided) to each group.

2. Ask the members of each group to smell their sample by opening the bag and wafting the odor towards their noses without removing the cotton, felt, or sponge from the bag.

3. The group should discuss what they believe the smell to be and record their guess by the appropriate number on the "Guess That Smell!" Observation Sheet.

4. Once each group has had a chance to record their guess, have someone in each group blow a little air into the bag, reseal it, and pass it on to another group. The groups should then repeat Steps 2 and 3 for each bag.

5. Once all the smelly bags have been tested by each group, compare the class results for each bag. Discuss why groups might have indicated different identifications, and then compare the class results to your answer key.

6. (optional) Have students prepare their own smelly bags and challenge other groups to identify the smell.

Part B: The Sniff Challenge

1. Give each group a scratch-and-sniff sticker.

2. Have each member of each group scratch and sniff the sticker without talking to each other and guess what the odor is. Once each member of the group has made his or her own guess, have the group discuss what they believe the odor is.

3. Have the groups report their findings and compare their results to what the package claims the odor is. Class discussion should focus not only on the identification of the smells, but also on why the stickers needed to be scratched to release the odor, how the stickers are made, and how the odor gets from the sticker to their noses. Challenge students to draw a picture of how they think the scratch-and-sniff would look if it were magnified. Compare these with the ideas proposed before the activity.

4. (optional) If the smell of the stickers matches any of the odors that were identified for the smelly bags, you might choose to have the students place the sticker next to the number of the smelly bag on their group's record sheet.

Variations and Extensions

1. Place the smelly bags on a bookshelf or long table. Have each student write his or her name on a sheet of paper and record a number on a line for each smelly bag. Write all the odors the students will smell on the board. Divide the class into teams of two. (The activity works well if each team is composed of a stronger learner and a more needy learner.) Have students smell the bags and record the identity of the odor. After all teams have smelled all the bags, record the number of correct answers for each smell on a graph. Use the graph to extract math information such as: How many students correctly identified coconut? How many students correctly identified vanilla? Is the number of students correctly identifying coconut greater than or less than the number of students correctly identifying vanilla? End the session with a discussion of why some smells might be more easily identified than others. If desired, give each student a commercial scratch-and-sniff sticker to help them remember the activity.

2. Use sheets of plastic bubble wrap to simulate the microencapsulation of smelly substances in scratch-and-sniff stickers. (See Figure 2.) Follow these steps: Inject flavored extracts into the bubble through the back of the sheet using a hypodermic syringe. (Insulin needles work well.)

 Be certain to do this step ahead of time. Students should NEVER have access to the syringe. Be careful not to stick yourself. Keep the needle covered with the plastic tip except when filling the needle or injecting the extracts. Store the syringe safely for future use.

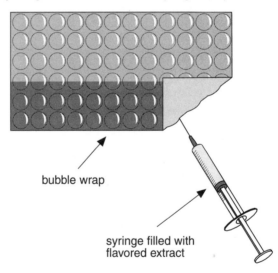

bubble wrap

syringe filled with flavored extract

Figure 2: Inject flavored extracts into bubble wrap.

Seal the hole soon after the injection is made. Transparent tape or hot-melt glue can be used as a sealer. A candle can be used to melt the glue if a glue gun is not available. Prepared bubbles can last several days if well-sealed. During the activity, the students pop the bubbles as they would when they usually play with bubble wrap. This extension closely simulates what happens when the students scratch and pop the tiny capsules on the stickers.

Explanation

 The following explanation is intended for the teacher's information. Modify the explanation for students as required.

All matter is made up of tiny particles. They are so small that under normal conditions they can't be seen. However, in some cases you can detect the presence of the particles by smelling them. Each of the extracts and other smelly substances used in this activity contains particles that have characteristic odors. When these smelly particles reach special receptors on the inside of our noses, a series of complex chemical reactions begins that ultimately results in the perception that you smell a particular substance.

When the smelly substances are encapsulated in the scratch-and-sniff stickers or the plastic bag, the smelly particles are for the most part sealed in. However, once the sticker is scratched or the bag is opened so that some of the encapsulated bubbles pop, some of the smelly particles evaporate (change from the liquid to the gaseous state). The gas particles quickly diffuse (spread out) through the air until some reach our noses.

Assessment

Have students draw pictures or act out the process of a "smell" getting to the nose. If doing an enactment, have several students surround another to "encapsulate" the "smell." Place a "nose" some distance away from the encapsulated sample. Break the "capsule." Have the "smell" travel to the "nose."

Cross-Curricular Integration

Home, safety, and career:
- Because sniffing glue and organic solvents continues to be a problem with dangerous consequences, you may wish to lead the class in a discussion of the dangers associated with such practices.

Language arts:
- Have students make scratch-and-sniff books using commercially available stickers.
- Have the students write stories or poems about smells that make them remember things that have happened to them.
- Have the students write or tell stories about a detective trying to find the source of a strange scent. These stories could be illustrated by gluing extract-soaked cotton balls at appropriate places in the stories.
- Have the students personalize a scent particle on a sticker by calling it "I" and write or tell a story about how "I" travel from the sticker to a child's nose. You can determine the level of students' understanding by reading their stories.
- Read aloud or suggest that students read one or more of the following books:
  - *Noses Are for Smelling Roses,* by Eve Morel (Grosset & Dunlap, ISBN 0448028085)
    By scratching and smelling pages, the reader shares some fragrances as a mother and her two children go through an ordinary day's activities.
  - *A Sniff in Time,* by Susan Saunders (Atheneum, ISBN 0689308906)
    One day in James' life is much like the next until a hungry wizard drops by for dinner and leaves James with the unsettling ability to smell into the future.

- *Sweet as a Rose,* by Albert Carr and Lawrence Lowery (Holt, Rinehart, & Winston, ISBN 0-03081170-8)
  A young child walks throughout his town and describes various smells he experiences. The reader can guess what the items are from clues provided.
- *What Your Nose Knows,* by Jane Belk Moncure (Children's Press, ISBN 0-51603255-0)
  Describes the many things your nose can identify throughout the year by their smells.
- *Your Five Senses,* by Ray Broekel (Children's Press, ISBN 0-516-0932-5)
  This book explains how the smells get to your nose and how the brain identifies the scent.

Life science:
- Demonstrate how the senses can work together by holding a tasting party. Have students taste the same foods while holding their noses and then not holding their noses.
- Study how a scent travels to the nose, how it is subsequently transmitted to the brain, and how the brain determines what it is. Hide one scent in the room and have students act as detectives to find the scent. Hide three scents in the room to demonstrate that after a period of time it is difficult to separate the different scents.
- Discuss how we use our sense of smell to detect and identify odors.

Math:
- Ask students to name their favorite smells and record the first 10 answers along the bottom of a graph. Have each student vote for the one of the 10 smells that is his or her favorite. Graph the results.
- Have students graph how long the smells last in the room or from the sticker.
- Have students walk toward the source of a scent and record the distance from which it is first detected.

Reference

Schultz, E. "Pop and Sniff Experimentation: A High-Sensory-Impact Teaching Device," *Journal of Chemical Education.* 1987, 64(9), 797–798.

Contributors

Theresa Applegate, Lincoln Heights Elementary School, Cincinnati, OH; Teaching Science with TOYS, 1993–94.
Opal Chambers, Taft Elementary School, Middletown, OH; Teaching Science with TOYS, 1990–91.
Cherie Kuhn, Tri-County North Elementary School, Lewisburg, OH; Teaching Science with TOYS, 1992.
Jean McCormack, Liberty Elementary School, Liberty, IN; Teaching Science with TOYS, 1991–92.
Diane Pieratt, Tri-County North Elementary School, Lewisburg, OH; Teaching Science with TOYS, 1992.

Handout Master

A master for the following handout is provided:
- Guess that Smell!—Observation Sheet

Copy as needed for classroom use.

Name _____   Date _____

THE SCRATCH-AND-SNIFF CHALLENGE

Guess that Smell!—Observation Sheet

Record your predictions.

1 ☆	2 ☆
3 ☆	4 ☆
5 ☆	6 ☆
7 ☆	8 ☆

If your prediction was correct, color the star in that box.

DENSITY BATONS

Students use the property of density to make beautiful toys.

Samples of Density Batons

GRADE LEVELS

Science activity appropriate for grades K–6
Cross-Curricular Integration intended for grades K–3

KEY SCIENCE TOPICS

- floating and sinking
- relative density

STUDENT BACKGROUND

Previous experience working with floating and sinking is helpful. This activity can be used to introduce or summarize a lesson on density.

KEY PROCESS SKILLS

• observing	Students observe the behavior of a gas and solids in a tube of liquid.
• measuring	Students measure time needed for various solids to sink in the Density Baton.

TIME REQUIRED

Setup	15	minutes
Performance	30	minutes
Cleanup	10	minutes

Materials

For the "Procedure"
Per class
- density toy such as a baton, keychain, necklace, or earrings filled with a liquid and glitter
- hot-melt glue gun and glue stick
- scissors or knife to cut the tubing
- (optional) washable marker
- (optional) small plastic or homemade paper funnels to pour glitter and sequins into tubing

Per student

- 12-inch length of ½-inch-diameter, clear, rigid plastic tubing

This tubing can be purchased in 3-foot lengths at an aquarium supply store or hardware store. Other sizes may be substituted, but tubing with a very large diameter may be difficult to seal.

- about 1 teaspoon of glitter, sequins, and/or small plastic objects
- water to fill tubing
- cork to fit tubing

For "Variations and Extensions"

❶ All materials listed for the "Procedure" plus the following:
Per student
- ribbon, string, or key chain
- loop of wire or jeweler's loop

❷ All materials listed for the "Procedure" plus the following:
Per class
- light Karo® syrup

❸ Per student
- clear plastic jar with lid
- sheets of materials similar to items used in Density Batons, such as a large piece of foil and a sheet of acetate
- water to fill jar
- scissors

Safety and Disposal

You should be the only one to handle the hot-melt glue gun and glue. Use caution in working with them.

Unwanted water/glitter mixtures can be filtered through tissue paper, with the solid disposed of in a trash can and the water poured down the drain.

Getting Ready

1. Cut the plastic tubing to desired length.

2. Using a hot-melt glue gun, completely seal one end of each piece of tubing.

3. For younger students, you may want to mark a line with washable marker on the tube at the 1-teaspoon level to help students gauge how much glitter to use.

Introducing the Activity

Show students a density toy. Explain that the liquid is water. Ask, "What else is in the baton?" *Air, glitter, sequins, etc.* Turn the toy. Ask, "Do the items move?" *Yes.* "Where does the air bubble go?" *The top.* "Where do the solids go?" *Most sink, but some may float.*

Procedure

1. Give each student a length of tubing with one end sealed. (See "Getting Ready.")

2. Have students add no more than 1 teaspoon of glitter and sequins to the tube.

3. Have students fill the tube with water to about 1–2 centimeters (cm) below the rim.
Leaving a small amount of air in the tube helps the glitter to move through the baton more freely.

4. Tell students to cork the open end of the tube and invert it. Ask them to observe their batons. Do the batons have enough glitter? Does the glitter swirl freely? If students are not satisfied with the result, they can add more glitter, pour out a little water to make room for more air, or discard the contents of the tube according to the recommended disposal procedure and start over.

5. When students are satisfied with the results, remove the cork and seal the top of the tube with the glue gun. Leave a small amount of air so the glitter can move freely.

6. Ask students to compare the homemade Density Baton to the commercial one. Are they similar?

Variations and Extensions

1. Use shorter lengths of tubing that have been modified as shown in Figure 1 to make key chains or necklaces.

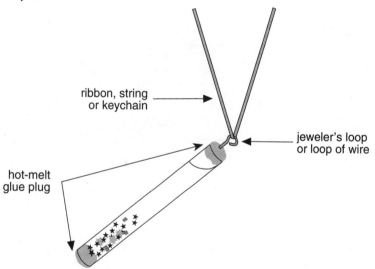

Figure 1: Use shorter lengths of tubing that have been modified.

2. Instead of pure water, use a 50/50 mixture of light Karo® or corn syrup and water in the baton to create a slower rate of flow.

3. Give each student a clear plastic jar with a lid. Have them fill the jars ¾-full of water. Pass out sheets of materials similar to the items used in the Density Batons. For example, to represent glitter, use a large piece of foil. To represent sequins, use acetate sheets (like overhead sheets). Have the students cut the foil and acetate sheets into several small pieces similar in size to the pieces of

glitter and sequins in their Density Batons. Have them cut several larger pieces about 5 to 10 times larger than the small pieces. Have the students predict whether the small pieces will sink or float when they are dropped into the water and record their predictions on the "Does It Sink or Float?" Data Sheet (provided). Then have them test their predictions by dropping several small pieces into their jars and recording their observations. Have the students predict whether the larger pieces will sink or float in water and record their predictions. Have them test their predictions and record their observations.

Explanation

 The following explanation is intended for the teacher's use. Modify the explanation for students as required.

Density batons, density key chains, and even density necklaces have become fashionable novelty items. If you examine some of the simpler ones, you can see that they contain a liquid (most often water), a small air bubble (helpful for agitating the solids when the tube is inverted), and various small solid items (including glitter, sequins, small plastic stars, moons, and other shapes.) When inverted, the materials in the tube shift and create a whirling, swirling motion that can mesmerize the observers. But what is the science behind these toys?

As the name of this activity implies, one of the most important factors in the behavior of the materials in the tube is their relative densities. Each kind of matter has a single characteristic density. Let's assume that the different types of matter we are considering are not soluble in each other. Because the densities of these different kinds of matter differ, some things float while others sink. Why do densities differ? All matter is made up of particles. The heavier and more closely packed these particles are, the denser the material is. Air, for example, is less dense than water. This accounts for the observation that the air bubble always moves to the top of the tube. Some of the solids in the tube may be less dense than water, and others may be more dense. The solids that are less dense will float in water. The solids that are more dense will sink in water.

Why do some of the denser materials sometimes move to the top of the baton? The agitation of the solids by the air bubble and the movement of the baton create currents in the water that may momentarily carry some of the denser materials to the top. The surface tension of the water may also allow small pieces of the denser solids to float. However, with time these items will also settle.

In Extension 2, students use a more viscous (thick) liquid, which slows the flow of the solid pieces. The 50/50 mixture of Karo® or corn syrup and water is also denser than pure water, so that some solids that previously sank may now float.

Extension 3 provides an interesting lesson that reinforces the fact that matter of a specific kind (for example, aluminum foil) has a single characteristic density that does not depend on the size of the piece of solid used.

Assessment

Options:

- Have students write three sentences describing what they learned in the activity.

- Invite the principal to visit the classroom and have the students explain how their Density Batons work.

Cross-Curricular Integration

Language arts:
- Have students pretend their Density Batons are magic wands and write stories about their wands. In their stories they should explain the activity of the items in their wands and who can use the wands. Each story should contain a "who," "what," "where," "when," and "how."

Math:
- Have students estimate the length of time it takes for objects to sink to the bottom of the tube and record estimates. Students should then use a stopwatch to time and record actual time of descent. Have students find the difference between predicted and observed times.

Physical education:
- As a movement activity, have students pretend they are the falling glitter in the Density Baton. When they reach the floor, have them pretend they are the bubble floating back to the top. Repeat several times.

Handout Master

A master for the following handout is provided:
- Does It Sink or Float?—Data Sheet

Copy as needed for classroom use.

DENSITY BATONS

Does It Sink or Float?—Data Sheet

Glue a sample of the object in the box. Predict what the object will do in water. In the picture on the left, draw the object where you think it will go when dropped in water.

Do the experiment. In the picture on the right, draw what you actually observe.

	Sample	**Predicted**	**Actual**
1. Small foil piece			
2. Large foil piece			
3. Small acetate piece			
4. Large acetate piece			

CLAY BOATS

Can a substance that typically sinks in water be made to float and even to carry a load?

Marbles, clay, and a clay boat

GRADE LEVELS

Science activity appropriate for grades 1–6
Cross-Curricular Integration intended for grades 1–3

KEY SCIENCE TOPIC

• density

STUDENT BACKGROUND

Students should have experience observing whether a variety of objects float or sink in water.

KEY PROCESS SKILLS

• estimating	Students estimate the optimum shape for their boats and the mass their boats can carry.
• investigating	Students test their boat's cargo-carrying capacity and use that data to modify the design.

TIME REQUIRED

Setup	5–10	minutes
Performance	30	minutes
Cleanup	5–10	minutes

Materials

For the "Procedure"
Part A, per group
• water
• ½ stick or about 60 grams (dry weight) of oil- or plastic-based clay
Be certain that the clay does not dissolve in water.

• a container deep enough to allow clay boats to be fully submerged, such as a clear plastic storage box or a dish pan

For Part B

All materials listed for Part A plus the following:

- 1 cup of 1 or more of the following "cargo":
  - marbles
  - pennies
  - washers
- (optional for older students) balance

For "Variations and Extensions"

❶ Per class
- water
- a container deep enough to allow clay boats to be fully submerged, such as a clear plastic storage box or a dish pan
- cargo listed in Part B
- aluminum foil
- disposable paper or plastic plate
- egg carton cups

❷ Per class
- water
- a container deep enough to allow clay boats to be fully submerged, such as a clear plastic storage box or a dish pan
- plastic lid
- graph paper
- pennies

❸ All materials listed for the "Procedure" plus the following:
Per class
- volume measure

❹ All materials listed for Part A plus the following:
Per student or group
- plastic straw
- notebook paper
- tape

❺ All materials listed for the "Procedure" plus the following:
Per class
- table salt

Safety and Disposal

No special safety procedures are required. Once the activity is completed, keep the clay in individual balls and store in individual plastic bags if possible. This will allow you to use the same clay from year to year while still maintaining equivalent amounts for each group. If washers are used, be sure to dry them once the activity is over to prevent subsequent rusting.

Introducing the Activity

This activity can be introduced by a discussion of the types and shapes of boats and the amount of cargo they carry, or the activity can be used as a lead-in to discussion of boats and boat design. It also provides an opportunity to review boat safety. Students could be asked to bring in pictures of boats to display and discuss their shapes and purposes.

Procedure

Part A: Clay Shapes

1. Work the clay to soften it and shape it into a ball. Ask students what they think will happen when the ball of clay is dropped into water. *It will sink.*

2. Have a volunteer drop the clay ball in the water and have the class observe as the clay ball sinks.

3. Ask if a smaller ball will float. *No.* Have a volunteer make a ball about half the size of the first and have the class observe again.

4. Ask students what shapes might float and have them work in groups to test a few of their ideas. Results of their tests may be shared with the class.

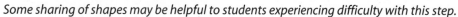 *Some sharing of shapes may be helpful to students experiencing difficulty with this step.*

Part B: Adding the Cargo

1. Challenge each group of students to design a clay boat that will hold the greatest load of "cargo" (such as marbles, pennies, or washers) without sinking.

2. Have the students test the cargo-holding capacity of their boats by counting and recording the number of pieces of a particular type of cargo (pennies, for example) the boat can hold without sinking; a "How Much Will Your Boat Carry?" Data Sheet is provided.

The data from three trials can be recorded on the Data Sheet.

3. (optional) Older students may use a balance to determine the mass of cargo each boat held.

4. Older students may wish to repeat Step 2 two or three more times using the same kind of cargo as used in Step 2. From these multiple trials, they can calculate an average load the boat will hold before it sinks.

5. Younger students may wish to repeat Step 2 using a different type of cargo.

6. Let students change the boat shape to see if it can carry more cargo. Does it help if the bottom is flatter? Does it help if the sides are higher?

7. Ask students to determine the variables (for example, shape of boat, height from which cargo is dropped, location of the cargo on the boat) that affect the outcome of the experiment.

Variations and Extensions

1. Use other materials such as a disposable paper or plastic plate, sections from an egg carton, or aluminum foil to construct the boat.

2. Determine effective cargo-loading strategies: Use a plastic lid as a boat. Place a piece of graph paper inside the lid. Load pennies in the "boat," using the graph paper as a guide. Record the placement of each penny. Compare different loading strategies. Which strategy allows you to load the most cargo?

3. For older students: Using the clay boats that successfully floated during the "Procedure," determine the volume of water each boat can hold before it sinks as follows: Fill a measuring cup and record the volume of water. Pour water from the measuring cup into the boat until the boat sinks. Next, find the volume of water that remains in the measuring cup. Subtract this number from the original volume of water in the container to find the volume of water required to sink the boat. Record this volume.

   To determine the volume of the objects held by the boat just before it sank, partially fill a measuring container (such as a measuring cup or graduated cylinder) with enough water to cover the objects. Record the volume of the water. Submerge the objects carefully so no water splashes out. Record the total volume of the water plus the objects. Subtract the initial volume of the water from the total volume of the water and objects to find the volume of the objects. Compare the volume of water that caused the boat to just sink with the volume of the greatest number of objects that the boat held before sinking.

4. Have students design and construct notebook-paper sails for their boats. Tape the sail to a plastic straw and stick the straw in the clay. Have sailboat races by having each student blow on his or her own sail.

5. Older students may wish to try this activity with ocean or salt water and compare the results with tap-water results.

6. For younger students: Let the students keep their boats for a second day and redesign them. Have them make predictions and test them.

Explanation

 The following explanation is intended for the teacher's information. Modify the explanation for students as required.

Generally, items that are denser than water sink in water, and items that are less dense than water float. The density of the clay used in this activity is approximately 1.9 g/mL while water's density is 1.0 g/mL. Thus it is not surprising that the ball or stick of clay sinks in water. So why does the clay boat float? In the boat shape, the clay holds some air, just like an "empty" cup holds air. As a result, the density of the clay/air "system" is less than the density of water. The same principle explains how ships, which are typically made of steel (density approximately 7.9–8.0 g/mL), can float. If too much of the air in the boat or cup is displaced with water or a denser cargo, the boat will sink.

The activity shows that there are several factors involved in designing a boat that floats while holding cargo. Besides the shape of the boat, other factors such as mass and placement of the cargo are involved. If a boat fills with too much cargo, it will eventually sink because the clay/cargo/air system eventually becomes denser than water. The amount of cargo you can load on your boat also depends on its placement in the boat. If the cargo is placed too close to the side of the boat, it will cause the boat to tip, allowing water to flow in and sink the boat. The density of the liquid in which the boat will travel is also a factor. The more salt that is dissolved in water, the denser the mixture becomes. The density of ocean water is about 1.03 g/mL. The density of water from the Great Salt Lake ranges from approximately 1.5–2.8 g/mL. In salty (and thus, denser) water, a boat can hold more cargo.

Assessment

Options:

- Have students complete the "Design Your Own Boat" Assessment Sheet (provided).

- Provide aluminum foil instead of clay for boat-making in the learning center. Have students report on aluminum foil's effectiveness versus clay's.

Cross-Curricular Integration

Language arts:
- Have students write a paper on boat safety.
- Read aloud or suggest that students read one or more of the following books:
  - *Boats,* by Anne Rockwell (E.P. Dutton, ISBN 0-525-44219-7)
    Depicts boats and ships of varying sizes and uses.
  - *Curious George Rides a Bike,* by H.A. Rey (Houghton Mifflin, ISBN 0-395-16964-X)
    Curious George rides his bike to a lake where he stops to make a boat and sets it afloat.

Math:
- Have students create a histogram of the number of items each boat held.

Social studies:
- Study the importance of canals in American history, the history of international shipping, the environmental dangers of shipping oil, and shipwrecks.
- Do this activity on Columbus Day or at Thanksgiving time and tie it in with the study of the voyages of Columbus or the *Mayflower.*

References

"Sink or Float;" *Elementary Science Study;* Webster Division McGraw-Hill: St. Louis, MO, 1989.

Paulu, N. *Helping Your Child Learn Science;* U.S. Department of Education: Washington, D.C., 1991.

Contributors

Mary Buck, Claymont Elementary School, Ballwin, MO; Teaching Science with TOYS, 1992.

Joyce Cook, Northwestern Elementary School, Kokomo, IN; Teaching Science with TOYS, 1992–93.

Willis E. Good, Frances Willard School, Rock Island, IL.

Diana K. James, Farmers Elementary School, Farmers, KY; Teaching Science with TOYS, 1991–92.

Marsha Jones, Springfield City Schools, Springfield, OH; Teaching Science with TOYS, 1991–92.

Pat King, Fairfield Central School, Fairfield, OH; Teaching Science with TOYS, 1992.

Gina Marchesini, Syre Elementary School, Seattle, WA; Teaching Science with TOYS, 1992.

Lorry Swindler, Holmes Elementary School, Wilmington, OH; Teaching Science with TOYS, 1992–93.

Julie Thompson, Syre Elementary School, Seattle, WA; Teaching Science with TOYS, 1992.

Handout Masters

Masters for the following handouts are provided:
- How Much Will Your Boat Carry?—Data Sheet
- Design Your Own Boat—Assessment Sheet

Copy as needed for classroom use.

Name _____   Date _____

CLAY BOATS
How Much Will Your Boat Carry? — Data Sheet

	Trial 1	Trial 2	Trial 3
10			
9			
8			
7			
6			
5			
4			
3			
2			
1			
0			

Draw a picture of each type of cargo.

Cargo 1	Cargo 2	Cargo 3

CLAY BOATS

Design Your Own Boat— Assessment Sheet

1. Below draw a picture of and describe your first boat design.

   _____

   _____

   _____

   _____

   _____

2. Now draw a picture of and describe your best boat design.

   _____

   _____

   _____

   _____

   _____

3. What advice would you give to next year's class on how to build a clay boat? What did you learn?

   _____

   _____

4. What did you find was the best way to load a boat?

   _____

   _____

5. **Predict.** Do you think a larger piece of clay will carry more or less weight? Why? Try it if you have time.

   _____

   _____

ARE MITTENS WARM?

How do mittens keep your hands warm?

Mitten with thermometer

GRADE LEVELS

Science activity appropriate for grades 1–6
Cross-Curricular Integration intended for grades 1–6

KEY SCIENCE TOPICS

- insulators
- temperature

STUDENT BACKGROUND

The students need previous experience using a thermometer and reading temperatures.

KEY PROCESS SKILLS

• collecting data	Students collect data on the ability of mittens to hold heat.
• controlling variables	Students control the experiment by using different types of mittens.

TIME REQUIRED

Setup	5	minutes
Performance	25	minutes
Cleanup	5	minutes

Materials

For the "Procedure"
Per class
- a clock with minutes marked

Per group
- metal cooking thermometer or alcohol thermometer with calibrations between 15–40°C (about 60–100°F)
- mitten (or glove)
- pencil

For "Variations and Extensions"

❷ All materials listed for the "Procedure" plus the following:
Per group
- glove made of the same material as the mitten

❸ All materials listed for the "Procedure" plus the following:
Per group
- mitten, glove, or piece of fabric made from each of the following fibers: wool, cotton, and polyester

❹ All materials listed for the "Procedure" plus the following:
Per class
- heating pad or electric blanket

Safety and Disposal

The use of mercury thermometers should be avoided because of the potential for breakage and the toxic nature of mercury. No special disposal procedures are required.

Introducing the Activity

The activity can be introduced by reading *The Mitten*, by Jan Brett (Scholastic, ISBN 0-399-21920-X). A discussion of the story and of appropriate clothing for different weather will lead the students to a prediction of how mittens keep our hands warm. You may wish to take some time to have students practice reading temperatures, "timing," and holding a thermometer properly. This activity is most appropriate during cold weather.

Procedure

1. Using a metal cooking (or alcohol) thermometer, have each group of students determine the air temperature in the classroom and record this temperature on their "Predict that Temperature" Data Sheet (provided).

 Remind students not to hold the bulb of the alcohol thermometer (or the stem of the metal cooking thermometer).

2. Ask the students to predict what will happen to the temperature if they place the stem (or bulb) of the thermometer in the palm of an open hand.

3. Have a student in each group carry out the experiment described in Step 2, leaving the thermometer in the palm of their hand for at least 2 minutes. Then without removing the thermometer, have another student from the group read the temperature and record it on the Data Sheet.

4. Ask the students to predict what will happen to the temperature if a fist is closed completely around the thermometer. Then instruct them to do this experiment, leaving the thermometer in place for at least 2 minutes. Remind them to keep their fists shut while reading the thermometers. Ask them why it is necessary to keep their fists shut. *To minimize the heat lost to the air.* Have the students record the temperature observed.

5. Ask the students to predict the temperature of an empty, not-recently-worn mitten. Instruct them to do the experiment leaving the thermometer in place for at least 2 minutes. Record the temperature.

6. Ask the students to predict what will happen to the temperature if a student were to put on the mitten and hold the thermometer inside the mitten on the palm.

7. Have a student in each group carry out the experiment described in Step 6, leaving the thermometer in position for at least 2 minutes. Then without removing the thermometer, have another student from the group read and record the temperature.

8. The following questions can be used to discuss the lesson.

   a. What was the room temperature? How does that compare to body temperature?

   b. What was the temperature when the thermometer was in the palm of your open hand? What was the temperature when your hand was closed into a fist?

   c. What were the temperatures on the inside of an empty, not-recently-worn mitten and an empty, just-worn mitten? Which of the two temperature readings was higher? Discuss reasons for the difference.

   d. What temperature was recorded with the mitten on? How does this compare to the other two temperatures recorded for the mitten? How does it compare to the temperature recorded in your open hand with no mitten?

   e. Why do you think wearing a mitten made your hand feel warmer?

   f. Discuss predictions versus experimentation—why we want to predict and why it's okay for predictions to be "wrong."

Variations and Extensions

1. To determine the effect of the air temperature on the activity, try the activity outside on a cold day and compare the temperatures recorded.

2. Try repeating this activity with gloves made from the same type of cloth as the mittens and compare the results.

3. To determine the effect of the kind of fabric used for the mitten or glove try repeating the activity with mittens, gloves, or pieces of fabric in wool, cotton, and polyester. Find out which type of fabric keeps you warmest (is the best insulator).

4. As a teacher demonstration to observe the effect of an external heat source, determine the temperature of a hand wrapped with a heating pad or electric blanket.

5. Have students rub their hands together for a minute and take the temperature with a closed fist. Does this reading differ from the reading taken before rubbing? *Yes.* Why? *Friction.*

6. To demonstrate insulation in a slightly different way, have students stand barefoot with one foot on a carpet or rug and the other on an uncarpeted surface such as tile, wood, or linoleum. Even though the carpeted and uncarpeted surfaces are at the same temperature, the uncarpeted surface feels colder because it conducts heat away from your body more rapidly.

Explanation

 The following explanation is intended for the teacher's information. Modify the explanation for students as required.

The goal of this activity is for students to discover that mittens are "warm" because they help to hold in heat from the body and minimize its loss into the air. In other words, mittens act as insulators. Humans are warm-blooded animals. We typically maintain a body temperature of 37°C, or 98.6°F. Except on very hot days, we usually lose some of our body heat to the air and our surroundings. This is because heat flows from materials with higher temperatures to materials with lower ones. One of the purposes of clothing is to hold in our body heat and minimize this heat loss. This is the reason we change the amount and kind of clothes we wear depending on weather.

In this activity, students are asked the question, "Are mittens warm?" Students typically know that mittens are worn in cold weather to keep their hands warm. Depending on their age and maturity, some students may believe that the warmth comes from the mitten itself. With further questioning and collecting of temperatures under various conditions, however, students discover the insulating ability of mittens and the role this plays in keeping their hands warm.

The first several temperatures are taken to allow students to discover that (a) air temperature is usually less than body temperature, and (b) the temperature of a hand (either open- or close-fisted) is typically below "normal" body temperature because heat is lost to the cooler surrounding air.

The final steps of the activity are done to show the insulating ability of the mitten. By itself the not-recently-worn mitten should have the same temperature as the air temperature. With your hand in the mitten, the temperature is higher because your hand is providing heat to warm the thermometer. This temperature is also greater than the previously recorded temperature of the palm without the mitten. The mitten prevents the cold air from the outside from making contact with your hand; the mitten insulates your hand from the cold surroundings. Thus, our hands are warmer when we have mittens on.

Assessment

Options:

- Have students complete one of the two Assessment Sheets (provided): "Temperature Levels" or "Are All Mittens Alike?"

- Ask students to predict what would happen to the temperature if a student put the thermometer in a mitten that's just been removed from a hand. Have them try this experiment and record and explain the results.

Home, safety, and career:
- Discuss how to dress to stay warm and how weather affects what we wear.

Language arts:
- Read aloud or suggest that students read the following book:
  - *Thumpity Thump Gets Dressed*, by Cyndy Szekeres (Western, ISBN 0307122034)
    A young rabbit changes clothes many times during the day as the weather also changes.

Life science:
- Discuss the ability of certain mammals, such as whales and penguins, to retain body heat in frigid water.

Math:
- Calculate changes in temperature.

Social studies:
- Start an aluminum can drive or other fund-raiser within your school. Use the money collected to purchase mittens and gloves for the needy.
- Discuss changing seasons, the weather in different locations, and adapting clothing to the weather.

Reference

Watson, B. "Teaching for Conceptual Change: Confronting Children's Experience," *Phi Delta Kappan.* May 1990, 680–685.

Contributors

Susan Brutsche, Bellevue City Schools, Bellevue, OH; Teaching Science with TOYS, 1991–92.
Diana James, Farmers Elementary School, Farmers, KY; Teaching Science with TOYS, 1991–92.
Sherril Newman, Huntsville Elementary School, Huntsville, OH; Teaching Science with TOYS, 1992–93.
Sandy Roser, Webster Elementary School, Hillsboro, OH; Teaching Science with TOYS, 1993–94.
Phyllis Wilkes, Harvey Rice School, Cleveland, OH; Teaching Science with TOYS, 1991–92.

Handout Masters

Masters for the following handouts are provided:
- Predict that Temperature—Data Sheet
- Temperature Levels—Assessment Sheet
- Are All Mittens Alike?—Assessment Sheet

Copy as needed for classroom use.

ARE MITTENS WARM?

Predict that Temperature—Data Sheet

Predict what the temperature will be and record the actual temperature.

Condition	Prediction	Actual Temperature	Was your prediction high or low?
Temperature in the room			
Temperature of your palm without mitten on			
Temperature of hand with closed fist (no mitten)			
Temperature of empty mitten			
Temperature of your palm with mitten on			

Use a red crayon to circle the warmest actual temperature. Use a blue crayon to circle the coolest actual temperature.

ARE MITTENS WARM?

Temperature Levels—Assessment Sheet

1. From your data sheet, record the actual temperature for each of these experiments.

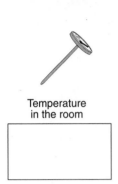  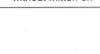 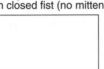

Temperature in the room	Temperature of your palm without mitten on	Temperature of hand with closed fist (no mitten)	Temperature of empty mitten	Temperature of your palm with mitten on

2. The following pictures represent Celsius thermometers. Color in the liquid to the level that corresponds to the temperatures for each case.

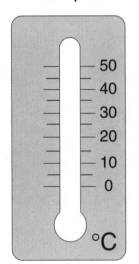 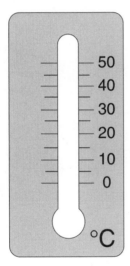 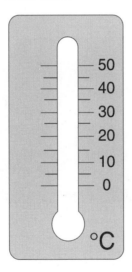 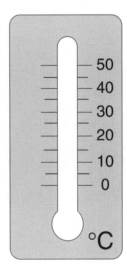 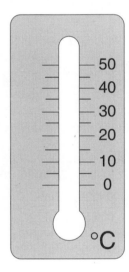

3. Which temperature is the highest? Why do you think this experiment had the highest temperature?

_____

_____

_____

_____

ARE MITTENS WARM?

Are All Mittens Alike?—Assessment Sheet

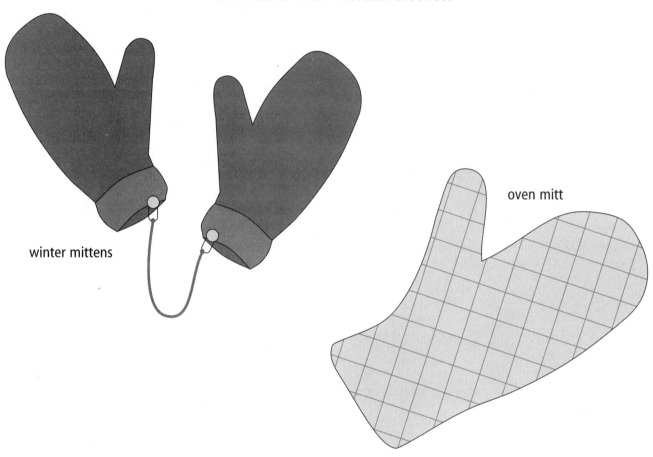

winter mittens

oven mitt

You may have observed an adult using an oven mitt to handle things from the oven. How is the oven mitt helpful? Describe its properties. Compare or contrast the oven mitt and the winter mittens.

_____

_____

_____

_____

_____

_____

_____

_____

MAGIC WORMS

What makes the paper worms "grow" when water is dropped on them?

Drinking straws and "Magic Worms"

GRADE LEVEL

Science activity appropriate for grades K–3
Cross-Curricular Integration intended for grades K–3

KEY SCIENCE TOPICS

- absorption
- capillary action

KEY PROCESS SKILLS

• observing	Students observe the behavior of various types of paper when they are wet.
• measuring	Students measure the length of their Magic Worms before and after addition of water.
• hypothesizing	Students hypothesize reasons for the motion of the paper worm.

TIME REQUIRED

Setup	5	minutes
Performance	30	minutes
Cleanup	10	minutes

Materials

For "Introducing the Activity"
Per student or group
- clear plastic cup
- about 1 cup water
- magnifying lens
- a strip of wax paper
- a strip of paper towel
- piece of sponge
- construction paper
- piece of writing paper
- (optional) scissors and paste (to cut and paste objects on "Which Will Absorb Water?" Data Sheet)
- (optional) crayons or markers (to color Data Sheet)

For the "Procedure"

Per student

- 2–3 straws with paper wrapping intact

You could have students bring these in. The paper wrapping on some straws may split when pushed down, so you may wish to have extra straws on hand.

- food color
- small cup to hold water
- 1–2 teaspoons water
- (optional) ruler

For "Variations and Extensions"

❶ Per class
- clear plastic cup
- about 1 cup water
- magnifying lens
- different brands of paper towels

❷ Per class
- food color
- stalk of celery or a white flower

Safety and Disposal

No special safety or disposal procedures are required.

Introducing the Activity

1. Have students make predictions about what will happen when they dip the paper towel, wax paper, construction paper, writing paper, and sponge in water. (Use the provided "Which Will Absorb Water?" Data Sheet to record predictions.) Ask, "What will happen to the water in the cup? What will happen to the water on the material?"

2. Have the students dip each strip (paper towel, wax paper, construction paper, writing paper, and sponge) in water. Have the students observe what happens to each strip and discuss. Ask, "How does each feel? Which soaked up the water the fastest?" Have the students use magnifying lenses to examine the five strips.

3. Define the word "absorb," meaning "to soak up." Ask, "Which strip absorbed the water fastest? What caused the water to be absorbed?"

Procedure

1. Give each student a straw with the paper covering intact and, if desired, the "Make a Magic Worm" Directions and Observations sheet (provided).

2. Have students hold the straws upright, with one end on the table or desk.

3. Have students grasp the paper covering at the top of the straw and push the paper firmly down to the bottom of the straw. (See Figure 1.)

Figure 1: Push the paper wrapper firmly
down the straw to make the "worm."

4. Have students carefully remove straws and examine their Magic Worms.

5. (optional) Have students measure the length of their Magic Worms.

6. Ask students to predict what will happen when a drop of water is added to the worm.

7. Have students use the straw to place a drop of water on the worm (See Figure 2) and then examine the expanded worm to find out if their predictions are correct. Discuss.

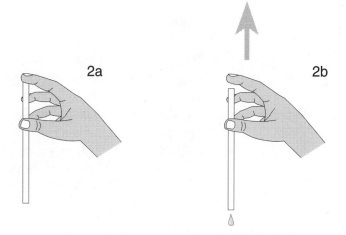

Figure 2: (a) Place one end of the straw in water and put your
finger over the other end. (b) Hold the straw over the worm
and lift your finger to place a drop of water on the worm.

8. (optional) Have the students measure the length of their worms again and complete "Willie's Growth Chart" Data Sheet (provided).

9. Have students repeat the activity using colored water.

Variations and Extensions

1. Try repeating "Introducing the Activity" with different brands of paper towels. Which brand is the most absorbent?

2. Place a stalk of celery or a white flower (with the bottom freshly cut) into food color to show how food color can be carried up the stem.

Explanation

 The following explanation is intended for the teacher's use. Modify the explanation for students as required.

When water comes in contact with a porous surface such as that of paper or a sponge, it tends to be absorbed (soaked up) into the pores of the material, moving throughout the material, even rising against the force of gravity. This is because the attractive force between the water molecules and the molecules in the paper or sponge is greater than the downward force of gravity on the water molecules. In a similar way, capillary action plays an important part in the growth of plants by allowing water from the soil to travel into the roots and up through the stem.

Assessment

Have students draw a picture of a dry Magic Worm and a wet Magic Worm and write a sentence about both.

Cross-Curricular Integration

Language arts:
- Read the book *Inch by Inch* by Leo Lionni (Mulberry, ISBN 0688132839) to the class. In this story, to keep from being eaten, an inchworm measures a robin's tail, a flamingo's neck, a toucan's beak, a heron's legs, and a nightingale's song. Discuss how an inchworm moves from place to place. Ask the students to imagine what problems they would have if they were inchworms. Then put together an inchworm book for each student:
   - Put two pieces of construction paper together, fold in half and staple.
   - Punch a hole in the center of each page.
   - Tie a knot in one end of an 8-inch piece of heavy green yarn. Pull the yarn through all the holes. Tie a knot in the other end of the yarn. This is how the inchworm inches his way through the book.

   Have the students finish the inchworm books (See Figure 3):
   - Draw small green inchworm heads near the holes on each right hand page.
   - Draw the background for the inchworms on each page.
   - Write a short sentence to go with each illustration.

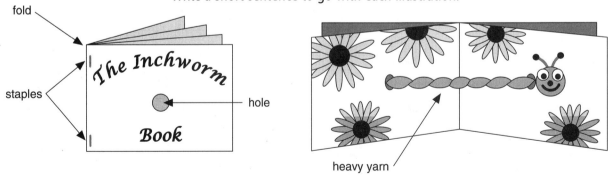

Figure 3: Fold and staple the book, then have students string heavy yarn between the holes.

Life science:
- Discuss how capillary action moves water up the stems of plants.

Math:
- Do Extension 1 and make a bar graph of the results.

Reference

"Two-toned Flower;" *Fun with Chemistry: A Guidebook of K–12 Activities;* Sarquis, M., Sarquis, J., Eds.; Institute for Chemical Education: Madison, WI, 1993; Vol. 2, pp 9–11.

Contributors

Charlotte Austin, Monroe Elementary School, Monroe, OH; Teaching Science with TOYS, 1993–94.

Pat King, Fairfield Central School, Fairfield, OH; Teaching Science with TOYS, 1992.

Kim Kline, Central Elementary School, Lawrenceburg, IN; Teaching Science with TOYS, 1992–93.

Carol Voss, Forest View Elementary School, Cincinnati, OH; Teaching Science with TOYS, 1991–92.

Gerri Westwood, Berkeley Elementary School, Spotsylvania, VA; Teaching Science with TOYS, 1992.

Handout Masters

Masters for the following handouts are provided:
- Which Will Absorb Water?—Data Sheet
- Make a Magic Worm—Directions and Observations
- Willie's Growth Chart—Data Sheet

Copy as needed for classroom use.

Name _____   Date _____

MAGIC WORMS

Which Will Absorb Water?—Data Sheet

❶ Predict which materials will absorb water. Color those objects blue.

❷ Predict which materials will not absorb water. Color those objects red.

❸ Now dip the real objects in the water.

❹ Cut and paste the pictures at the bottom of this page onto the chart below to represent the results of your experiment.

These absorb water:	These do not absorb water:

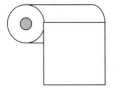
paper towel

wax paper

construction paper

writing paper

sponge

MAGIC WORMS

Make a Magic Worm—Directions and Observations

Materials:

- straw with paper covering
- water

Directions:

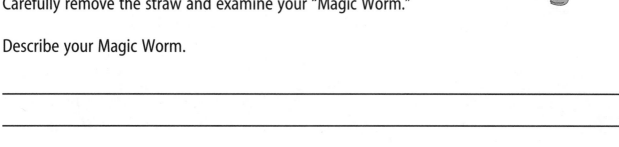

1. Hold your straw upright with one end on the table or desk.

2. Grasp the paper covering at the top of the straw and push the paper firmly down to the bottom of the straw.

3. Carefully remove the straw and examine your "Magic Worm."

   Describe your Magic Worm.

   _____

   _____

   _____

4. What do you think will happen when you add a drop of water to your worm?

   _____

   _____

   _____

5. Use your straw to place a drop of water on your worm.

   Describe what happened to your Magic Worm.

   _____

   _____

   _____

   _____

MAGIC WORMS

Willie's Growth Chart—Data Sheet

Color in a segment on Willie Worm for each centimeter your "Magic Worm" grew. Use another color for the rest of Willie. Compare your worm with that of a friend! Graph all your friends' worms. Whose grew the most? The least?

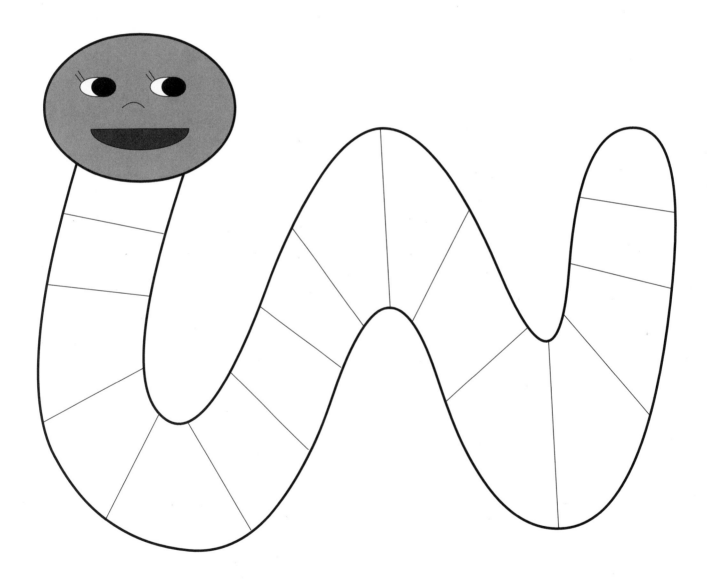

FORTUNE-TELLING FISH

How does a Fortune-Telling Fish work?

A cellophane Fortune-Telling Fish

GRADE LEVELS

Science activity appropriate for grades K–6
Cross-Curricular Integration intended for grades K–3

KEY SCIENCE TOPICS

- absorption
- nature of paper/cellophane

KEY PROCESS SKILLS

• inferring	Students infer that cellophane absorbs water by observing its behavior in their hands and in water.
• hypothesizing	Students solve the riddle of the Fortune-Telling Fish by observing its behavior under different conditions.

TIME REQUIRED

Setup	5	minutes
Performance	10–15	minutes
Cleanup	5	minutes

Materials

For the "Procedure"
Per group
- water
- 1 zipper-type plastic bag
- 1 Fortune-Telling Fish

 The Fortune-Telling Fish (# 747) can be purchased from GTA, 2201 107th Lane NE, Blaine, MN 55434; (800) 328-1226.

Safety and Disposal

No special safety or disposal procedures are required.

Getting Ready

Put each fish into a zipper-type plastic bag and seal.

Introducing the Activity

Discuss the sweat glands in the hand. Tell students that the moisture from sweat glands will cause the cellophane fish to move. Introduce the word hygroscopic. "Hygro" means water, and "scopic" means to view or find. Hygroscopic means to find water. Tell students that cellophane will readily absorb water.

Procedure

1. Give each group a Fortune-Telling Fish in a zipper-type plastic bag.

2. Have one student in each group take the Fortune-Telling Fish out of the bag and place it in the palm of the hand. The group should make observations, pass the Fortune-Telling Fish around so each member has a try, and record their observations. (The fish curls up and moves around.)

3. Have each group return the Fortune-Telling Fish to the plastic bag and pass the bag around the group, giving each member a chance to place the fish in the bag in the palm of their hand as in Step 2. The group should record their observations. (The fish does not curl up or move around.)

4. Have students propose reasons for the difference in the behavior of the fish inside and outside of the bag. (Students will probably suggest that either moisture or heat from the hand could be causing the changes.)

5. Challenge the students to design an experiment that could rule out one of these factors. If they place the plastic bag on the palm and the fish on top of the plastic bag, they will observe that the fish does not curl up. (The plastic provides a barrier to the moisture from the hand but not to the heat; therefore, we can rule out heat as a cause of the fish's behavior.)

Explanation

The following explanation is intended for the teacher's information. Modify the explanation for students as required.

The Fortune-Telling Fish curls, twists, and bends in the palm of your hand because the cellophane absorbs moisture from your hand. As the side of the fish toward your hand absorbs moisture, the paper begins to swell (like a flattened sponge swells when it gets wet). This causes the ends of the Fortune-Telling Fish to curl up, away from your hand. The lightness of cellophane makes it very susceptible to air currents, which adds to the effect as the Fortune-Telling Fish seemingly dances in your hand.

This type of movement does not occur when the Fortune-Telling Fish is inside the plastic bag. The plastic bag presents a barrier that prevents the absorption of water from your palm by the cellophane. As a result, the Fortune-Telling Fish does not move.

Teaching Chemistry with TOYS

Assessment

Options:

- Invite the principal into class and have the students lead him or her through the activity. Encourage the students to ask the principal questions as they present the activity to be sure he or she understands their explanation.

- Have the students write a sentence about the source of energy that drives the movement of the Fortune-Telling Fish.

Cross-Curricular Integration

Language arts:

- Have students write a set of fortunes to replace those which come with the fish.

Life science:

- Explore the nature of sweat glands and their location in the body.

Reference

White, L.B. *Investigating Science with Paper;* Addison-Wesley: Reading, MA, 1970; pp 54–55.

Contributor

Pat Williams, Forest View Elementary School, Cincinnati, OH; Teaching Science with TOYS, 1988–89.

PAINT WITH WATER BOOKS

How do different solvents affect the paint in Paint with Water books?

A Paint with Water book

GRADE LEVELS

Science activity appropriate for grades K–12
Cross-Curricular Integration intended for grades K–3

KEY SCIENCE TOPICS

- dissolving
- polar/nonpolar substances
- solubility
- solvents

KEY PROCESS SKILLS

- classifying — Students classify the ability of different solvents to dissolve paint from a Paint with Water picture.

- inferring — Students develop ideas of solubility from experimenting with Paint with Water pictures.

TIME REQUIRED

Setup	5	minutes
Performance	10–20	minutes
Cleanup	5	minutes

Materials

For the "Procedure"
Per student
- 1 page from a Paint with Water book
- 1 piece of regular white notebook or writing paper

Per group of students
- magnifying lens
- 4 labels or masking tape
- 4 cotton swabs (such as Q-tips®)
- 4 small containers (such as baby food jars or plastic or paper cups)

➤ *Do not use polystyrene.*

- (optional) ruler
- water
- vegetable or baby oil
- 2 or more of the following solvents:
  - vinegar
  - rubbing alcohol (70% isopropyl alcohol)

- milk
- colorless or light-colored soda pop or juice
- bubble solution

For "Variations and Extensions"

❶ Per student
- ball-point pen
- fine-tip markers that contain water-soluble ink
- piece of white, unlined paper

❷ All materials listed for the "Procedure" plus the following:
- goggles
- substitute 2 or more of the solvents below for the solvents in the "Procedure":
  - 91–99% isopropyl alcohol
  - ethyl rubbing alcohol (70% ethyl alcohol)
  - acetone-containing fingernail polish remover
  - non-acetone-containing fingernail polish remover

 All of these solvents should be available from a drug store.

Safety and Disposal

Because of the volatile nature of some of the solvents used, adequate ventilation is necessary. Be sure the students do not taste the solvents used. Isopropyl alcohol is flammable; keep flames away. Goggles should be used if concentrated isopropyl alcohol or acetone-containing solutions are used. Unused solvents can be saved or flushed down the drain. If you choose to use liquids other than those listed in "Materials," test them ahead of time. Some household items should not be included because of their reactivity, flammability, or toxicity. DO NOT USE:
- toilet cleaners, drain cleaners, or other household bases which react with cleaners containing ammonia or chloramines to generate ammonia gas;
- hypochlorite ("chlorine") bleach (such as Clorox®) which reacts with acids found in vinegar, soft drinks, citrus drinks, and some cleaners to produce highly toxic chlorine gas; or
- antifreeze that contains ethylene glycol. (Ethylene glycol tastes sweet but is very toxic, and ingestion can be fatal.)

Getting Ready

For younger children, the teacher may want to prepare the page from the Paint with Water book as described in Step 1 of the "Procedure."

Label the containers for the solvents and fill them with a small amount of the appropriate liquid.

Introducing the Activity

Ask students if they have ever used plain water to color a piece of paper. Allow them to discuss this question. Then take out the Paint with Water books and point out the name. Ask them what this means. Distribute a Paint with Water sheet and a regular piece of paper to each student or group of students. If they've never seen a Paint with Water book before, let them examine a page. Give each group a magnifying lens and let them examine the page closely. Ask them how the pages differ, but don't answer the question yet. Allow them to swab some water onto the plain paper and observe that there is no color change. Then allow them to do the same on the Paint with Water page. Discuss possible reasons for the differences.

Procedure

1. Have the students divide the Paint with Water pictures into quarters using a pencil and ruler or by folding the paper in half lengthwise and then in half widthwise.

2. Have students write the name of a different solvent to be used in each of the four sections of the picture. (See "Materials" for recommended solvents.)

3. Instruct the students to use a cotton swab which has been dipped into the appropriate solvent to paint each section. They should use a different cotton swab for each solvent and should not mix the swabs and containers.

4. While the pictures are still wet, have students use a magnifying lens to examine the four sections and observe the differences in the appearance of the paper and color of the paint. (A "Wet and Dry Pictures" Observation Sheet is provided.)

5. Allow the pictures to dry and again have the students examine the paper and colors. Compare the observations to those made in Step 4. Also compare results with others in the class.

Variations and Extensions

1. Have students try making their own Paint with Water pictures: First, draw a picture with a pencil or ballpoint pen. Then place small dots of ink from fine-tipped markers that contain water-soluble ink. Once the picture has dried, paint the picture with water or test it with the solvents used in the "Procedure."

Certain liquids are inappropriate for use in this activity. DO NOT USE bleach, antifreeze, ammonia, or household bases. See "Safety and Disposal." Fingernail polish remover should be dispensed from its original container, paper cup, or other container which must first be checked to ensure it is not made of a material which will dissolve in the polish remover.

2. Older students may wish to paint with liquids containing different amounts of water to determine if there is an observable difference in the ability of the liquids to dissolve the paint. For example, students could use different types of alcohol solutions or different concentrations of alcohol solutions:

   • rubbing alcohol (70% isopropyl alcohol)
   • 91–99% isopropyl alcohol
   • ethyl rubbing alcohol

   They might also test acetone-containing and non-acetone-containing types of fingernail polish remover.

3. Set up a Paint with Water station in your classroom where students can create their own Paint with Water pictures during free time.

Explanation

 The following explanation is intended for the teacher's information. Modify the explanation for students as required.

Most books use inks which are not water soluble (do not dissolve in water). As a result, the ink will not run even if you brush water on it. In contrast, the colored inks on the page of a Paint with Water book are water soluble. These water-soluble colors are applied as small dots inside the dark lines outlining the picture. Of course, these dark lines are made from water-insoluble inks. When water is applied with a paint brush or cotton swab, the water dissolves some of the paint and the brush or swab spreads the color across the page.

Besides testing the effect of water on these water-soluble inks, this activity tests the effects of other solvents. Not surprisingly, solvents that contain large amounts of water (for example, milk, soda, and juice) give similar results to the water. In contrast, oil has very little effect on water-soluble inks. As a "rule of thumb," one substance will dissolve in another if the two substances are similar—hence the expression, "Like dissolves like." As a result, the students can conclude that the water-soluble inks do not dissolve in oil because they are not similar to oil.

Chemists often describe the nature of solvents in terms of being "polar" or "nonpolar." Water (a polar substance) dissolves other polar materials, such as acetic acid (found in vinegar) and sugar, as well as ionic substances such as salts. Oil, on the other hand, is nonpolar. Oil dissolves other nonpolar substances such as some inks, grease, and some types of dirt; it does not dissolve salt or sugar.

Students may note another interesting phenomenon when oil is tested as a solvent. Oil affects the nature of the paper itself and causes it to appear almost transparent. (This effect is similar to that observed when paper is coated with wax to make wax paper.) This phenomenon is not very well understood. Some sources suggest that reflection of light from white paper is due in part to light scattering from the unbonded surfaces of the fibers in the paper. The various liquids poured on the paper somehow change this unbonded nature, so that the light is scattered less, hence reflectance decreases, allowing the light to penetrate. Other sources suggest that because paper is made of many layers of tiny fibers with air in between, the speed of light constantly changes as it passes through the material. When oil (or another similar liquid) is added, the molecules of liquid move into the spaces between the fibers. The light passes through oil and paper at about the same speed, and as a result, less light is scattered and the paper appears more transparent. Most papers contain sizing materials which reduce the ability of water to wet the sheet. As a result, water does the poorest job of making the paper transparent. The sizing materials seem to have little effect on oils and certain other organic liquids.

Assessment

Ask students to explain why Paint with Water books have that name. Ask them to make up a name for a book that includes an oil-soluble ink.

Art:
- Bring in a paper sample book from a Japanese paper company. The paper is usually made of mulberry fibers and often is translucent with tiny flowers or other items embedded in it. You can order a book with 150 3½-inch by 6¾-inch samples from Aiko's Art Materials, 3347 North Clark Street, Chicago, IL 60657; (312) 404-5600.
- Have students tear pictures out of coloring books and dot them with water-soluble markers. When the pages are dry, have the students paint them with water. For Valentine's Day, have the students cut heart shapes out of coffee filters, dot them with water-soluble markers, and paint them with water. After the filters have dried, have students write valentine messages on them with markers.

Social studies:
- Have the students research the history of paper. Where and when was it first developed? What types of fibers can be used to make paper? Paper companies will provide swatch books free of charge that contain many interesting paper samples.
- Find out how the translucent paper used in Japanese sliding doors (shoji) is made.

References

Barrett, T. *Japanese Paper Making: Traditions, Tools, and Techniques;* Weatherhill: New York, 1992.

Pulp and Paper Chemistry and Chemical Technology Vol. III; Casey, J.P., Ed.; John Wiley and Sons: New York, 1981.

Handout Master

A master for the following handout is provided:
- Wet and Dry Pictures—Observation Sheet

Copy as needed for classroom use.

Name _____   Date _____

PAINT WITH WATER BOOKS
Wet and Dry Pictures—Observation Sheet

Solvent Name _____

Wet _____

_____

_____

Dry _____

_____

_____

Solvent Name _____

Wet _____

_____

_____

Dry _____

_____

_____

Solvent Name _____

Wet _____

_____

_____

Dry _____

_____

_____

Solvent Name _____

Wet _____

_____

_____

Dry _____

_____

_____

WEATHER BUNNIES

*Can we "see" humidity? No, but try making bunnies (or other patterns)
that reflect changes in humidity by changing color.*

A Weather Bunny

GRADE LEVELS

Science activity appropriate for grades 2–8
Cross-Curricular Integration intended for grades 2–6

KEY SCIENCE TOPICS

- chemical reaction
- humidity
- water

STUDENT BACKGROUND

Students should be aware that humidity is the amount of
moisture in the air.

KEY PROCESS SKILLS

- observing — Students observe the color changes of their "Weather Bunnies."

- collecting data — Students collect data to relate the color of the Weather Bunny to the known humidity.

TIME REQUIRED

Setup	15	minutes
Performance	30	minutes
Cleanup	5	minutes

Materials

For the "Procedure"
Per student
- white blotter paper
- scissors
- small piece of magnetic strip
- white glue
- (optional) decorations for figures

Per class
- several patterns (for example, bunnies, flowers, or umbrellas)
- 25–50 milliliters (mL) 10% aqueous cobalt chloride solution (See "Getting Ready.")

➤ *Cobalt chloride hexahydrate crystals are available from Flinn Scientific, P.O. Box 219, Batavia, IL 60510, (708) 879-6900, and other science education suppliers.*

- spray bottle for cobalt chloride solution
- shallow container such as a box or aluminum pie pan

➤ *If you use a pie pan for this activity, do not use it for food again.*

- containers for measuring and mixing mixtures
- water
- (optional) spray bottle for water
- (optional) hair dryer
- goggles

For "Variations and Extensions"

❷ Per student
- circle of filter paper
- pipe cleaner
- square of tissue paper
- 10% cobalt chloride solution

Safety and Disposal

Cobalt chloride ($CoCl_2$) is harmful if swallowed. It is also a possible skin irritant. Remind students not to taste it and to wash well if skin contact occurs. Goggles must be worn while spraying the cobalt chloride solution, and spraying should be done into a shallow container or box and away from observers.

Unused solution may be stored for future use.

Getting Ready

Prepare 10% cobalt chloride solution by dissolving 5 grams (g) (about 1 teaspoon) cobalt chloride hexahydrate crystals ($CoCl_2 \cdot 6H_2O$) in 50 mL (about ⅕ cup) water.

Procedure

1. Have each student trace a bunny, flower, or other pattern on white blotter paper and cut it out.

2. Have students glue or stick a magnetic strip onto the back of the figure so that it can be attached to a refrigerator, and then have them place the figures in a shallow container.

Students should not be allowed to do this step. Eye protection must be worn while spraying the cobalt chloride solution and spraying should be done into a shallow container or box and away from observers. See "Safety and Disposal" for additional cautions.

3. Spray the figures with the 10% cobalt chloride ($CoCl_2$) solution, taking precautions not to direct it toward any bystanders.

4. Allow the figures to air dry or dry with a hair dryer. Have students observe what happens when the figures dry.

   Avoid handling the figures while wet. Be sure to wash your hands after handling.

5. (optional) Once the figures are dry, the students may wish to decorate them (for example, use pom poms and wiggly eyes to decorate the bunny).

6. Have the students place the dry figures in different locations and observe them for several days.

7. (optional) Spray the figures with a fine mist of water and observe what happens. Use the hair dryer to dry the toy and observe.

Variations and Extensions

Make flowers from filter paper, tissue paper, and pipe cleaner as shown in Figure 1. Spray or dip the filter paper in the 10% cobalt chloride solution and dry as in the activity.

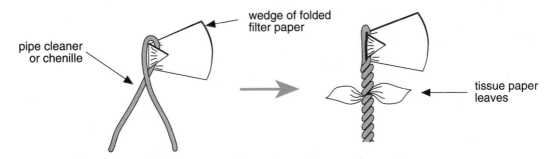

Figure 1: Make flowers from filter paper and pipe cleaners.

Explanation

The following explanation is intended for the teacher's information. Modify the explanation for students as required.

The colors observed in this activity are a result of the loss or gain of water. Anhydrous (without water) cobalt chloride ($CoCl_2$) is blue while cobalt chloride hexahydrate ($CoCl_2 \cdot 6H_2O$) is pink. The blue cobalt chloride is observed when little or no water is present (for example, very dry air). The pink color is observed when the amount of water present is great (for example, humid air or aqueous solutions). A purple color represents a combination of the anhydrous and hydrated form indicating a moderate level of water. The chemical reaction can be represented as follows:

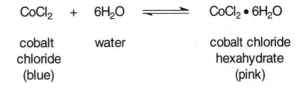

$$CoCl_2 + 6H_2O \rightleftharpoons CoCl_2 \cdot 6H_2O$$

| cobalt chloride (blue) | water | cobalt chloride hexahydrate (pink) |

This reversible reaction provides a method for observing changes in the humidity—pink indicates humid days and blue indicates dry days.

Assessment

Options:

- Have students create pictures of a very humid place, a very dry place, and an in-between place. Give each student a pink, blue, and purple Weather Bunny and ask them to place their colored bunny in the setting that most closely mimics the behavior of the Weather Bunnies under these actual conditions.

- Have the students write a story about giving a Weather Bunny as a gift to a friend and how the friend might use it.

Cross-Curricular Integration

Earth science:

- Use the Weather Bunnies as part of a weather station (a barometer made from the Teaching Science with TOYS activity "Under Pressure" can also be used in the weather station), and discuss how weather predictions are made.
- Have students use the "Is Your Bunny Pink or Blue?" Observation Sheet (provided) to observe and analyze the weather.

Home, safety, and career:

- Study careers in meteorology at the weather bureau and at television stations (weather forecasting).

Language arts:

- Write stories or poems about individual humidity indicators (what if they could talk? …walk?…, or "the day my indicator tried to…").
- Read aloud or suggest that students read one or more of the following books:
  - *A Wet Monday*, by Dorothy Edwards (William Morrow, ISBN 0688320813)
    On one particular rainy Monday, all the members of a family have a difficult day.
- Have the students write descriptive stories about uses of humidity indicators or instructions on how to make humidity indicators.

Reference

"Weather-or-not Flowers;" *Fun with Chemistry: A Guidebook of K–12 Activities;* Sarquis, M., Sarquis, J., Eds.; Institute for Chemical Education: Madison, WI, 1991; Vol. 1, pp 95–98.

Contributor

Julie Klinefelter, Morgan Elementary School, Hamilton, OH; Teaching Science with TOYS, 1991–92.

Handout Master

A master for the following handout is provided:
- Is Your Bunny Pink or Blue?—Observation Sheet

Copy as needed for classroom use.

WEATHER BUNNIES

Is Your Bunny Pink or Blue?—Observation Sheet

Record your observations of the weather and your Weather Bunny each day for five days. Fill in the date, day of the week, and time. Then, based on what color your bunny is, color the blue box blue, or the pink box pink. Describe the day's weather with words or pictures. Record the temperature at the time of your report and the day's relative humidity from your local news or The Weather Channel. Did your bunny predict the weather?

Weather Reporting Chart					
Date and day	Time	Color of your bunny (pink, purple, or blue)	Describe the weather.	Temperature	Relative humidity

Use your chart to answer the following questions. Color a blue box for each blue bunny day, a pink box for each pink bunny day, and a purple box for each purple bunny day.

How many days was the bunny blue?

How many days was the bunny pink?

How many days was the bunny purple?

TWIRLY WHIRLY MILK

Students observe the effect soap (or detergent) has on the movement of food color in milk.

GRADE LEVELS

Science activity appropriate for grades 1–8
Cross-Curricular Integration intended for grades 1–3

KEY SCIENCE TOPICS

- milk fat
- soap and detergent

KEY PROCESS SKILLS

- observing — Students observe the movement of food color in milk and the effect of soap on the movement.

- controlling variables — Students determine the effect of different percentages of milk fat on the flow of food color.

TIME REQUIRED

Setup	5	minutes
Performance	20	minutes
Cleanup	5	minutes

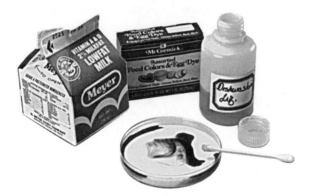

Twirly Whirly Milk materials

Materials

For the "Procedure"

Per student or group

- very small plastic cup or petri dish
- about ¼ cup whole milk
- several different food colors in dropper bottles
- 2–3 cotton-tipped swabs (such as Q-tips®)
- a few drops of dishwashing liquid (soap or detergent)

For "Variations and Extensions"

❶ All materials listed for the "Procedure" except
- substitute ¼ cup water for the milk

❷ All materials listed for the "Procedure" except
- substitute ¼ cup of each of the following for the whole milk:
  - 2% milk
  - skim milk
  - half-and-half
  - cream

❸ Per student
  • 30 mL cold whipping cream
  • small glass jar with lid

Safety and Disposal

Caution students not to drink the milk used in this activity. No special disposal procedures are required.

Procedure

1. Pour about ¼ cup milk into each group's plastic cup or petri dish.

Have the students do the following:

An optional "What Happens to Your Milk?" Observation Sheet containing student directions is provided.

2. Place a drop of food color on the surface of the milk without stirring. Add two or more drops of different colors. Watch to see whether the colors spread out or stay together in the milk.

3. Touch one end of a dry cotton swab to a food color drop and observe what happens.

4. Wet the other end of the swab with dishwashing liquid and touch it to the food color drops. Observe the movement of colors and the milk.

Variations and Extensions

1. Repeat the activity using water instead of milk.

2. To determine the effects of different percentages of milk fat, have students repeat the experiment with 2% milk, skim milk, half-and-half, and cream. Have them describe the differences.

3. A natural extension of this activity is any butter-making activity. One way to make butter is to pour about 30 mL of cold whipping cream into a small glass jar, screw the lid on tightly, and shake the jar vigorously. After about 5 minutes, butter will form.

Explanation

The following explanation is intended for the teacher's information. Modify the explanation for students as required.

When the food color is placed on the surface of the milk, the drops remain essentially intact with little to no spreading. This lack of spreading is due to the fact that the water-based food color does not readily mix with milk. This is because milk is a suspension of fat globules in water and the food color is a water-soluble dye. In general, fat globules and water (and thus food color) do not dissolve in each other. As a result, there is little mixing. In contrast, food color placed in water (Extension 1) diffuses throughout the water and colors it.

When soap (or detergent) is added to the surface of the milk, the soap spreads out over the surface and causes the food color to swirl about. Several factors need to be considered to understand the cause of the swirling motion, including the nature of soap and fat molecules.

Figure 1 shows the structure of sodium stearate, a common soap molecule. Soap (and detergent) molecules have two distinctly different parts. The long chain of carbon and hydrogen atoms is referred to as the nonpolar tail and the charged group on one end is called the polar head.

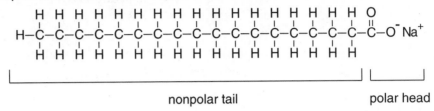

nonpolar tail   polar head

Figure 1: Sodium stearate, a common soap molecule, has a polar head and a nonpolar tail.

Like the nonpolar tail of soap, fats and oils also contain large numbers of carbon and hydrogen atoms. This similarity in structure allows the nonpolar tail of soap to dissolve in globules of fats and oils, creating structures called micelles. Micelles look much like oranges with cloves poked through the rinds. (See Figure 2.) Part of the swirling and churning motion you see when you add soap to your dish of milk is a result of the attraction between the soap molecules and the fat molecules in the milk.

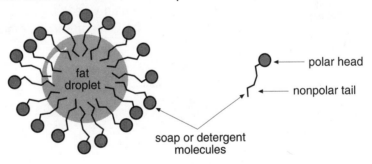

Figure 2: Soap forms a micelle around a fat droplet.

As the soap spreads across the surface of the milk, more and more fat globules are pulled to the spreading soap. As these fat globules congregate, the water in the milk is pushed away, taking the food color with it. The movement in the milk will subside as the soap becomes "used-up" (forming micelles). The addition of more soap can often reactivate the swirling and churning motion. Eventually however, the system will reach equilibrium (uniform distribution of fat globules-soap micelles), and the motion will stop.

Assessment

Have students complete the "Milk and Fat" Assessment Sheet.

Cross-Curricular Integration

Art:
- Have students create cartoons or posters persuading others to eat low-fat foods.

Language arts:
- Read aloud or suggest that students read one or more of the following books:
  - *From Grass to Butter* by Ali Mitgutsch (Carolrhoda, ISBN 0-87614-156-4)
    This book explains how milk is made, from grass to finished product.
- Interview a grandparent, great-grandparent, or another older member of the family about how milk was obtained and packaged when they were young. Did they buy it in the store? Did they milk cows? Was milk packaged the way it is today?
- Have students write creative stories about spending a day at a dairy farm.
- Have students write funny or serious poems about low-fat diets.

Life science:
- Discuss the different milk-fat content in skim milk, whole milk, and cream.
- Discuss the nutritional value of dairy products and the health dangers of a high-fat, high-cholesterol diet.
- Have students plan a low-fat menu.
- Take the class on a tour of a dairy farm if one is nearby.
- Visit a grocery store and check the fat content on various food labels.

Music:
- Show "A Day at Old McDonald's Farm," a Viewmaster Sing-Along Video, Warner Brothers, Together Again Video Production (approximately 30 minutes). This would be suitable for first and second grades.

References

Alexander, A.; Bower, S. *Science Magic;* Prentice-Hall: New York, 1986; pp 34–35.

Cassady, T. et al. "Food Colors in Milk;" Henkel Corporation—Emery Group; *Partners for Terrific Science*, Terrific Science: Middletown, OH.

"Mixable Unmixables;" *WonderScience;* November 1987; Vol. 1, No. 4, pp 2–3.

Sarquis, M.; Kibbey, B.; Smyth, E. "A Jar Full of Mystery;" *Science Activities for Elementary Classrooms;* Flinn Scientific: Batavia, IL, 1989; pp 1–4.

Contributors

Carol Schelbert, Randall Elementary School, Peru, IN; Teaching Science with TOYS, 1993–94.

Jean Wagner, Demmitt Elementary School, Vandalia, OH; Teaching Science with TOYS, 1989–90.

Handout Masters

Masters for the following handouts are provided:
- What Happens to Your Milk?—Observation Sheet
- Milk and Fat—Assessment Sheet

Copy as needed for classroom use.

Name _____   Date _____

TWIRLY WHIRLY MILK

What Happens to Your Milk?—Observation Sheet

1. Pour ¼ cup milk into the plastic cup. Drop two different food colors onto the surface of the milk. DO NOT STIR! Observe. Describe what happened. Draw a picture on a separate sheet of paper of what you observed or write a sentence telling what you observed. _____

   _____

   _____

2. Touch one end of the cotton swab to a drop of food color. Describe what happened in a sentence, or draw a picture on a separate sheet of paper. _____

   _____

   _____

3. Wet the other end of the cotton swab with dishwashing liquid and touch it to a food color drop. Describe what happened in a sentence, or draw a picture on a separate sheet of paper.

   _____

   _____

4. Now repeat this same procedure using 2% milk, skim milk, cream, and water. Record your findings in the table below.

Liquid	Describe the activity of the drops of food color.

5. In which liquid in Step 4 did the food color drops exhibit the greatest activity? What was the difference? Explain. _____

   _____

   _____

6. Can you think of another exciting name for this experiment?

   _____

Name _____   Date _____

TWIRLY WHIRLY MILK
Milk and Fat—Assessment Sheet

1. Write three sentences telling what you learned from this lesson.

    _____

    _____

    _____

    _____

    _____

    _____

2. How could you use what you have learned to help you choose which milk is better for your health?

    _____

    _____

    _____

    _____

    _____

3. On a separate piece of paper, create a poster to encourage people to eat foods that are low in fat.

4. Write a poem to encourage others to adopt a low-fat diet. Your poem can be funny or serious.

    _____

    _____

    _____

    _____

    _____

Activities for Grades 4–6

Temperature Mixing

Under Pressure

Water Fountain in a Jar

The Amazing Balloon Pump

Pencil Hydrometers

Plastics Do Differ!

Shape Shifters

Pop the Hood

Things that Glow in the Dark

A Collection of Surface Tension Activities

One-Way Screen

Mysterious Sand

Sumi Nagashi

Chromatography Color Burst

TEMPERATURE MIXING

Students experiment to determine that when different amounts of water are mixed, the volumes are additive but temperatures are not.

Temperature mixing

GRADE LEVELS

Science activity appropriate for grades 2–12
Cross-Curricular Integration intended for grades 2–6

KEY SCIENCE TOPICS

- heat energy
- temperature
- volume

STUDENT BACKGROUND

Students should have prior experience using the scientific method, measuring volume, and using and reading thermometers.

KEY PROCESS SKILLS

- predicting — Students predict the final temperature which will result from mixing samples of water of known temperatures.

- controlling variables — Students systematically change the amounts of hot and cold water used in the mixtures.

TIME REQUIRED

Setup	10	minutes
Performance	45	minutes
Cleanup	5	minutes

Materials

For "Getting Ready"
- 3 clear, plastic cups with a capacity of at least 100 milliliters (mL) for each group
- volume measure calibrated in 10-mL graduations, such as a graduated cylinder
- permanent marker
- masking tape

For the "Procedure"

Per group of 3–4 students
- 3 clear plastic, graduated cups prepared in "Getting Ready"
- 1 alcohol or metal cooking thermometer graduated in Celsius degrees

Per class
- volume measure calibrated in 10-mL graduations, such as a graduated cylinder
- cold or ice water
- hot water (from a faucet or coffee maker)
- (optional) 2 appropriately insulated containers to store the hot and cold water until use

Safety and Disposal

Because of the potential breakage of thermometers, alcohol or metal cooking thermometers should be used rather than mercury thermometers. Caution students about the handling of hot water.

No special disposal procedures are required.

Getting Ready

1. Using clear plastic cups with at least 100-mL capacity, prepare three graduated cups for each group as follows: Pour 10 mL water into each cup, and mark the 10-mL line with a permanent marker. Continue adding 10-mL portions of water and mark each as before until you reach 100 mL. Label the marks in 20-mL increments. Label the three cups "hot," "cold," and "mixed." (See Figure 1.)

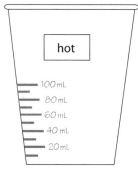

hot

100 mL
80 mL
60 mL
40 mL
20 mL

Figure 1: Mark each cup in 10-mL increments
and label it in 20-mL increments.

2. Be sure that hot and cold water are readily available. If stored for long periods of time, the water should be stored in appropriately insulated containers, such as thermos bottles or ice buckets.

Introducing the Activity

Review the use of a thermometer and temperature and volume measurements with the students. A paper thermometer, blackboard drawing, or overhead transparency may be useful to discuss how a thermometer works and to practice reading a thermometer. Blackboard or overhead transparency drawings can be used to show students the correct way to measure volume by using the lines on the measuring container.

Procedure

1. Distribute the "What's the Temperature?" Data Sheet (provided) to each group of students. Explain to students they will measure volume and temperature for both hot and cold water and record predictions and observations on the Data Sheet. Then have each group complete the following steps.

 Water above 60°C can burn or scald if not handled carefully. Due to the risk of spillage, water above 60°C should not be used with younger students.

2. Pour 30 mL hot water (either hot tap water or water heated in a coffee maker) into the cup labeled "hot."

3. Pour 30 mL cold or ice water into a second cup labeled "cold." Be certain no ice is transferred.

4. Measure and record the temperature of each water sample on the Data Sheet.

5. Predict and record both the volume and the temperature that will result when the cold water is added to the hot water.

6. Pour the cold water into the hot water, mix, and read and record the temperature and volume of the mixture.

7. Have each group of students record its data on the Class Data Chart (provided) and discuss the results of the experiment.

8. Have the students repeat Steps 2–7 above using 20 mL hot water and 40 mL cold water.

9. Have the students repeat Steps 2–7 above using 40 mL hot water and 20 mL cold water.

10. Challenge the students with summarizing questions such as, "Why do you think that you got the measurements that you did from mixing the different volumes of water at the different temperatures? Why didn't all the hot and cold mixtures result in the same temperature? Were your predictions closer to the actual temperature with your first, second, or third trial? Why or why not?"

Variations and Extensions

1. Have the students collect additional data, varying the amount and the temperature of the hot and cold water samples.

2. Have students design an experiment to determine if the order of mixing affects the outcome of the experiment.

Explanation

 The following explanation is intended for the teacher's information. Modify the explanation for students as required.

In this activity, students observe that when mixing samples of water, the volumes are additive, but temperatures are not. To say that volumes are additive means that the final volume of water can be accurately predicted by adding the two volumes that are mixed together. (For example, 30 mL water + 30 mL water = 60 mL water.) However, students observed that in this mixing, the temperature of the final mixture was not the addition of the two starting temperatures. (For example, equal volumes of 10°C water + 40°C water result in about 25°C water, not 50°C.) To address this issue, let's first discuss the term "temperature."

While temperature is a difficult term to precisely define, we all have an intuitive idea of what it means. It is a relative measure of the "hotness." A hot object has a higher temperature than a cold object. If these two objects were placed next to each other, the hot object would become cooler and the cold object would become warmer. These temperature changes result from a loss or gain of heat energy.

Heat flows from things that are warmer to things that are cooler. When two samples of water at different temperatures are mixed, the final water sample will have a temperature somewhere between the two original temperatures. The resulting temperature depends on both the original temperatures and the relative amounts of water in the original samples.

For example, if equal volumes of hot and cold water are used, the resulting temperature should be halfway between the two original temperatures; however, if a greater amount of hot water than cold water is used, the final temperature should be closer to the original temperature of the hot water. Similarly, when more cold water is used, the final temperature should be closer to the original temperature of the colder water.

While the mathematical relationship to determine the final temperature may not be appropriate for class discussion, you might find it useful to know that one exists. The temperature can be estimated by the following relationship:

$$(T_{cold})\left(\frac{V_{cold}}{V_{total}}\right) + (T_{hot})\left(\frac{V_{hot}}{V_{total}}\right) = T_{final}$$

where T_{cold} is the temperature of cold water, V_{cold} is the volume of cold water, T_{hot} is the temperature of hot water, V_{hot} is the volume of hot water, V_{total} is the total volume after mixing, and T_{final} is the temperature of the final mixture. For example, assume you have 20 mL 10°C water which you mix with 40 mL 50°C water. The final temperature would be

$$(10°C)\left(\frac{20mL}{60mL}\right) + (50°C)\left(\frac{40mL}{60mL}\right) = 37°C$$

The relationship above is derived from the more general relationship for heat transfer that uses the temperature, mass, and specific heat of the substances mixed. (Specific heat is a measure of the ability of a substance to absorb heat.) Note that the actual final temperature will be less than calculated as some heat is lost to the cup and air. Don't worry about getting exactly the temperature predicted by the formula; in general, it will be a little lower than predicted due to loss of energy to the container and surroundings.

When discussing the results, you may find it helpful to use blocks to reinforce the concepts. A 1-cm x 1-cm x 30-cm block has a volume of 30 cm³ (volume = l x w x h). If the block was hollow it could hold 30 mL water (1 cm³ = 1 mL). Laying two such blocks each containing 30 mL water next to each other would show the final volume is double that of the initial. The issue of temperature could be addressed by pointing out the temperature can't get any hotter than the hotter block nor colder than the colder block. (See Figure 2.)

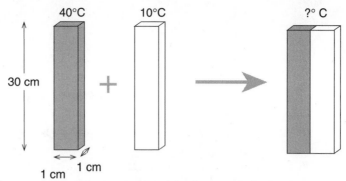

Figure 2: Use blocks to reinforce the concepts.

Assessment

Options:

- Use the completed Data Sheet as a group assessment.

- Adapt the Data Sheet to challenge students to predict what would happen if they mixed water at different temperatures than in the "Procedure."

- Individually question students on such topics as: What happens to the temperature of the water when you mix hot and cold water? What happens to the volume of the water when you mix hot and cold water? An individual written assessment, including completion of the "What Happens to the Water?" Assessment Sheet, is an option for older students.

Cross-Curricular Integration

Math:
- The students add the volumes of water mixed in the experiment.

References

"The Third Degree;" *SAVI/SELPH;* Center for Multisensory Learning; University of California: Berkeley, CA, 1982.

Woodward, L. *Temperature and Thermometers*, University of Southwestern Louisiana, Lafayette, LA, personal communication.

Contributors

Pat Carlin, Pierremont Elementary School, Manchester, MO; Teaching Science with TOYS, 1992.

Julie Klinefelter, Ross Local Schools, Ross, OH; Teaching Science with TOYS, 1991–92.

Jan Rugge, Henry School, Manchester, MO; Teaching Science with TOYS, 1992.

Handout Masters

Masters for the following handouts are provided:
- What's the Temperature?—Data Sheet
- Temperatures and Volumes—Class Data Chart
- What Happens to the Water?—Assessment Sheet

Copy as needed for classroom use.

TEMPERATURE MIXING

What's the Temperature?—Data Sheet

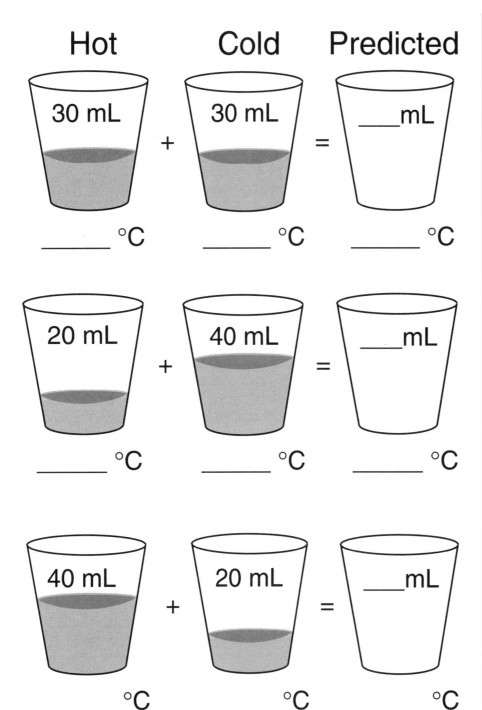

Hot		Cold		Predicted		Actual
30 mL	+	30 mL	=	___mL		___mL
___°C		___°C		___°C		___°C
20 mL	+	40 mL	=	___mL		___mL
___°C		___°C		___°C		___°C
40 mL	+	20 mL	=	___mL		___mL
___°C		___°C		___°C		___°C

TEMPERATURE MIXING

Temperatures and Volumes—Class Data Chart

This is a smaller version of a large chart that would be used to record the results of each group. Whole class discussion on the results would follow. Were predictions the same? Were results the same? If there were differences, can you explain the differences?

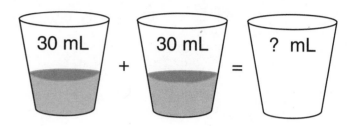

Group Number	Predicted Temperature	Predicted Volume	Actual Temperature	Actual Volume
Group 1				
Group 2				
Group 3				
Group 4				
Group 5				

Name _____   Date _____

TEMPERATURE MIXING

What Happens to the Water?—Assessment Sheet

You have 20 mL water at 40°C and 20 mL water at 60°C. You mix them together.

What will the final temperature be? _____

What will the final volume be? _____

Draw a diagram to show what you think would happen.

Explain your answer. _____

_____

_____

_____

_____

_____

_____

_____

_____

_____

UNDER PRESSURE

Build a simple barometer and use it to observe and predict weather changes.

A homemade barometer

GRADE LEVELS

Science activity appropriate for grades 1–6
Cross-Curricular Integration intended for grades 1–6

KEY SCIENCE TOPICS

- atmospheric pressure
- barometer

KEY PROCESS SKILLS

- observing   Students observe the movement of the barometer pointer under different weather conditions.

- investigating   Students investigate the effects of air pressure changes on their barometer.

TIME REQUIRED

Setup	none
Performance	10 minutes (plus several days to observe)
Cleanup	5 minutes

Materials

For the "Procedure"
Per class (works best as a demonstration)
- large-mouthed glass jar (such as a peanut butter, mayonnaise, or pickle jar)
- 9-inch or larger balloon
- straw or piece of linguine pasta
- scissors
- rubber band
- sheet of construction paper or cardboard
- tape or glue

For "Variations and Extensions"
❸ All materials listed for the "Procedure" plus the following:
Per class
- very hot tap water
- ice water

❹ Per class
 • small baby food jar
 • 1-quart, wide-mouthed jar
 • 2 9-inch balloons
 • glue
 • flat toothpick
 • 2 rubber bands to fit tightly over necks of jars

❺ Per class
 • commercial barometer or other source of atmospheric pressure readings (for example, TV or radio weather report)

Safety and Disposal

No special safety or disposal procedures are required.

Introducing the Activity

Discuss the devices that scientists use to forecast the weather. One device, invented by the seventeenth-century Italian physicist Torricelli, is called the barometer. A barometer measures the pressure, or push, on the earth caused by our atmosphere. Introduce the idea that the class will make a barometer and use it to determine what effect weather has on atmospheric pressure.

Procedure

1. Use a pair of scissors to cut a large flat piece of rubber from a balloon.

2. Stretch the piece of rubber tightly over the mouth of the empty jar and secure it with a rubber band as shown in the photo on page 1. The seal must be tight.

3. Flatten a straw to make a needlelike pointer.
   Some plastic straws do not flatten well. If necessary these can be cut apart to produce a flat needle. A piece of linguine pasta can be used as an alternative.

4. Tape or glue the end of a flattened straw or linguine in the center of the balloon membrane. The straw should extend over the edge of the jar to be used as the "needle" of the barometer. (See photo.)

5. Fold the construction paper or cardboard lengthwise into three equal portions. Unfold and tape the edges together to form a triangular tower. (See Figure 1.)

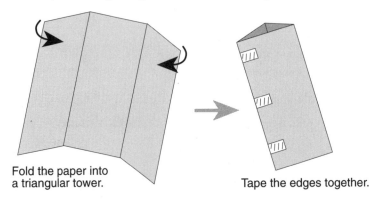

Fold the paper into a triangular tower.

Tape the edges together.

Figure 1: Make a triangular tower.

Teaching Chemistry with TOYS

6. Stand the paper tower beside the jar so that it is just behind the end of the barometer "needle" as shown in the photo at the beginning of the activity.

   If the triangular tower does not stand securely, you may need to tape it to a cardboard base or to the table to provide additional support or prop it up some other way.

7. Photocopy and cut out the scale at the end of the activity (Figure 5) and tape or glue it to the paper tower such that the needle lines up with the zero. (See Figure 2.)

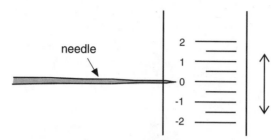

Figure 2: Before securing, adjust scale so that the needle lines up with zero.

8. On the "How's the Weather?" Record Sheet (provided), record the date, the time, and a description of the weather.

9. Place the barometer where it will be undisturbed and away from drafts, windows, and heating and air-conditioning registers.

   Keep the barometer away from extreme temperature changes, as temperature changes can also affect the movement of the needle.

10. Have the students observe the barometer daily and record their observations.

11. See if students can determine why the "needle" changes position. Can they make weather predictions based on the barometer reading?

Variations and Extensions

1. Ask students, "How can we use our own senses to determine weather and weather changes?" (*Hearing—thunder, wind; smell—moisture or pollen in the air; touch—feel the temperature of the air, feel rain and snow, feel changes in wind direction; sight—stormy skies, trees bending in the wind.*)

2. As another weather-predicting activity, make humidity-detecting bunnies or flowers in the Teaching Science with TOYS activity "Weather Bunnies."

3. Determine the effect that temperature has on the volume of the air in the homemade barometer by placing the jar into very hot water and in ice water.

4. The following modification of the barometer activity can be used to allow the teacher (or students) to directly change the external pressure instead of relying on changes in atmospheric pressure.

   • Cut off the top of a balloon. (See Figure 3.)
   • Stretch the bottom section of the cut balloon over the mouth of the baby food jar and secure with a rubber band.
   • Glue the large end of the toothpick to the rubber lid and allow it to dry.
   • Place the small jar inside the wide-mouth jar.
   • Tie the neck of a second balloon.
   • Cut the bottom from this second balloon.

- Stretch the top over the mouth of the large jar and secure the balloon with a rubber band.
- Observe the toothpick on the small jar as you pull up and push down on the balloon stretched across the large jar.

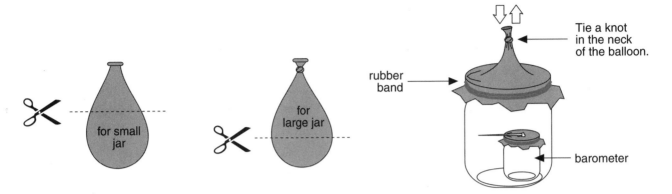

Figure 3: Modify the barometer activity.

5. Compare readings from the homemade barometer with those of a commercial barometer. How good is the homemade barometer at indicating pressure changes?

6. Take students to the playground to play on the seesaw and discuss the similarities between this barometer and a seesaw. (See the "Explanation.") A "Barometer Seesaws" Extension Sheet is provided.

Explanation

> *The following explanation is intended for the teacher's information. Modify the explanation for students as required.*

Because the amount of air inside the jar stays relatively constant, and assuming there are no large fluctuations in temperature, the pressure inside the jar does not change much over the time of the experiment and can be assumed to be about constant. The atmospheric pressure, however, does change with movements of weather fronts. The change in atmospheric pressure causes the pointer of the homemade barometer to move.

The homemade barometer works like a seesaw. Initially, the pressure inside the jar is equal to the pressure outside the jar. (See Figure 4a.) The balloon is flat and the needle points straight out. When the air pressure outside the jar increases, the pressure of the air outside the jar is greater than that on the inside. This excess pressure on the outside pushes down on the surface of the stretched balloon, causing the balloon to become concave (See Figure 4b), and the needle goes up. When the air pressure outside the jar decreases, the pressure of the air trapped inside the jar is greater and so pushes up on the balloon, causing the balloon to become convex (See Figure 4c), and the needle goes down. You can show the relationship between needle position and outside air pressure by collecting data over several weeks or a month. Get the barometric pressure daily from a weather station and read and record the needle position. The higher the barometric pressure, the higher the needle points.

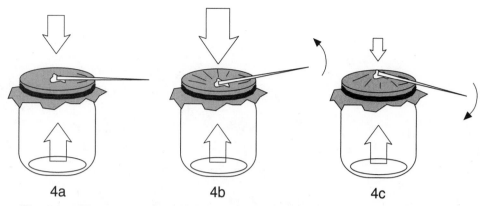

Figure 4: The barometer made in this activity works like a seesaw. Note that the pressure of the air trapped inside the jar stays about constant.

Why does air pressure change? One variable that affects air pressure is altitude. You could measure this effect if you carried a barometer from sea level to the mountains. The gas particles that make up the atmosphere exert force on the surface below, and at sea level, there are more gas particles above you than there are at higher altitudes. Thus, the air pressure is greater at sea level. As you go to higher elevations, there are fewer gas molecules above you, so the pressure is less.

However, you probably aren't hiking from the sea to the mountains with your barometer during this activity—you stay at the same altitude. At a given altitude, air pressure changes with the movement of air masses, the edges of which are called "fronts." As you know from listening to weather reports, when fronts move, the weather usually changes. Typically, high pressure means the incoming air is cool and dry. Commonly, low pressure means that the incoming air is warm and moist, which usually brings bad weather.

It is important to note that the homemade barometer built in this activity is also affected by changes in temperature (Extension 3). Temperature changes can cause the trapped air inside the jar to expand or contract. An increase in temperature increases the volume of the gas, while decreasing the temperature decreases the volume. When the volume increases, the rubber is stretched above the mouth of the jar and the needle drops. When the volume decreases, the rubber is stretched below the mouth of the jar and the needle rises. Thus, if the temperature in the room changes frequently, your pressure data may not correlate with the weather report data.

Assessment

Options:

- Have the students draw pictures showing the position of the barometer needle when the pressure in the room increased and when it decreased.

- After observing the barometer for several weeks, have the students write three sentences telling what they learned about their homemade barometer.

Cross-Curricular Integration

Earth science:

- Use the barometer as part of a weather center, and discuss how weather predictions are made. Have the students chart the weather on weather charts. (The master for a "How's the Weather?" Record Sheet is provided.)

Home, safety, and career:

- Study and discuss careers at the National Weather Service.
- Write a class letter to a weather forecaster and ask him or her to visit your classroom.
- Ask students, "What careers require knowledge of weather conditions and predictions?" *Pilots, outdoor sports, boaters, farmers, truckers, gardeners, house painters, police officers.*

Life science:

- Make a class poster as follows: Discuss the importance of dressing for the weather. Divide a large piece of paper or poster board into four sections and label "Hot," "Cool," "Cold," and "Wet." Have the students look through magazines to find examples of people dressed for these conditions, cut them out and paste them in the appropriate sections.

Social studies:

- Point out Italy on a world map and set the scene as in the seventeenth century. This may give students a better appreciation for Torricelli's work.

Reference

Caney, S. *Steven Caney's Toy Book;* Workman: New York, 1972.

Contributors

Lynn Hogue (activity developer), Winton Woods High School, Cincinnati, OH; Teaching Science with TOYS staff member.

Marilyn Lanich, Springcreek Elementary, Piqua, OH; Teaching Science with TOYS, 1991–92.

Ann Veith, Rosedale Elementary, Middletown, OH; Teaching Science with TOYS, 1991–92.

Handout Masters

Masters for the following handouts are provided:

- How's the Weather?—Record Sheet
- Barometer Seesaws—Extension Sheet

Copy as needed for classroom use.

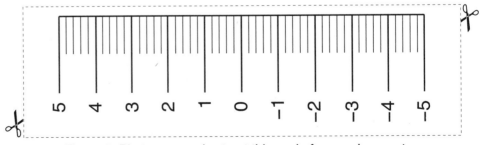

Figure 5: Photocopy and cut out this scale for your barometer.

Name _____   Date _____

UNDER PRESSURE

How's the Weather?—Record Sheet

Record the date and time for each reading. Record the barometer reading in the third blank. In the fourth blank, draw ↑, ↓, or → (no change) to show the change of the barometer needle.

Look for patterns!

Date _____ Time _____ The barometer reading is _____ The barometer went _____

Date _____ Time _____ The barometer reading is _____ The barometer went _____

Date _____ Time _____ The barometer reading is _____ The barometer went _____

Date _____ Time _____ The barometer reading is _____ The barometer went _____

Date _____ Time _____ The barometer reading is _____ The barometer went _____

Date _____ Time _____ The barometer reading is _____ The barometer went _____

Date _____ Time _____ The barometer reading is _____ The barometer went _____

Date _____ Time _____ The barometer reading is _____ The barometer went _____

Date _____ Time _____ The barometer reading is _____ The barometer went _____

Date _____ Time _____ The barometer reading is _____ The barometer went _____

UNDER PRESSURE

Barometer Seesaws—Extension Sheet

High (heavy) pressure

Make a happy child (sunny weather).

When atmospheric pressure is high, it pushes down on our barometer, and the needle goes up.

Low (light) pressure

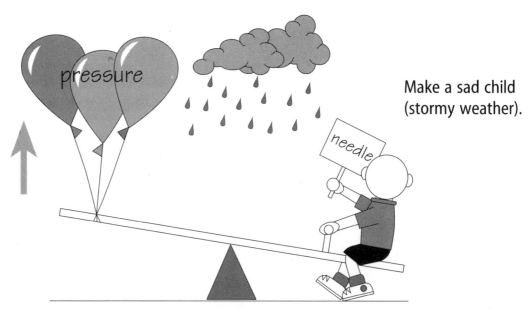

Make a sad child (stormy weather).

When atmospheric pressure is low, the opposite happens.

WATER FOUNTAIN IN A JAR

Make an interesting water fountain to demonstrate the effect of air pressure.

Water fountain apparatus

GRADE LEVELS

Science activity appropriate for grades 5–12
Cross-Curricular Integration intended for grades 5–6

KEY SCIENCE TOPICS

- atmospheric pressure
- siphoning

STUDENT BACKGROUND

Students should be familiar with the concepts of states of matter, air pressure, and siphoning.

KEY PROCESS SKILLS

- inferring   Students infer reasons why some fountains did not work.

TIME REQUIRED

Setup	10–20	minutes
Performance	10–20	minutes
Cleanup	5	minutes

Materials

> ### For "Getting Ready" only
> *These materials are intended for teacher use only.*
>
> - hammer and nail (or punch) or drill and drill bit (sized to make straw-diameter-sized hole)
> - (optional) food color
> - (optional) materials to make a sample fountain

For the "Procedure"
Part A, per group of 3–4 students
- 2 jars or bottles, 1 with a tight-fitting lid

Baby-food jars with safety button lids, canning jars, and juice bottles with metal lids work well. Ask students to bring in clean jars or bottles from home.

- 2 thin, clear plastic straws
- scissors
- oil-based clay or hot glue gun and glue

Part B, per group of 3–4 students
- fountain apparatus made in Part A
- plastic container or tub
- container filled with about 1 L water

 A "pop-beaker" made from a cut-off plastic 2-L soft-drink bottle works well.

For the "Variation"
All materials listed for the "Procedure" plus the following:
Per group
- shallow pan such as a pie pan

For the "Extension"
All materials listed for the "Procedure" plus the following:
Per group
- different-sized straws and/or different-sized jars
- (optional) tubing

Safety and Disposal

The metal edges around the holes in the lids are sharp. If using glass containers, caution students to handle them carefully. If you use hot glue instead of clay, you should be the only one to use the glue gun. The gun and glue are hot and can burn skin and/or melt the straws. No special disposal procedures are required.

Getting Ready

1. Check that the lid fits tightly on one jar of each set by filling the jar with water and inverting it. No water should leak out. (A steady stream of air bubbles indicates a leak.)

2. Make the holes in the jar lids: With the lid off the jar, use the hammer and nail or drill and drill bit to put one hole through the top in the center and one hole about ½ inch to the side. (See Figure 1.)

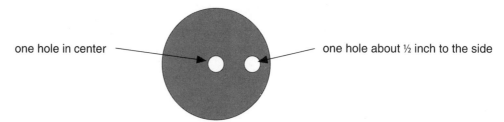

Figure 1: Make holes in the jar lid.

3. (optional) Fill each group's container of water and, if desired, put 3–4 drops of food color into each container.

4. (optional) Construct one fountain as directed in the "Procedure" for students to use as a model as they make their own.

Introducing the Activity

Options:

- Present one or more demonstrations such as a common siphon or "Fountain in a Flask." (See Liem reference.)

- Show students the materials with which they will be working. Ask questions such as, "How could we make a fountain using these jars?"

Procedure

Provide students with a copy of the Student Instruction Sheet (provided) and/or have an actual fountain for students to use as a model.

Part A: Preparing the Fountain

1. Have each group identify the two jars: Jar 1 has no lid and will end up on the bottom, and Jar 2 has the lid and will end up on top.

2. Have each group cut one straw about 1 inch longer than Jar 1 is tall. Tell them not to cut the other straw.

3. With the lid on Jar 2, have students push about 1 inch of the cut straw through the hole in the center.

4. To verify the appropriate amount of protruding straw, students must invert Jar 1 over the straw and onto the lid and adjust the straw as necessary so that it is close to, but not touching, the bottom of Jar 1. (See Figure 2.)

 The closer the straw is to the bottom of Jar 1, the longer the fountain will last.

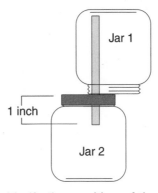

Figure 2: Verify the position of the center straw.

5. Have students remove Jar 1.

6. Have students push about ¼ inch of the uncut straw through the other hole.

 The gun and glue are hot and can burn skin and/or melt the straws.

7. Without disturbing the straw positions, form tight seals between the straws and the lid, either by molding the clay on both sides of the lid or by putting glue on the top side with a glue gun. (See Figure 3.)

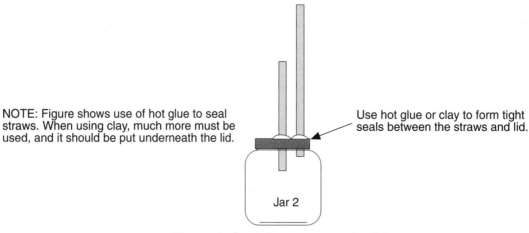

NOTE: Figure shows use of hot glue to seal straws. When using clay, much more must be used, and it should be put underneath the lid.

Use hot glue or clay to form tight seals between the straws and lid.

Jar 2

Figure 3: Seal the straws to the lid.

Part B: Operating the Fountain

1. Have each group pour about 1½ inches of water into Jar 2.

2. Have each group put the lid securely on the jar without disturbing the straws.

3. Have the students nearly fill Jar 1 with water and place it on the edge of a table.

4. Have each group position the plastic container or tub on the floor to catch the water that will be coming out of the long straw.
   Alternatively, students can hold the fountain apparatus over a container placed on the table.

5. Have each group turn Jar 2 upside down with the center straw inside Jar 1 and the other straw outside Jar 1. (See Figure 4.) Ask, "What happens to the water in Jar 1?"

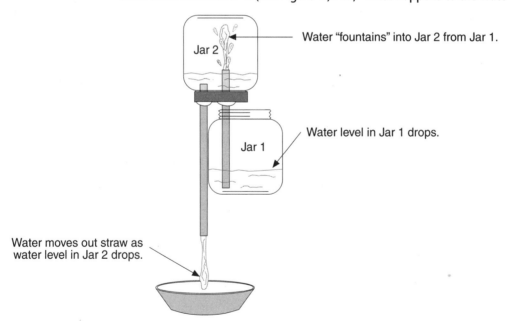

Water "fountains" into Jar 2 from Jar 1.

Jar 2

Water level in Jar 1 drops.

Jar 1

Water moves out straw as water level in Jar 2 drops.

Figure 4: Operate the fountain.

6. Lead students in a discussion of what took place. Ask, "What might be some reasons why some fountains did not work?" *Seals are not tight around the straws or between the lid and jar; the uncut straw is protruding too far into Jar 2, preventing enough water from running out; there are holes in the straws' sides.*

Explanation

 The following explanation is intended for the teacher's information. Modify the explanation for students as required.

The water fountain in this activity is a special kind of siphon. A siphon is a device with which liquid is pushed up and then deposited at a lower level. To create a simple siphon, a tube (usually flexible) is first filled with liquid and then positioned in an inverted "U-shape" (or "J-shape") so that one end is in a container of liquid and the other end is outside and lower.

A simple siphon works because of differences in pressure (water pressure plus atmospheric pressure) on each side. Atmospheric pressure is the force that the Earth's atmosphere exerts on the Earth's surface. This pressure is produced by the mass of the matter that makes up the atmosphere being pulled toward the Earth's surface by gravity. Although atmospheric pressure can change with altitude or with the weather, it will generally remain constant during the time period of this activity.

Figure 5 illustrates a simple siphon. When the water begins flowing out of the tube into the lower container, the atmospheric pressure upon the surface of the water in the upper container forces the water up the short end of the tube. The fluid nature of water allows it to flow in one continuous stream from container A, through the tube, and into container B. The flow continues until the water level in container A drops below the end of the tube (or until the two water levels are the same).

A siphon will only work if the open end of the tube is lower than the end in the liquid. If the open end of the tube is higher than the end in the liquid, water will not continually siphon through the tube. To understand why, assume each end of the tube is in a separate container of liquid. (See Figure 5.) The same atmospheric pressure is exerted on the surface of both containers. But the water pressure inside each side of the tube is different. This pressure is directly proportional to the water height between the bend and each corresponding end. Because there is less water pressure in the shorter side, atmospheric pressure can more easily push the liquid up the shorter side of the bend. If you lowered container A and raised container B, the flow would be reversed. If you held container A and B exactly even, the flow would stop.

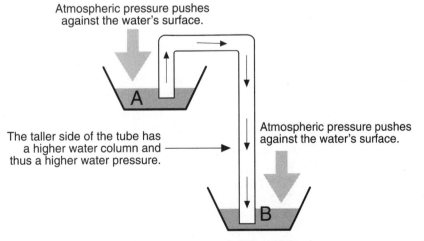

Figure 5: A simple siphon works because of differences in pressure on each side.

In the water fountain, Jar 2 corresponds to the top of a siphon tube and the straws correspond to the two sides. Before starting the fountain, the air pressure inside Jar 2 is equal to the atmospheric pressure. When Jar 2 is inverted, the force of gravity causes some of the water to flow out. Now the air in Jar 2 has a larger volume to occupy. Gases always expand to fill the available volume. When a gas expands, the pressure the gas exerts on the container decreases (at constant temperature). So the air pressure in Jar 2 is less than atmospheric pressure. As a result, the atmospheric pressure now exerts enough pressure on the surface in Jar 1 to force water up the straw (overcoming gravity) and into Jar 2. As long as water keeps flowing out of Jar 2 (keeping the air pressure in the jar less than atmospheric pressure) and the water level in Jar 1 stays above the bottom of the straw, the fountain will continue. If the lid of Jar 2 has a leak, the fountain will not work because air will rush in as the water falls out, which prevents the lowering of air pressure in the jar.

Variation

If the water outlet straw is cut so it does not protrude below Jar 1 (but below the straw inside the jar), the fountain can be placed in a shallow pan to catch the water flowing out.

Extension

Redo the activity by changing one variable at a time: change the diameter and/or length of straws, replace straws with tubing, change the size and/or relative positions of jars, and/or change the amount of water. Time how long the fountain runs for each change in variable.

Cross-Curricular Integration

Earth science:
* Have students investigate the relationship between weather and atmospheric pressure.

Language arts:
* Have students write a paragraph to demonstrate their understanding of atmospheric pressure.
* Have students write a paragraph describing how they would use a siphon or write an advertisement for their siphon products.
* Read aloud or suggest that students read one or more of the following books:
  ○ *Hatchet,* by Gary Paulsen (Puffin, ISBN 0-14-032724-X)
    After a plane crash, a boy survives in the wilderness with the aid of a hatchet. The story includes two topics related to this activity: air pressure in airplanes and a tornado.
  ○ *The Magic School Bus at the Waterworks,* by Joanna Cole (Scholastic, ISBN 0-590-40360-5)
    When Ms. Frizzle's class visits the waterworks, they learn about siphons as well as hydraulics, pipes, pumps, and drains.

Math:
- Practice metric measurement.
- Graph flow times versus straw diameters and/or lengths.

Social studies:
Have students investigate historical and agricultural uses of siphons.

References

Liem, T.L. *Invitations to Science Inquiry;* 2nd ed.; Ginn: Lexington, MA, 1987; p 18.

Walpole, B. *175 Science Experiments to Amuse and Amaze Your Friends;* Random House: New York, 1988; p 64.

Contributor

Jo Parkey, Smith Middle School, Vandalia, OH; Teaching Science with TOYS peer writer.

Handout Master

The master for the following handout is provided:
- Student Instruction Sheet

Copy as needed for classroom use.

WATER FOUNTAIN IN A JAR

Student Instruction Sheet

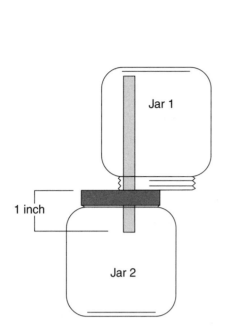
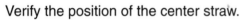

1 inch

Verify the position of the center straw.

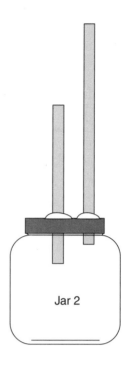

Seal the straws to the lid.

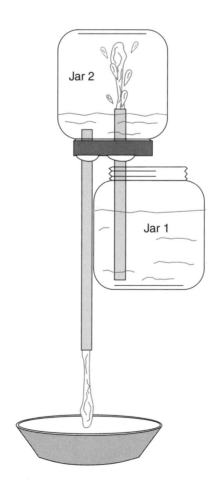

Operate the fountain.

THE AMAZING BALLOON PUMP

How is a balloon pump different from a bicycle pump? In this activity, students find the answer to this question while learning about air pressure and valves.

A balloon pump

GRADE LEVELS

Science activity appropriate for grades 4–12
Cross-Curricular Integration intended for grades 4–6

KEY SCIENCE TOPICS

- air pressure
- gases

STUDENT BACKGROUND

Students should have experience with activities that explore the concept of air pressure.

KEY PROCESS SKILLS

- comparing/contrasting — Students observe the operations of different pumps and compare the effectiveness of the pumps.

- hypothesizing — Students form hypotheses to explain the balloon pump's amazing behavior.

TIME REQUIRED

Setup	5	minutes
Performance	20–30	minutes
Cleanup	5	minutes

Materials

For "Getting Ready" only

These materials, intended for teacher use only, are needed to cut a viewing "window" in a second pump the first time the activity is done. These materials are needed only if the ends of the pump cannot be removed and reattached.

- drill
- saw

For the "Procedure"

Per class
- 1 bicycle pump
- 3 balloons
- 1 rubber band

Per group of 3–4 students
- 1 balloon pump with screw ends (so it can be disassembled and reassembled)

If your balloon pumps do not have screw ends, or if you have only one balloon pump, Part B can be done as a demonstration.

For the "Extensions"

❷ Per class
- air-driven drill or other air-driven tool

Safety and Disposal

The drill and saw used in "Getting Ready" and the air-driven tools used in Extension 2 are intended for teacher use only and should be handled according to manufacturers' specifications. No special disposal procedures are required.

Getting Ready

Ideally, the balloon pump used in this activity should have removable screw ends (allowing the ends to be removed for viewing internal workings and then reattached to make the pump functional again). If the ends of the pump are sealed with glue, try twisting to loosen the glue; however, ends sealed with glue may not be easily reattached. If the ends of the pump cannot be removed and reattached, two pumps will be needed—one to serve as a working pump in Part A and one that has been cut open to provide a viewing "window" that reveals the inner workings for Part B. (Cut a 1-inch x 6-inch viewing window into the side of the pump with a drill and saw.)

Introducing the Activity

Use your mouth to blow up a balloon in the normal fashion, and ask the students to describe in detail what you did. If students do not mention that you held the balloon shut between puffs, blow it up a second time in an exaggerated fashion, using short puffs. After each puff, make a point of having to hold the end of the balloon so that the air in the balloon does not leak out. Ask students if they noticed anything more when you blew the balloon up the second time.

Procedure

Part A: What's Amazing About the Balloon Pump? (demonstration)

1. Ask students to imagine they have to blow up hundreds of balloons for a big party. "What tool could help you out?" *A pump.*

2. Show students a bicycle pump. "Does anyone recognize this? What does it do?" Attach a balloon to the pump (secure with a rubber band if necessary to obtain a tight fit) and ask students to watch the size of the balloon very carefully as you pump. Alert them to watch the balloon on both the upstroke and the downstroke. "What happened?" *The balloon got bigger on the downstroke, but did not change size on the upstroke.*

3. Tell the students that you have another kind of pump to try out. Show the students the balloon pump. Attach a balloon to the pump nozzle, and ask students to watch the size of the balloon very carefully as you pump. Alert them to watch the balloon on both the upstroke and the downstroke. "What happened?" *The balloon got bigger on both the upstroke and the downstroke.*

4. Ask students to compare the processes of filling balloons by mouth and with each type of pump. Challenge them with the following questions: "How are the two pumps different? How does the balloon pump force air into the balloon? What prevents the air from coming out?" Have students form hypotheses about the internal workings of the balloon pump to explain its "amazing" behavior.

Part B: Exploring the Balloon Pump

If your balloon pumps cannot be disassembled and reassembled, your students cannot do Part B as a hands-on activity.

The nozzle breaks off of the piston rod rather easily. If this happens, the pump will still pump air, but inflating balloons will be more difficult.

1. Have each group of students disassemble a balloon pump to observe its inner workings at various pumping positions (especially noting the gaskets at each end as well as the O-ring gasket on the piston).

2. Have each group reassemble their pump.

3. Lead a discussion that revisits some of your original questions including, "How does a balloon pump force air into a balloon?" Also lead students to consider other issues such as "What is the biggest complication of a tool that uses air pressure?" *Leaks!* Ask, "Why is blowing up a balloon with the balloon pump more efficient than blowing up a balloon by mouth or with a bicycle pump?" *Because the balloon pump pumps air on both up and downstrokes.*

Explanation

This explanation is intended for the teacher's information. Modify the explanation for students as required.

To understand how a balloon pumps works, we must first examine the key components. Figure 1 illustrates the key components of the balloon pump, including the following: the cylindrical body, a hollow piston, a hollow piston rod connected to a nozzle, and three rubber gaskets. Two flat, round gaskets cover holes at each end of the body; an O-ring gasket covers several holes within a somewhat larger groove around the edge of the piston, separating the inside of the body into two compartments.

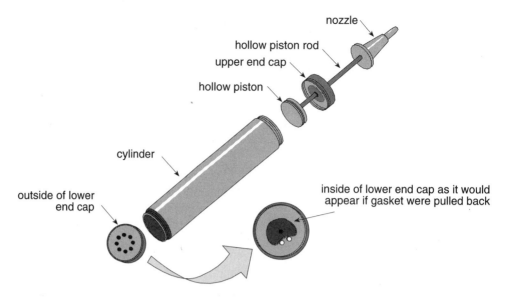

Figure 1: Examine the key components of a balloon pump.

Unlike the more common tire-type pumps that expel air only on the downstroke, balloon pumps expel air on both the up and downstrokes. The events that occur when the piston rod is pulled up are outlined below and shown in Figure 2.

a. The increasing pressure in the top compartment pushes the top gasket over the holes in the upper end cap.

b. The O-ring piston gasket is forced down, exposing the holes in the piston to the top compartment.

c. This increased pressure (caused by the decrease in volume) is relieved as air is forced through the piston holes and hollow piston rod into the balloon.

d. At the same time, a decreasing pressure (caused by the increase in volume) is created in the bottom compartment, so the greater outside air pressure pushes open the bottom gasket.

e. The bottom compartment fills with air.

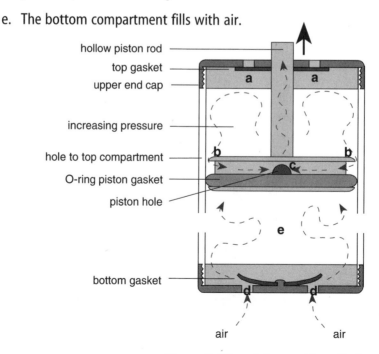

Figure 2: The piston rod is pulled up.

Pushing the piston rod down also forces air into the balloon. The events that occur are outlined below and shown in Figure 3.

a. The increasing pressure in the bottom compartment (caused by the decrease in volume) pushes the bottom gasket closed.

b. The O-ring piston gasket is forced up, exposing the holes to the bottom compartment.

c. This increased pressure is relieved as air again is forced through the piston holes into the hollow piston rod and the balloon.

d. At the same time, a decreasing pressure is created in the top compartment (caused by the increase in volume) so the greater air pressure pushes open the top gasket.

e. The top compartment refills with air.

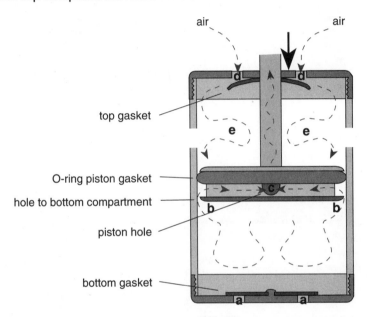

air   air

top gasket

O-ring piston gasket

hole to bottom compartment

piston hole

bottom gasket

Figure 3: The piston rod is pushed down.

The opening and closing of the gasket valves due to increased pressure and the accompanying movement of the fluid (in this case, air) is analogous to the operation of a squirt gun.

Extensions

1. After blowing up the balloon, lay down the pump (with the balloon still attached) and allow the air to escape. (The energy stored in the stretched rubber propels the pump.)

2. Compare the workings of a balloon pump to that of a tire pump, air-driven drill, or other air-driven tool; see *How Things Work* by Steve Parker (Random House, ISBN 0-679-80908-2).

3. Compare the rate at which two balloons fill, using a balloon pump and another type of pump. (Keep both pump strokes uniform.)

Home, safety, and career:
- Provide students with materials that describe engine valves and pistons; how tires are inflated; and the impact of low air pressure on auto safety, gas mileage, and tire wear.

Language arts:
- Read aloud or suggest that students read one or more of the following books:
  - *Balloons—Building and Experimenting with Inflatable Toys,* by Bernie Zubrowski (Beech Tree, ISBN 0-688-08324-2)
    Text and experiments introduce scientific principles that can be demonstrated with balloons and other inflatable toys.
  - *The True Confessions of Charlotte Doyle,* by Avi (Orchard, ISBN 0531084930)
    Air pressure builds into a hurricane at sea.

Life science:
- Have students study the heart as a pump and compare its valves and chambers to the valves and chambers of the balloon pump.
- Have students compare and contrast how the lungs work with how a bicycle pump or a balloon pump works.

Math:
- Have students measure and graph the time of pumping (constant rate) versus balloon circumference.

References

Jennings, T. *The Young Scientist Investigates Air;* Children's Press: Chicago, 1982.

Koff, R.M. *How Does It Work?;* Doubleday: Garden City, NY, 1961; pp 165–168.

Contributor

Jo Parkey, Smith Middle School, Vandalia, OH; Teaching Science with TOYS peer writer.

PENCIL HYDROMETERS

Students compare how objects float in tap water and in salt water.

Pencil Hydrometer

KEY SCIENCE TOPICS

- density
- displacement

STUDENT BACKGROUND

Students should have previous experience with the concept of relative density.

KEY PROCESS SKILLS

• collecting data	Students collect data by placing the hydrometer in various solutions.
• making graphs	Students graph their data.

TIME REQUIRED

Setup	5	minutes
Performance	20	minutes
Cleanup	5	minutes

Materials

For the "Procedure"
Per group of 3 students
- 1 pencil about 8 centimeters (cm) long

If you do not have enough short pencils, you can use straws cut to 8-cm lengths.

- 3 cups (24 ounces) water
- 3 10-ounce clear plastic cups (about 10 cm high)
- 2 stirrers
- permanent marker
- pea-sized piece of oil-based or plastic modeling clay
- tablespoon measure
- paper towels
- 1-cup (8-ounce) measuring cup
- 4 tablespoons table salt
- metric ruler

For "Variations and Extensions"

❸ All materials listed for the "Procedure" plus the following:
- more clay
- balance

❹ All materials listed for the "Procedure" except
- substitute the following substances for the salt-water solution:
  ◦ 4–5 sugar-water solutions of different concentrations
  ◦ several types of "flat" soft drinks

Safety and Disposal

No special safety or disposal procedures are required.

Getting Ready

1. Using a permanent marker, mark the pencils with horizontal lines drawn at 0.5-cm intervals, starting at the pointed end. (See Figure 1.)

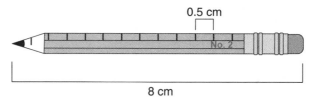

Figure 1: Mark the pencil.

 Students must use the same pencil for each of the three trials.

2. Label each set of three cups with the amount of salt: no salt, 1 tablespoon salt, and 3 tablespoons salt.

Introducing the Activity

Ask students to predict whether a pencil will float or sink in water. Have the students test their predictions. Ask students how the pencils could be made to float upright. After listening to their suggestions, give students some clay and challenge them to use the clay to make the pencils float upright. Then ask them to cause the pencil to float at different heights (by varying the amount of clay).

Procedure

Have each group do the following:

1. Pour 8 ounces tap water into each of the three labeled plastic cups.

2. Add the appropriate number of level tablespoons of salt into the labeled cups and stir to mix.

3. Place a pea-sized ball of clay securely on the eraser end of the pencil. (While some pencils will float vertically in water without the clay, the modeling clay is needed to keep the Pencil Hydrometer floating vertically even when it is placed in the more buoyant salt water.) Place the pencil clay-side down into the cup of

water to check that it floats vertically and does not touch the bottom of the cup. (See Figure 2.) Adjust the amount of clay if needed.

➤ *Have the "Floating Pencils" Data Sheet (provided) and an extra pencil ready to record measurements.*

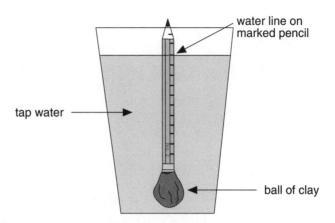

water line on marked pencil

tap water

ball of clay

Figure 2: Place the hydrometer in tap water.

4. Read and record the number of lines on the pencil that remain above the surface of the tap water. Remove the pencil and pat dry with a paper towel.

5. Predict how high the point of the Pencil Hydrometer will float above the solution with 1 tablespoon salt. Record your prediction.

➤ *Do not change the amount of clay on the Pencil Hydrometer between steps.*

6. Lower the marked pencil into the solution with 1 tablespoon salt. Read and record your observation.

7. Repeat Steps 5 and 6 using the solution that contains 3 tablespoons salt.

8. Graph the height the Pencil Hydrometer extends above the liquid versus the number of tablespoons of salt in the solution.

Variations and Extensions

1. Have students use solutions of different densities and compare the results.

2. Let the water evaporate from the cup containing salt water. (This may occur more quickly if the cup is placed in a window where the sun shines in.) The salt makes interesting crystal patterns in the plastic cups.

3. Have students determine the effect the mass of the Pencil Hydrometer has on how high it floats by adding different amounts of clay to the pencil, determining the mass of the hydrometer, and comparing this to the height at which it floats.

4. For upper-level students, have them make and determine the concentrations of a series of 4–5 different sugar-water solutions of increasing concentration. Determine the floating point of the Pencil Hydrometer in each solution. Plot the concentration of the sugar-water solution versus the floating point. Then determine the floating point of the hydrometer in different types of "flat" soft drinks to determine the sugar concentration in each. Be sure the soft drinks are at room temperature.

Explanation

 The following explanation is intended for the teacher's information. Modify the explanation for students as required.

Objects either sink or float in a liquid because of their density relative to the density of the liquid. All things in the universe are made of tiny particles. The density of an object depends on two factors: the mass of the individual particles and how closely packed the particles are. The heavier the particles are and the closer they are packed together, the more dense the object. An object which is more dense than the liquid sinks. An object which is less dense than the liquid floats. When salt is dissolved in water, the solution becomes more dense; the more salt dissolved, the greater the density of the solution. Thus, an object that sinks in tap water might float in a salt-water solution.

A floating object displaces a volume of solution that has a mass equal to that of the object. This is known as Archimedes' principle. Because salt water is more dense than tap water, a given mass of salt water will occupy less volume than the same mass of water. (In other words, a volume of salt water will have a greater mass than the same volume of tap water). Therefore, the volume of salt water that is equal in mass to the hydrometer is less than the volume of tap water; this is graphically represented by Figure 3. The Pencil Hydrometer needs to displace less volume of salt water to float, so less volume of the hydrometer is submerged in the salt water than in the tap water. Thus the observation made in the activity: the Pencil Hydrometer floats highest in the most-concentrated salt water and lowest in the tap water.

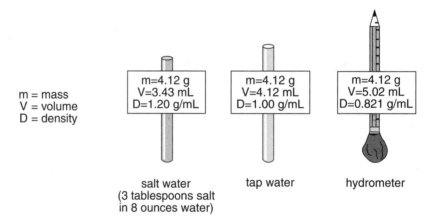

Figure 3: This representative drawing shows the relative volumes of equal masses of salt water, tap water, and the hydrometer.

Assessment

Have the students write a paragraph and/or draw a diagram to predict the outcome of an experiment in which the Pencil Hydrometer was placed in a series of four salt-water solutions with different amounts of salt dissolved.

Cross-Curricular Integration

Life science:
• Discuss the kinds of plant and animal life that might live in salt water versus fresh water.

Math:
- Have students graph the results of the activity. (See the "Procedure," Step 8.)

Social studies:
- Discuss the Great Salt Lake with the students. Explain that the Great Salt Lake is a large lake with very salty water (about six times as salty as ocean water). Many small mountain rivers flow into the Great Salt Lake carrying large amounts of dissolved salt from the mountains. Once the water runs into the Great Salt Lake, it generally remains because the lake has no outlets. However, some of the water evaporates, but the salt remains. Therefore, the amount of salt in the lake is always increasing even though the water is evaporating. This causes the concentration of salt in the lake to increase. After students have done the activity, ask them to predict how Pencil Hydrometers would behave when dropped into 8 ounces of water from Great Salt Lake. *The hydrometers would float higher than they did in salt water of lower concentrations.*
- The Dead Sea is another example of an inland salt lake that might be used. Compare the salinity of the Dead Sea and the Great Salt Lake.
- Ask students to predict how the salinity of ocean water will affect a big ship. Explain that ocean water is very different from tap water. Ocean water contains many different kinds of minerals that have been dissolved from the soil and carried into the ocean. (Water that falls on the land as snow and rain goes back to the ocean with a small amount of minerals dissolved in it.) When ocean water evaporates, the minerals remain, and the water gets saltier. Then explain that a ship floats at different levels depending upon the salinity of the water, the weight of the cargo, and the temperature of the water. It floats lower in fresh water than in salt water, and lower in warm water than in cold water. The mark called the "Plimsoll line" shows the safe-float level for a fully loaded ship in different types of water. A Plimsoll line is now required by law on ships of all nations. It is sometimes called the "International Load Line."

References

Growing Up with Science; H.S. Stuttman: Westport, CT, 1987; Vol. 15, p 1334.

Hackett, J.K.; Moyer, R.H.; Adams, D.K. *Science 4;* Merrill: Columbus, OH, 1989.

Smith, S. *Discovering the Sea;* Stonehenge: London, 1981.

Taylor, B. *Sink or Swim!;* Random House: New York, 1991.

World Book Encyclopedia; World Book: Chicago, 1991; Vol. 15, p 575.

Contributor

Mary Davis, Miami East South Elementary School, Troy, OH; Teaching Science with TOYS, 1991–92.

Handout Master

A master for the following handout is provided:
- Floating Pencils—Data Sheet

Copy as needed for classroom use.

PENCIL HYDROMETERS

Floating Pencils—Data Sheet

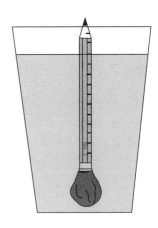

How high does your Pencil Hydrometer float? Use the chart below to make your predictions and record your observations.

	Trial 1: No Salt — Height above the water		Trial 2: 1 Tablespoon Salt — Height above the water		Trial 3: 3 Tablespoons Salt — Height above the water	
cm	Predicted	Actual	Predicted	Actual	Predicted	Actual
6						
5.5						
5						
4.5						
4						
3.5						
3						
2.5						
2						
1.5						
1						
0.5						
0						

PLASTICS DO DIFFER!

Physical properties are used to distinguish between three readily available plastics: high-density polyethylene (HDPE), polyethylene terephthalate (PET or PETE), and polystyrene (PS).

HDPE, PET, and PS

GRADE LEVELS

Science activity appropriate for grades 4–9
Cross-Curricular Integration intended for grades 4–6

KEY SCIENCE TOPICS

- physical properties
- relative density
- separating plastics for recycling

STUDENT BACKGROUND

Students should understand physical properties and why objects sink or float.

KEY PROCESS SKILLS

• collecting data	Students collect sink and float data.
• interpreting data	Students use sinking and floating data to determine the relative densities of polymers.
• investigating	Students identify an unknown polymer.

TIME REQUIRED

Setup	10–15	minutes
Performance	15–30	minutes
Cleanup	5–10	minutes

Materials

For the "Procedure"
Per class
- 1-L container such as a plastic soft-drink bottle
- saturated salt solution made from the following:
  - 360 g table salt (sodium chloride, NaCl)
  - water

Per group of 3–4 students
- 250 mL water
- scissors
- 2 wide-mouthed 250-mL or larger containers, such as:
  ○ 250-mL beakers
  ○ cut-off plastic 1- or 2-L soft-drink bottles
  ○ jars
- 1 of each of the following plastic items:
  ○ polyethylene terephthalate (PET), recycle code 1, such as a soft-drink bottle

➤ *If the bottle has a plastic base cup, do not use the base cup since it is made from a different type of plastic.*

  ○ high-density polyethylene (HDPE), recycle code 2, such as a milk bottle
  ○ polystyrene (PS), recycle code 6, such as a clear lid from a yogurt container or a clear salad bar or deli container
- permanent marker

For the "Variation"
All materials listed for the "Procedure" plus the following:
Per group
- 40–60 g sugar
- 200 mL water

For the "Extensions"
❶ All materials listed for the "Procedure" plus the following:
Per group
- various plastics such as:
  ○ polyvinyl chloride (PVC), recycle code 3, such as a cooking oil bottle
  ○ low-density polyethylene (LDPE), recycle code 4, such as an Elmer's® Glue bottle
  ○ polypropylene (PP), recycle code 5, such as a yogurt container

❷ All materials listed for Extension 1 plus the following:
Per group
- 1 or more of the following solutions made in the proportions noted:
  ○ 100 mL rubbing alcohol (70% isopropyl alcohol) and 40 mL water
  ○ 80 mL rubbing alcohol and 40 mL water
  ○ 75 g sugar and 150 mL water
- a container for each solution

Safety and Disposal

The rubbing alcohol used in Extension 2 is intended for external use only. No special disposal procedures are required.

Getting Ready

1. For each group, label one 250-mL (or larger) container "water" and the other "saturated salt solution."

2. Prepare the saturated salt solution (about 200 mL for each group) as follows: measure about 360 g sodium chloride into a 1-L container and add water to

the 1-L mark. Stir intermittently for about 10–20 minutes, allowing sufficient time for the salt to dissolve. Some solid salt should remain undissolved; this indicates the solution is saturated. Allow the undissolved salt to settle to the bottom of the container. Carefully pour or decant about 200 mL of the clear liquid (the saturated salt solution) into the container labeled "saturated salt solution."

3. Fill the other 250-mL container with water.

4. (optional) Students may be more excited about the activity if they bring the plastic items from home. If you choose this option, introduce the plastic recycling code and show students how to identify the plastics they need to bring for the activity.

5. (optional) Cut pieces of plastics as described in Step 1 of the "Procedure."

6. (optional) Cut pieces of plastics for the "unknowns" and mark them with code numbers.

Introducing the Activity

Options:

- If you have not already done so, introduce the plastic recycling code as a means of identifying plastics.

- Discuss or brainstorm ways of distinguishing between unknown solids without decomposing them or subjecting them to chemical modification.

- If the students are not familiar with polymers and monomers, introduce these concepts.

Procedure

1. Have each group use scissors to cut out two equal-sized pieces from each of the three types of plastic. Have them use a permanent marker to label each with its recycle code.

2. Students should investigate the physical properties of these plastic pieces and record their observations on the Observation Sheet (provided). The physical properties include:
   - visual appearance (transparent or translucent, colored or colorless, shiny or dull);
   - feel and texture (waxy, slippery, smooth, etc.);
   - flexibility (does it bend easily; does it remain bent, hold a partial curl, or return to its original shape; does it crack, etc.); and
   - sound made when dropped onto a solid surface (dull or high ring).

3. Have the students determine the relative densities of the plastic pieces to water by submerging one piece of each plastic in water; it will either sink (more dense) or float (less dense).

If the pieces of plastic do not sink immediately, have students tap them lightly with a pencil. (Surface tension can make something float that actually is more dense than the liquid it is in.)

4. Similarly, have the students determine the relative density of the plastic pieces to saturated salt solution by submerging one piece of each plastic in salt solution.

5. (optional) Give each team an "unknown" (coded) piece of plastic to identify by repeating Steps 2–4.

Explanation

 The following explanation is intended for the teacher's information. Modify the explanation for students as required.

The focus of this activity is using physical properties to differentiate between three common plastics: polyethylene terephthalate (PET), high-density polyethylene (HDPE), and polystyrene (PS). Such plastics belong to a group of giant molecules (or macromolecules) called polymers. Polymers are comprised of hundreds to thousands of repeating units. ("Poly" means "many" and "mer" means "units.") The small units from which a polymer is made are called monomers. ("Mono" means "one.") These three polymers are but a small sample of the many types of polymers that are so much a regular part of our lives. We can scarcely imagine living without such items as polymer-based synthetic fabrics, construction materials, food packaging, and vehicle components. One of the reasons polymers are so useful is their variety. This variety is possible because of the many types of monomers and the many ways in which they can be joined.

The selection of a polymer for a particular job is based on its set of properties—polymers may be flexible or rigid; transparent, translucent, or opaque; heat resistant or not; waterproof or water-soluble; electrical insulators or conductors; hard or soft; elastic or stiff. In this activity, students use the physical properties of appearance, texture, flexibility, sound, and density. (Physical properties are those that can be measured or observed without changing the identity of the substance.) Table 1 provides some data representative of that collected on the Observation Sheet. Since an important feature of appearance is whether the plastic is translucent or transparent, you may want to introduce these terms in advance. (Light passes through both translucent and transparent plastic, but in the former, the light is diffused enough so that objects beyond cannot be clearly seen.) Of all common plastics, only PS gives a distinctive sound: a high, metallic "clink" or ring when dropped onto a solid surface.

Table 1: Representative Data			
Test	PET (1)	HDPE (2)	PS (6)
Appearance	transparent, shiny	translucent, shiny	transparent or translucent
Texture	waxy	waxy	smooth
Flexibility	bends, holds shape	stiff, holds partial curl	bends, but cracks in the process
Sound	dull	dull	high "clink" or ring
Floats in water?	no	yes	no
Floats in salt solution?	no	yes	yes

The final physical property utilized is density (which is a measure of the ratio of a material's mass to its volume). Because density is determined by the nature of the particles of which it is comprised, each material has a characteristic density. The three plastics of this activity have the following values: PET 1.3–1.4 g/mL; HDPE 0.95–0.97 g/mL; PS 1.04–1.06 g/mL.

As shown by this activity, however, measuring relative densities is sufficient to distinguish between these three materials. The two liquids serve as the reference materials. Because the salt solution has particles of salt dissolved in the water, it is more dense than water alone. (The salt solution is called a saturated solution because the maximum amount of solute—salt—is dissolved in the solvent—water.) Relative to these liquids, each plastic is either more dense (in which case it will sink) or less dense (in which case it will float). These two liquids were chosen to give the maximum of three distinguishing flotation combinations: sink, sink; float, float; and sink, float. Since PET sinks in both liquids, it is more dense than either liquid; since HDPE floats in both, it is less dense than either liquid; since PS floats in salt solution but sinks in water, its density is between that of the two liquids.

In the "Variation," a sugar solution is substituted for the salt solution but the flotation behavior is the same. The increased number of liquids of Extension 2 allows for more flotation combinations, although the plastics do not encompass all possible density ranges.

Variation

Replace the saturated salt solution with a 20–30% sugar solution (density 1.08–1.13 g/mL) made from 40–60 g sugar in 200 mL water.

Extensions

1. Increase the challenge of the activity by adding these plastics to both known and unknown groups:
   - PVC, density 1.16–1.35 g/mL;
   - LDPE, density 0.92–0.94 g/mL; and
   - PP, density 0.90–0.91 g/mL.

2. Should you choose to do Extension 1, you may also choose to add additional density solutions to provide ample float/sink data to help students identify unknown samples. Three possible solutions are listed below. See Kolb and/or Sarquis references for additional solutions.
   - 100 mL 70% isopropyl rubbing alcohol and 40 mL water (density 0.91 g/mL)
   - 80 mL 70% isopropyl rubbing alcohol and 40 mL water (density 0.93 g/mL)
   - 75 g sugar and 150 mL water (density 1.14 g/mL)

Cross-Curricular Integration

Art:
- Have students make posters persuading others to recycle plastics.

Home, safety, and career:
- Have students bring in items (or pictures of items) from home made of synthetic polymers (plastics) and natural polymers. Label and list advantages and disadvantages of each for a specific use.
- Bring in a speaker to inform students of careers in the world of plastics. Not only is it important to inform students about science careers, it may meet state education requirements regarding career education.
- Have students draw and/or build (individually or in lab teams) a new item or model of an item made of plastic. Have them share their ideas and creation with the class and be ready for questions: Which type plastic would you use? Why? Would many people have a need for your item? Will you make your first million dollars on your creation?

Language arts:
- Have students develop a plan for automating the separation of plastics using physical properties. Have them list the many uses of plastics and write reasons why plastics are used instead of other materials (less breakable, lightweight, strong, durable, recyclable, water repellent, etc.).

Social studies:
- Ask students how we can balance our concerns about conserving fossil fuels with our need for the products that plastics make possible.

References

Conway, L. *ENERGY: A Good Apple Science Activity Book/Grades 5–8+;* Superific Science Series Book XI; Good Apple: Carthage, IL, 1985; pp 5, 8–10.

Kolb, K.E.; Kolb, D.K. "Method for Separating or Identifying Plastics," *Journal of Chemical Education,* 1991, 68, 348.

Modern Plastics Encyclopedia; McGraw-Hill: New York, 1983; Vol. 60, No. 10A.

"Identifying Polymers by Density and a Flame Test;" *Fun with Chemistry: A Guidebook of K–12 Activities;* Sarquis, M., Sarquis, J., Eds.; Institute for Chemical Education: Madison, WI, 1993; Vol. 2, pp 107–112.

Contributor

Jo Parkey, Smith Middle School, Vandalia, OH; Teaching Science with TOYS peer writer.

Handout Master

A master for the following handout is provided:
- Observation Sheet

Copy as needed for classroom use.

Names _____   _____

_____   _____

PLASTICS DO DIFFER!
Observation Sheet

	1 PET	**2** HDPE	**6** PS	code number UNKNOWN
look (appearance)				
touch (texture)				
bend (flexibility)				
listen (sound when dropped)				
floats in water?				
floats in salt solution?				

SHAPE SHIFTERS

Watch pieces of polystyrene film become curling, shrinking Shape Shifters.

Shape Shifters

GRADE LEVELS

Science activity appropriate for grades K–12
Cross-Curricular Integration intended for grades 4–6

KEY SCIENCE TOPICS

- heat
- polymers
- thermoplastics

STUDENT BACKGROUND

It is helpful if students are familiar with the effects of heat.

KEY PROCESS SKILLS

• measuring	Students use rulers to measure the polystyrene.
• collecting data	Students collect data about the size of the polystyrene before and after heating.
• investigating	Students collect and analyze data and draw conclusions about the effects of heat on polystyrene.

TIME REQUIRED

Setup	5–10	minutes
Performance	30–90	minutes
Cleanup	5–10	minutes

Materials

For the "Procedure"

Part A, per group of 3–4 students

- clear clean polystyrene (PS) containers (#6 recycle code) such as clear yogurt cup lids and deli containers

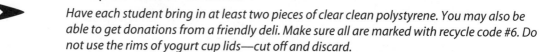

Have each student bring in at least two pieces of clear clean polystyrene. You may also be able to get donations from a friendly deli. Make sure all are marked with recycle code #6. Do not use the rims of yogurt cup lids—cut off and discard.

- several different-colored, fine- or medium-point permanent markers

Markette and Sanford brands work very well.

- scissors
- ruler

Part B, per class
- Shape Shifters from Part A
- (optional) 2 or more Shrinky-Dinks® designs
- hot pad or oven mitt
- aluminum foil
- cookie sheet or metal tray
- smooth item such as a board or cardboard
- (optional) sandpaper
- (optional) garbage bag of various plastic items
- conventional oven or toaster oven

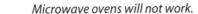*Microwave ovens will not work.*

For the "Variation"

❶ All materials listed for the "Procedure" plus the following:
Per group
- graph paper

For "Extensions"

❶ All materials listed for the "Procedure" plus the following:
Per group
- water
- 200 mL saturated salt solution
- balance

❷ All materials listed for the "Procedure" except
- substitute foamed vegetable trays of more than one color for the clear polystyrene containers

❸ All materials listed for the "Procedure" plus the following:
Per group
- other plastic films and/or different forms of polystyrene

Safety and Disposal

Allow the shrunken polystyrene designs to cool before handling. For students too young to handle all heating aspects, you will need an adult helper to operate the oven. You may want to use sandpaper to smooth points or sharp edges on the shrunken pieces. Polystyrene designs can be saved by students or recycled along with all polystyrene scraps.

Getting Ready

1. Primary teachers may choose to cut the polystyrene ahead of time.

2. Since oven temperatures can vary, test the oven you plan to use in advance to determine the best baking time. A toaster oven may take less time (a minute or less at 325°F) than a conventional oven (about three minutes at 325°F). Avoid using an institution-sized oven if it has a large internal fan that could blow Shape Shifters around.

3. (optional) Prepare "before" and "after" samples using commercial Shrinky-Dinks® or Shape Shifters of your own design.

Introducing the Activity

Options:

- Ask students for examples of how heat can change different items and show some common examples such as melted crayons and the hot melt glue from a glue gun.

- To emphasize recycling, dump a garbage bag full of plastic items on the floor in front of the class to initiate a discussion about plastic and how plastic can be reused. This can then lead to a discussion of the recycling code system and classification of plastic containers that use this system.

- Have students name items made of polymers or plastics. Discuss how plastics differ in ways such as appearance, strength, and texture. Ask the students to brainstorm reasons why these different characteristics are useful in different situations.

- Show "before-heating" and "after-heating" polystyrene samples and ask students what caused the change.

- You may wish to remind students they are to measure the widest and tallest parts of their design both before and after shrinking, and that the Shape Shifter will curl before it flattens.

Procedure

Part A: Making the Shape Shifters

Have each student do Steps 1–5.

1. Use permanent markers to create a design on polystyrene.
   Colors will be more intense on the shrunken design. Be sure the polystyrene is free of dust, since dust particles are also more noticeable after shrinking.

2. Cut out the design.

3. Measure and record the length and width of the polystyrene at the longest and widest parts.

4. Put your initials on the back of the Shape Shifter.

5. If ample polystyrene is available, cut 10 flat strips (about 0.5 cm x 1 cm) of polystyrene from the scrap; reserve for use in Part B, Step 7.

Part B: Heating the Shape Shifters

1. Preheat the oven to 325°F.

2. Cover a cookie sheet or metal tray with aluminum foil and place the Shape Shifters on the foil.

3. Use an oven mitt or hot pad to place the tray of Shape Shifters in the oven and heat them until the objects have ceased shrinking (usually a minute or less).

   Adult supervision is required during heating, removing the hot objects, and handling immediately after.

4. Use an oven mitt or hot pad to remove the hot tray from the oven.

Because oven temperatures can vary, watch shrinking time carefully. Pieces of polystyrene will typically first curl and then lie flat as they shrink upon heating. (If the curled edges touch, they may stick. Should this happen, using extreme caution, pull them apart while still warm and reheat as needed to flatten.) The Shape Shifters might need to be flattened while still warm with a smooth item such as a board or cardboard.

5. After the shrunken polystyrene has cooled, remove it from the cookie sheet.

6. (optional) Sandpaper sharp edges.

7. Instruct students to measure and record the length and width of the shrunken polystyrene. Have them use the strips from Part A, Step 5 to determine how many strips it takes to match the thickness of the shrunken piece.

8. Have students compare the shrunken design with the original design.

Explanation

The following explanation is intended for the teacher's information. Modify the explanation for students as required.

Commercial Shrinky-Dinks® and the Shape Shifters in this activity are made of polystyrene, a common polymer. Depending upon how they are manufactured, polystyrene and certain other polymers can have the ability to shrink when heated. When the shrinkable polystyrene is heated at low temperatures, it does not decompose to form new products; the molecules merely return to their original (not stretched) configurations. This means that no change in mass is expected.

One classification scheme of polymers involves their response to heating. Thermoplastic polymers soften on heating, are unaltered chemically in this heating process, and can be heated and melted any number of times. Thermosetting polymers are set into the desired form during polymerization and cannot be reformed; extensive heating can cause them to degrade or decompose. Polystyrene is a thermoplastic in that it softens during heating. But what causes the shrinking?

The shrinking ability of polystyrene is somewhat unusual. Most common solids, when heated, either expand before they melt into liquids (for example, metals) or decompose (for example, wood into charcoal). Polystyrene and other shrinkable plastics exhibit their shrinking nature due to the way they are manufactured. As they are produced, these plastics are heated, stretched out into a film, then quickly cooled. The sudden cooling "freezes" the molecules of the polymer in their stretched-out configuration. To visualize this process, imagine how a person might appear if suddenly asked to freeze while in the middle of doing jumping jacks. When the plastics are heated once again, the molecules within them are released from their "frozen" configurations; they return to their original dimensions, resulting in the observed shrinkage.

Foams (used in Extension 2) are made by adding a blowing agent (low-boiling liquid such as pentane) during the polymerization of the styrene. The resulting polystyrene-pentane mixture is then exposed to the effects of steam. Steam heats the polystyrene to its softening point, allowing the cells within the solid matrix to expand due to the permeating steam and the expansion of the pentane as it vaporizes into a gas. With time, air replaces the pentane (at least in part). When the foam is again heated, as in Extension 2, air pressure and gravity (or any other external force) will collapse the cells, and the solid shrinks.

Variation

For younger students, have each group cut a pattern of a rectangle on graph paper. This pattern should be large enough to fit on a flat piece of the polystyrene sample (and about three times larger than the intended finished product). Have the students measure the length and width. Shrink. Measure the decreased length and width and compare with the original dimensions.

Extensions

1. Students can make additional measurements before and after shrinking the polystyrene:

   a. Have students carry out flotation measurements on the polystyrene (See the Teaching Science with TOYS activity "Plastics Do Differ!") using water and a saturated salt solution.

   b. Have students measure the mass of the polystyrene.

2. Using foam vegetable trays of more than one color, have students cut pieces to fit like a puzzle. Do the pieces still fit together after shrinking?

3. To show that looks can be deceiving and the need for recycle codes for plastic containers, compare the shrinking behavior of polystyrene film to other plastic films and/or different forms of polystyrene (for example, foamed polystyrene, which gives a bumpy, opaque, brittle product, or opaque polystyrene, which only shrinks in one direction) and/or compare the properties (such as pliability) of the shrunken piece to the original. Two clear pieces can be different and a clear piece and a cloudy piece can have the same basic composition.

Assessment

Options:

- Conduct a lab practical to test students' ability to classify. Students sort pieces of plastic into one of four categories:

  A—usable for Shape Shifters (#6),
  B—usable for Shape Shifters but less desirable (#6 foam),
  C—unusable for Shape Shifters (not #6),
  D—may be usable for Shape Shifters (not coded).

- Have students answer in writing the following questions about the categories listed previously:

  ○ Describe an experiment that would help you decide whether the items in category D can be assigned to one of the other categories. *Test a small piece.*

  ○ Why is coding of plastics important? *Recycling.* Should the government require that manufacturers always put a code on plastic products? Should there be incentives to do so and/or penalties if not done?

Cross-Curricular Integration

Art:
- Design "Shrinky" art or jewelry. Plan for shrinkage in creating the design so that a clasp can be glued on the back. Try hanging necklaces, earrings, or key rings on narrow ribbon. Determine the correct placement and size of the hole. Clear polyurethane spray can be used to add gloss. To make beads, roll small pieces of shrunken foam that have slightly cooled around toothpicks to form beads. Then remove the toothpick and string for a bracelet, necklace, etc. Use scraps for art by arranging scraps (after students have colored them) together on a tray so they overlap. When heated, the scraps will link together.
- Plan a "shrunken zoo" or "circus under the little top" for which students make animals, trees, cages, snakes, etc. This will take a great deal of teamwork!

Home, safety, and career:
- Plan a field trip to a local company that makes or uses polystyrene film or foam. (Florists and meat packagers use shrinkable plastic film.)

Language arts:
- Read aloud or suggest that students read one or more of the following books:
  - *Alice in Wonderland,* by Lewis Carroll (any version)
    Alice eats a magic food and shrinks.
  - *Flat Stanley,* by Jeff Brown (Trophy, ISBN 0-06-440293-2)
    A boy becomes flat and can slip easily under doors.
  - *George Shrinks,* by William Joyce (Scholastic, ISBN 0-590-45031-X)
    A boy shrinks to mouse-size.

Math:
- Extend this activity to deal with ratios, areas, similar figures/polygons, measuring (including metric), and weighing.

Social studies:
- Introduce the saying, "Reduce, reuse, recycle." For more on recycling plastic, see *50 Simple Things Kids Can Do to Save the Earth*, by John Javna (The Earth Works Group, Andrews and McMeel, ISBN 0836223012).
- Have the students study stained glass designs of different periods and create their own versions with shrinking crafts.

References

Modern Plastics Encyclopedia; McGraw-Hill: New York, 1983; Vol. 60, No. 10A, pp 72–74, 224–226.

Rodriguez, F., "Classroom Demonstrations of Polymer Principles," *Journal of Chemical Education.* 1990, 67, 784–788.

"Shrinkable Plastics;" *Fun with Chemistry: A Guidebook of K–12 Activities;* Sarquis, M., Sarquis, J., Eds.; Institute for Chemical Education: Madison, WI, 1991; Vol. 1, pp 101–105.

Contributor

Jo Parkey, Smith Middle School, Vandalia, OH; Teaching Science with TOYS peer writer.

POP THE HOOD

Use a "Convertable" toy car to demonstrate the effect of heat on a metal.

Hot Wheels® Convertable

GRADE LEVELS

Science activity appropriate for grades 4–6
Cross-Curricular Integration intended for grades 4–6

KEY SCIENCE TOPICS

- conduction of heat
- metals and their physical properties
- thermal expansion and contraction

STUDENT BACKGROUND

Students should be familiar with the conduction of heat. You may wish to do this activity in conjunction with or after the Teaching Science with TOYS activity "Color-Changing Cars," so the cars' color change does not distract from the metal expansion property being investigated.

KEY PROCESS SKILLS

• observing	Students observe the car's behavior in cold and warm water.
• inferring	Students infer reasons for the car's behavior.

TIME REQUIRED

Setup	5–10	minutes
Performance	10–25	minutes
Cleanup	5	minutes

Materials

> **For "Getting Ready" only**
>
> *The drill and bit, intended for teacher use only, are needed to disassemble the Convertable the first time the activity is done.*
>
> - drill and ⅛-inch bit

For the "Procedure"

Per group of 3–4 students
- Convertable (a Hot Wheels® toy car by Mattel®)

Although the Hot Wheels® Convertable is not currently being manufactured, you or one of your students may have one in a car collection.

- container of cold tap water wide enough to hold car

A "pop-beaker" made from a cut-off plastic 2-L soft-drink bottle works well.

- container of very warm tap water wide enough to hold car

Be sure the water is not too hot. The manufacturers of liquid crystal toys usually caution against exposing the toys to extremely hot water and sunlight.

Per class
- 1 disassembled Convertable
- (optional) expandable ball and ring set, thermocouple and heat source, and/or jumping disk

Expandable ball and ring sets are available from Frey Scientific, (800) 225-FREY (#F01164), and other science education suppliers. Jumping disks are not currently being manufactured.

For the "Extension"

All materials listed for the "Procedure" plus the following:
- water at different temperatures
- alcohol thermometer

Safety and Disposal

Exercise caution when working with an open flame in "Introducing the Activity." No special disposal procedures are required.

Getting Ready

The first time the activity is done, prepare one car by drilling out the heads of the two rivets that hold the bottom of the car in place. The bottom can now be removed to expose the spring.

Introducing the Activity

Options:

- Demonstrate an expandable ball and ring set to demonstrate the concept of thermal expansion of metals.

- Demonstrate a jumping disk.

Procedure

1. Have the students carefully observe the Convertable and note its physical features such as color and shape. Record observations.

2. Have each group place the car in the warm water for a few seconds, then remove it and carefully observe and record any changes in the car.

 Although the liquid crystal color change is the most obvious physical change, it is not the focus of this activity. Lead students to note the change in shape of the car.

3. Have students alternate putting the car into cool and warm water and observe and record changes. Challenge them to propose a reasonable explanation for the movement of the plastic part(s).

4. Use the disassembled Convertable to show the spring. Lead the students to include this in their explanation.

5. Through a facilitated discussion, lead students to understand that the expandable ball and ring seen in "Introducing the Activity" also works by thermal expansion and contraction.

Explanation

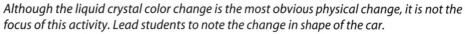 *The following explanation is intended for the teacher's information. Modify the explanation for students as required.*

In this activity, students observe two significant changes that result from heating and then cooling the Convertable toy car—its color and its shape. These are both physical changes, in that they occur without altering the identity of the substance.

An external plastic piece moves when the temperature changes because the plastic piece rests upon an interior lever linked to a coiled metal spring. When the spring is warmed by the water, it expands and pushes on the lever, and the external plastic piece rises above the surface of the body of the car. When the spring is cooled, the process is reversed. The properties of heat conduction and thermal expansion and contraction account for this result. The property of being a good heat conductor is one characteristic of metals. Other characteristic properties of metals include conduction of electricity, lustrousness (shininess), malleability (ability to be pounded into shapes without breaking), and ductility (ability to be drawn into wires). The thermal expansion and contraction observed in this activity is a property of metals and many other materials. For example, concrete sidewalks and roads expand and contract with temperature changes. Because of this, expansion joints must be used to prevent cracking.

Thermal expansion is also shown in "Introducing the Activity" with the metal ball and ring set. Originally, the metal ball has a larger diameter than the inside of the metal ring, which prevents it from passing through the ring; however, when the ring is heated, the metal expands, its diameter increases, and the ball passes through. If the ball is heated, it will also expand and again have too large a diameter to pass through the ring.

The jumping disk toy, which is made of two different metals joined together, demonstrates that different metals expand differently. (It is cut out of a bimetallic strip, analogous to a thermocouple). When the disk is held and the label side is pushed in, the metal on the label side expands more from the warming than the metal on the reverse side, and the disk holds its inverted shape. When the disk is placed on a flat surface, it cools, and the metal on the label side contracts more than the metal on the reverse side, pulling the disk back into its original shape. This causes the disk to "jump" off the surface.

Although color change is not the focus of this activity, students will certainly be interested in it. The paint on the cars contains liquid crystals that change color with a change in temperature. Liquid crystals comprise a rather small set of unique compounds whose molecules change orientation with changes in temperature (and sometimes with changes in other factors, such as pressure) and thus reflect light differently. (For a more detailed explanation of liquid crystals, see the Teaching Science with TOYS activity "Color-Changing Cars.")

Extension

Repeat the experiment using water at various temperatures to determine the minimum temperature needed to produce movement; record temperatures with thermometers.

Cross-Curricular Integration

Math:
- Students use measuring skills in the Extension.
- Have students graph the results of the Extension.

Contributor

Richard Pfirman, Sycamore High School, Cincinnati, OH; Teaching Science with TOYS, 1992.

THINGS THAT GLOW IN THE DARK

Students investigate two different processes by which objects glow.

Glow-in-the-dark products

GRADE LEVELS

Science activity appropriate for grades 1–12
Cross-Curricular Integration intended for grades 4–6

KEY SCIENCE TOPICS

- electrons
- energy and energy levels
- light

STUDENT BACKGROUND

Students should be familiar with light and energy.

KEY PROCESS SKILLS

• observing	Students observe various fluorescent and phosphorescent materials.
• communicating	Students report and discuss their findings.
• classifying	Based on their observations, students classify objects as fluorescent, phosphorescent, or neither.

TIME REQUIRED

Setup	15	minutes
Performance	25–40	minutes
Cleanup	5	minutes

Materials

For the "Procedure"
Part A, per class
- fluorescent and phosphorescent products, toys, and books

 To generate student interest, have students bring their own items from home.

- fluorescent posterboard
- 1 of the following phosphorescent (glow) "boards":
  - "Magic Glow in the Dark Playboard"
  - Glow-in-the-dark phosphorescent vinyl

 Available from Hanovia, Inc., 100 Chestnut St., Newark, NJ 07105; (201) 589-4300; (201) 589-4430 (FAX).

- room that can be almost completely darkened or a learning station made from the following:
  - blanket
  - box or table
- (optional) overhead projector

Part B, per group of 3–4 students
- 1 or more fluorescent materials, such as the following:
  - posters
  - highlighters
  - crayons
  - detergent with optical brighteners (such as Tide)
- 1 or more phosphorescent materials (identified as "glow-in-the-dark" or "luminous")
- various light sources: fluorescent lamp, incandescent lamp, flashlight, "black" light or other ultraviolet (UV) light lamp

For the "Variations"

❶ All materials listed for Part B plus the following:
- stopwatch
- graph worksheets

❷ Per group or class
- piece of particle board about 1 foot square
- primer
- fluorescent paint or fluorescent posterboard
- phosphorescent paint

Phosphorescent paint is available from art and/or craft stores. The paint is expensive.

Safety and Disposal

The UV light emitted from a black light or other UV light source can cause severe eye damage: Use carefully so that no one can look directly at the light. No special disposal procedures are required.

Getting Ready

1. If you are using the adhesive phosphorescent vinyl instead of the Playboard, you can cut a piece of fluorescent posterboard to match the size of the vinyl and place the vinyl strip on the back of the posterboard to form a single board. Keep the phosphorescent side facedown until doing the "Procedure."

2. If a room that can be completely darkened is not available, set up a learning station by covering a large box or table with a blanket. Leave a small opening for observation.

Lower-grade-level options:

- Begin without introduction to enhance the surprise.

- Have students bring out their fluorescent and phosphorescent products. Turn off the lights. Explain that the activity will explore the mystery of the "magic" light.

Upper-grade-level option:

- Discuss energy levels of electrons.

Procedure

Part A: Introduction to Glowing

Part A can be done as a demonstration or as a hands-on activity if a sufficient number of phosphorescent and fluorescent surfaces are available.

1. Position the students so that all can see the glow board.

2. Darken the room.

3. Turn the phosphorescent side faceup and place your hand on the board with your fingers spread. DO NOT REMOVE YOUR HAND!

4. Have someone turn on the lights. (Alternatively, an overhead projector can be used as the light source. Place your hand on the board so it is between the light source and the board.)

5. Ask someone to turn out the lights (or the overhead) to again darken the room.

6. Remove your hand from the board and hold the board so the students can see the phosphorescent side (a black handprint appears on a glowing surface).

Be very careful that the UV light does not shine in anyone's eyes.

7. (optional) If a UV source is available to demonstrate fluorescence:

    a. In the darkened room, shine the UV light on the fluorescent surface. (The surface will appear "neon bright".)

    b. Turn off the UV light. (The surface will immediately be dark.)

8. Have the lights turned on again and have the students examine the phosphorescent and fluorescent surfaces.

9. Discuss students' observations. Lead them to conclude that phosphorescent materials continue to glow after the lights are turned out while fluorescent materials do not.

Part B: Exploration

1. Allow each student or student group to observe and experiment with the available items and light sources and record their observations on the Data Sheet (provided), using one sheet for each object.

Caution students not to look directly at the UV or black lights.

2. Have the students use what they learned in Part A to sort the available items into fluorescent and phosphorescent groups.

3. Have the students report and discuss their findings.

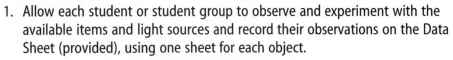

Explanation

The following explanation is intended for the teacher's information. Modify the explanation for students as required.

The "glowing" materials used in this activity glow by one of two different processes. Fluorescence involves the object emitting light immediately after absorbing it. When the light source is removed, the object immediately ceases to glow. With the second process, termed phosphorescence, the object continues to glow for some time even after the light source has been removed. This is why phosphorescent objects are said to "glow in the dark." It is this process that is responsible for perhaps the most dramatic part of this activity—the black handprint on the phosphorescent surface. The hand print is visible because the visible light was blocked from reaching the phosphorescent surface underneath your hand and so this portion of the surface will not glow when your hand is removed.

A phosphorescent surface exposed to visible light continues to glow even after the light is turned off because the energy absorbed from the light is released over a period of time. In contrast, the fluorescent surface behaves the same as any other normal surface. When the light source is turned off, nothing can be seen. This is because the fluorescent surface gives up its light immediately; once the light source is turned off, the fluorescent surface no longer glows. Thus, the area blocked by your hand and the rest of the surface appear exactly the same—no glow. In summary, both phosphorescent and fluorescent objects must be "energized" by light; only the former continues to glow after the light source is turned off.

While phosphorescent materials can be activated by visible light, fluorescent materials typically require ultraviolet (UV) radiation (or "black light") to produce the characteristic glow. Some fluorescent materials (such as Dayglow paint and some specialty glow papers) do fluoresce with near-ultraviolet light (wavelengths of light very close to the visible range) and so can glow even without the use of a UV light.

More Advanced Levels

Fluorescence and phosphorescence are not the only processes by which matter emits light. The following classification scheme (as suggested in 1888 by Eihard Wiedemann) shows the relationship of the processes of this activity to the others. (See Figure 1.) "Hot" light, or incandescence, refers to light that a substance emits solely as a result of its high temperature. (The filament inside a regular incandescent light bulb emits light as it is heated electrically.) "Cold" light, or luminescence, refers to light that a substance emits without a rise in temperature, and of which there are several subcategories. Light that is emitted as a result of adding mechanical energy is triboluminescence (as evidenced by crushing wintergreen Lifesavers or pulling apart adhesives, such as Curad®-brand bandage wrappers). As discussed above, light emitted as a result of light falling on a substance (incident radiation) is either fluorescence or phosphorescence. (Inside a fluorescent light bulb is mercury vapor: while the bulb is electrified, radiations are emitted that the inside white coating absorbs and re-emits as white light.) A substance that converts the energy from a chemical reaction into light exhibits either bioluminescence (if occurring in a living organism) or chemiluminescence (if not).

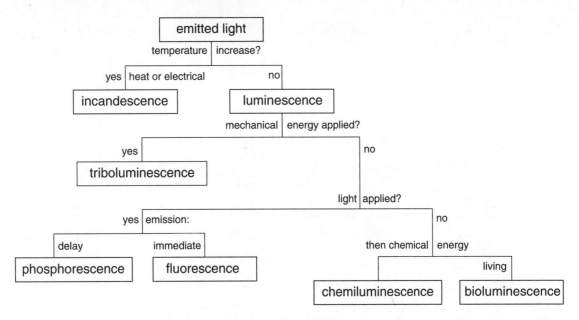

Figure 1: This flow chart shows the relationships among several processes by which matter emits light.

The emission of light by matter can be explained by the arrangement and behavior of electrons in the atom. At normal temperatures, the electrons in an atom reside in the lowest-possible energy levels. Such an electron configuration (or arrangement) is called the ground state. It is possible, however, for the atom to absorb energy from an external source. (The energy can be in the form of heat, light, or chemical, biochemical, electrical, or mechanical energy.) This energy can cause one or more of the electrons to move to a higher energy level, called an excited state. Because excited states are unstable, they typically are very short-lived. The excited electrons return to a lower energy level and give up their excess energy in the process. Regardless of how the energy came in, this excess energy is given off in the form of light.

Substances that either fluoresce or phosphoresce do so because their electrons are easily excited to higher energy levels upon exposure to light; however, they differ in the timing of their electrons returning to the ground state. In fluorescence, the excited electrons go back to the ground state in one second or less. In phosphorescence, the excited electrons drop to a lower but still excited intermediate level before eventually returning to the ground state. This multistep process results in the observed emission of light even after the original light source has been turned off.

Variations

1. Have teams illuminate phosphorescent items for 1–5 seconds; then record the time of glowing (rounding to the nearest minute). Team or entire group data can be tabulated and the relationship between time of exposure to time of glowing examined.

2. Make a glow board with particle board and fluorescent and phosphorescent paints:

   a. Apply a primer first to minimize the amount of glow paint needed.

   b. Apply the phosphorescent paint as instructed on its container.

   The oil-based phosphorescent paint is difficult to apply and does not adhere well to many surfaces.

c. When the phosphorescent paint is dry, paint the other side of the board with the fluorescent paint.

d. When dry, keep phosphorescent side facedown until use.

Extensions

1. Have the students name some practical uses for fluorescent and phosphorescent objects. (Examples include fluorescent decorations for running shoes, other apparel, and bicycles, and phosphorescent markings on light switches.)

2. Have the students identify other toys or objects that glow (that were not used in the activity) and identify them as fluorescing or phosphorescing.

3. Do chemiluminescence activities with lightsticks or luminol. One source is the Teaching Science with TOYS activity "Investigating the Effect of Temperature on Lightsticks."

4. Plan a field trip to a place like the SciTrek Museum in Atlanta or the Exploratorium in San Francisco. They have a phosphorescent-painted room in which a strobe light flashes every 10 seconds or so; the "captured shadows" are quite impressive.

Cross-Curricular Integration

Art:
- Have students use fluorescent and phosphorescent paints to create artworks.

Earth science:
- Discuss phosphorescent minerals and the use of this characteristic in identifying mineral samples.
- Use peel-and-stick, glow-in-the-dark paper stars to make the night sky in the classroom or suggest students and parents do this at home. (*The Glow-in-the-Dark Night Sky Book,* by C. Hatchett, Random House, 1988, ISBN 0-394-89113-9; *Glow in the Dark Constellations,* by C.E. Thompson, Brooke House, ISBN 0-448-09070-8.)

Home, safety, and career:
- Discuss the ways in which fluorescent materials are used for personal safety (such as fluorescent orange vests for road workers, hats for hunters, and Halloween costumes). Challenge students to think of new ways to use fluorescent and phosphorescent materials for personal safety.

Language arts:
- Read aloud or suggest that students read one or more of the following books:
  - *James and the Giant Peach,* by Roald Dahl (Knopf, ISBN 0-394-81282-4)
    James is given a sack of glowing objects that are magical.
  - *My Teacher Glows In the Dark,* by Bruce Coville (Minstrel, ISBN 0-671-72709-5)
    Peter Thompson finds out that his teacher glows in the dark.

Math:
- In Variation 1, students use math and graphing skills.

Reference

Laidler, K. "The Story of Chemiluminescence," *CHEM 13 News*. March 1991, 202, 8.

Contributors

Thomas Lanich, Springcreek Elementary School, Piqua, OH; Teaching Science With TOYS, 1991–92.
Kathe Lindner, Cedarville High School, Cedarville, OH; Teaching Science With TOYS, 1988–89.
Clifton Martin, Northmont High School, Clayton, OH; Teaching Science With TOYS, 1988–89.
Jo Parkey, Smith Middle School, Vandalia, OH; Teaching Science With TOYS peer writer.

Handout Master

A master for the following handout is provided:
•   Things that Glow in the Dark—Data Sheet
Copy as needed for classroom use.

THINGS THAT GLOW IN THE DARK

Data Sheet

For each object you are testing, record the indicated information.

Name of object tested:					
List light sources used.	Describe the appearance of the object in the light.				Turn the light off. Does the object glow? (Yes or No)

Conclusion: The object is _____ fluorescent _____ phosphorescent _____ neither

A COLLECTION OF
SURFACE TENSION ACTIVITIES

*Select one or more of the nine activity parts
to allow students to investigate some interesting effects of surface tension.*

How full is full?

GRADE LEVELS

Science activity appropriate for grades K–12
Cross-Curricular Integration intended for grades 2–6

KEY SCIENCE TOPICS

- attractive forces
- surface tension
- water and its properties

KEY PROCESS SKILLS

- communicating   Students describe observations of surface tension experiments.

- predicting   Students predict the effect of soap on surface tension.

TIME REQUIRED

Setup	10–15	minutes
Performance	5–10	minutes per part
Cleanup	5–10	minutes

Materials

For the "Procedure"
Per class
- water

Generally tap water can be used; however, sometimes water with a high mineral content ("hard" water) can affect those parts of the activity that involve the addition of soap. If you have trouble, try using distilled water in place of tap water.

- droppers
- 1 cup of 50/50 soap-water solution made from the following:
  - ½ cup water
  - ½ cup dishwashing liquid

Part A, per group
- small container
- waxed paper

Part B, per group
- clear plastic cup
- pennies or paper clips

Part C, per group
- penny

Part D, per group or per class
- clear plastic cup
- powder (talcum, baby powder, pepper)
- 1 toothpick
- 3–4 drops dishwashing liquid
- 3–4 drops rubbing alcohol

Part E, per group or per class
- clear plastic cup
- 2 toothpicks
- 3–4 drops rubbing alcohol
- 3–4 drops dishwashing liquid

Part F, per group or per class
- pie pan
- 24–30 inches of thread
- scissors
- 1 toothpick
- 4–5 drops dishwashing liquid

Part G, per group or per class
- clean pie pan
- paper or index card
- scissors
- 1 toothpick
- 3–4 drops dishwashing liquid

Part H, per group or per class
- pie pan
- paper or index card
- scissors
- 1 toothpick
- 3–4 drops dishwashing liquid

Part I, per group or per class
- clear plastic cup
- needle
- magnifying lens
- waxed paper
- (optional) tissue paper
- (optional) sharp pencil

Safety and Disposal

Handle needles and toothpicks with care. No special disposal procedures are required.

Getting Ready

Prepare a 50/50 solution of dishwashing liquid and water by mixing equal volumes of each liquid.

Procedure

Some of these activities are more appropriately done as student hands-on activities, while others are useful as teacher demonstrations. Our recommendations appear in parentheses following the title of each part.

Part A: Drops on Waxed Paper (activity)

1. Use a dropper to place a few drops of water onto a piece of waxed paper. Observe the shape of the drops.

2. Cause several drops to run together by tilting the waxed paper, and observe any changes in the shape of the water.

3. Repeat Steps 1 and 2 with the 50/50 soap-water solution (prepared in "Getting Ready") and compare observations.

Part B: How Full Is Full? (activity)

1. Fill a clear plastic cup (free from any soap residue) with water to the rim. Note the water level in the cup.

2. Predict what will happen when a penny (or other small object, like a paper clip) is carefully placed into the cup. Will the water spill over? Add a penny and see what happens. (See Figure 1.)

3. Predict how many pennies you can add before the water spills. Try the experiment and see.

4. Have the groups compare results. What shape does the top of the water have just before it spills? Discuss why the number of pennies varies.

> *Variables include how full the cup was before the pennies were added, the angle of entry, the distance the pennies fell before they reached the water, the force with which the pennies were dropped, the diameter of the top of the glass, and cleanliness of the pennies.*

5. Repeat the activity several times with the 50/50 soap-water solution (prepared in "Getting Ready"). Compare the results with results obtained in Steps 2–3.

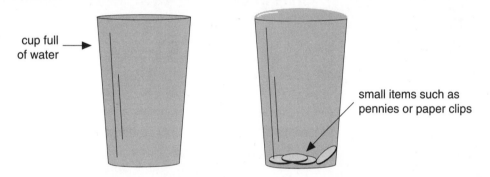

cup full of water

small items such as pennies or paper clips

Figure 1: Drop small items into the water until the water spills out of the cup.

Part C: Drops on the Head of a Penny (activity)

1. Predict how many drops of water can be placed on the head of a penny. Record your prediction.

2. Use a dropper to carefully place drops of water onto the penny. Count as you go. Record the number of drops you added before water spilled off the penny.

3. Discuss the variables that affect the number of drops you could place on the penny.

> *Variables include the size of the drops, placement of the drops, and distance the drop falls before it reaches the water.*

4. Repeat Step 2 several times and compare results.

5. Repeat the activity several times with the 50/50 soap-water solution (prepared in "Getting Ready"). Compare the results with those obtained in Steps 2 and 4.

Part D: Floating Powder (activity or demonstration)

> *If doing as a demonstration, Parts D–I are best done on an overhead projector to allow all the students to view at once. Substitute a glass pie pan or petri dish for the plastic cup.*

1. Fill a plastic cup (free from any soap residue) about ¾-full of water and gently shake the powdered substance onto the surface until the entire surface is covered evenly.

2. Dip the end of a toothpick into dishwashing liquid and touch the toothpick to the surface. Observe what happens.

3. Substitute rubbing alcohol for the dishwashing liquid and repeat Steps 1 and 2 using a dropper to deliver the rubbing alcohol.

4. Repeat the addition of rubbing alcohol several times.

5. (optional) Repeat Steps 1–4 with different powders.

Part E: Moving Toothpicks (activity or demonstration)

1. Fill a plastic cup (free from any soap residue) just to the rim with water. Float two toothpicks in the water so that they are parallel to one another.

2. Using a dropper, drop a few drops of rubbing alcohol between the toothpicks and observe.

3. Repeat Steps 1 and 2 substituting dishwashing liquid for the rubbing alcohol.

Part F: Thread Loop (activity or demonstration)

1. Fill a pie pan (free from any soap residue) with water.

2. Tie the ends of a 12–15-inch piece of thread together to make a loop.

3. Float this loop of thread in the water.

4. Put dishwashing liquid on a toothpick and touch the toothpick to the surface of the water within the area of the thread loop.

5. Observe the shape of the loop.

6. Thoroughly rinse out the pie pan.

7. Repeat Steps 1–3 with a new piece of string.

8. Ask students to predict what will happen if you add soap outside of the loop.

9. Put dishwashing liquid on a toothpick and touch the toothpick to the surface of the water just outside the loop.

Part G: Boat Propellant (activity or demonstration)

1. Fill a pie pan (free from any soap residue) with water.

2. Cut a small "boat" from a piece of paper or index card so that it is about 3 inches long. (Use Figure 2 as a model.)

3. Carefully float the boat on top of the water with the notch at the edge of the pie pan.

4. Put some dishwashing liquid on a toothpick and touch the toothpick to the notch at the rear of the boat. Observe the boat.

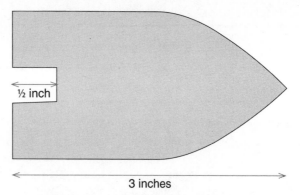

½ inch

3 inches

Figure 2: Cut a boat out of paper.

Part H: Spinning Spiral (activity or demonstration)

1. Fill a pie pan (free from any soap residue) with water.

2. Cut a circle from a piece of paper or an index card. Then make a spiral as shown in Figure 3.

3. Float the spiral on top of the water. Put dishwashing liquid on a toothpick and touch the toothpick to the center of the spiral. Observe the behavior of the spiral.

Figure 3: Cut a small spiral strip out of paper.

Part I: Floating Needle (activity or demonstration)

1. Fill a cup (free from any soap residue) with water.

2. Drop a needle, point-first, into the water and observe.

3. Carefully lower a needle horizontally into the water and observe.
The needle should float; if you have trouble, try one of these ideas:
- *Rub it on your forehead, being careful not to prick yourself, then try to float it. Why might this change the behavior?*
- *Float a piece of tissue paper on the surface of the water. Gently place the needle on the paper. Using the point of a sharpened pencil, push the paper under the water. The needle should remain on the surface.*

4. Have the students use a magnifying lens to examine the surface of the water where the needle is touching. They should see a depression in the water.

5. While the needle is floating, use a dropper to add several drops of the 50/50 soap-water solution (prepared in "Getting Ready") to the surface of the water near the needle.

Extension

Try the Teaching Science with TOYS activity "One-way Screen."

Explanation

➤ *The following explanation is intended for the teacher's information. Modify the explanation for students as required.*

This series of activities demonstrates the high surface tension of water. Surface tension causes the surface of a liquid to act like a thin, invisible "skin." Liquids with high surface tension generally bead up when dropped onto highly waxed surfaces (as observed in Part A, Steps 1 and 2) or form a dome well above the rim of a glass (Part B) or on the head of a penny (Part C).

The high surface tension of water allows it to support not only objects that are less dense than water (such as powder, string, paper, and toothpicks), but also objects that are more dense than water (such as the needle in Part I). The high surface tension of water results from the very strong attraction water molecules have for each other. This tendency for particles of a liquid to be attracted to each other is called cohesion. Figure 4 provides a graphical illustration of the cohesive forces in a sample of water. Water molecules in the middle of a drop or glass of water are attracted equally in all directions. Those water molecules on the surface, however, are only attracted to water molecules within the sample. This creates the force across the surface which accounts for the observations in Parts A, B, and C, as well as the domed droplets of dew on leaves. Water molecules are not attracted to a waxed surface or the air that surrounds the outer layer.

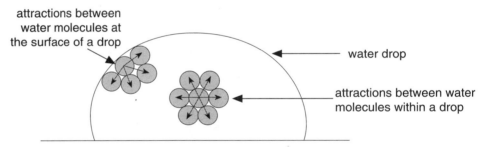

Figure 4: Molecules in the middle are attracted equally in all directions, but molecules on the surface are attracted only to other water molecules. This is an extremely simplified representation; a drop of water actually contains millions of water molecules which are slipping and sliding over and around one another.

Surface tension can be reduced by introducing a surfactant (a surface-acting agent) such as soap, which interferes with the attractive forces between the water molecules. The addition of the soap alters the behavior of the water at the point where the soap is introduced. Soap spreads out rapidly in all directions across the surface of the water from the point of entry and reduces the surface tension.

In the "Procedure," the addition of soap causes the less-dense, floating item to move away from the point of entry of the surfactant: the pepper spreads to the sides of the container; the boat moves forward, away from the soap; the spiral

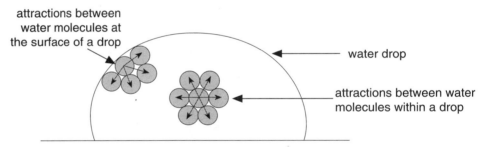

174

rotates; the thread loop spreads out when the soap is placed inside; and the toothpicks move apart. The more-dense needle (in Part I) sinks as the surfactant lowers the surface tension of the water. While less effective than soap or detergent, rubbing alcohol also lowers the surface tension of water. It also causes the powder and toothpicks to spread.

Assessment

Options:

- Challenge the students to design an experiment to determine at least one variable that affects the number of drops of water that can be placed on the head of a nickel. (Possible answers include the size of the drop, the height from which the drop is released, the cleanliness of the coin, impurities in the water, and the presence of contaminants on students' hands that interfere with the penny, dropper, or water.)

- Give a writing assignment as a possible portfolio entry: Certain insects, including water striders, use the principles of surface tension in order to travel across the water surface. Choose one of these insects and report on how its use of surface tension helps the creature to move, to hunt, or to carry out another aspect of its life.

Cross-Curricular Integration

Earth science:
- Observe the shapes of dew drops on leaves.

Life science:
- Have students study water striders and how they move across the surface of water.

References

Carle, M., Sarquis, M., Nolan, L. *Physical Science: The Challenge of Discovery;* D.C. Heath: Lexington, MA, 1991.

Herbert, D. *Mr. Wizard's Supermarket Science;* Random House: New York, 1980; p 46.

Strongin, H. *Science on a Shoe String;* Addison-Wesley: Menlo Park, CA, 1976.

"Surface Tension of Water," *WonderScience.* October 1989, 3(3).

Contributors

Rainel Dargis, Milford South Elementary School, Milford, OH; Teaching Science with TOYS, 1992.

Steven King, Northeastern High School, Springfield, OH; Teaching Science with TOYS, 1988–89.

Mark Rohrig, Milford South Elementary School, Milford, OH; Teaching Science with TOYS, 1992.

Donita Sheets, South Side Middle School, Anderson, IN; Teaching Science with TOYS, 1992–93.

ONE-WAY SCREEN

A screen-covered jar is filled by pouring water into it. But when it is inverted, the water remains inside! Students discover what makes this phenomenon possible.

One-Way Screen apparatus

GRADE LEVELS

Science activity appropriate for grades 1–12
Cross-Curricular Integration intended for grades 4–6

KEY SCIENCE TOPICS

- adhesion and cohesion
- atmospheric pressure
- intermolecular forces of attraction
- properties of water
- surface tension
- gravity

STUDENT BACKGROUND

Before doing this activity students should have previous experience with other activities that involve surface tension, air pressure, and gravity (such as the Teaching Science with TOYS activity "A Collection of Surface Tension Activities").

KEY PROCESS SKILLS

- observing

  Students observe the One-Way Screen apparatus as they manipulate it in different ways.

- communicating

  Students describe what happens in the activity and discuss their observations.

TIME REQUIRED

Setup	10	minutes
Performance	5–10	minutes
Cleanup	10	minutes

Materials

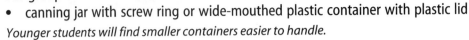

For "Getting Ready" only
Per group of 3–4 students
- canning jar with screw ring or wide-mouthed plastic container with plastic lid

Younger students will find smaller containers easier to handle.

- mesh screen (large enough to cover the jar mouth) used for window screens
- scissors to cut screen
- marker

For the "Procedure"
Per group of 3–4 students
- One-Way Screen apparatus prepared in "Getting Ready"
- card (large enough to cover the jar mouth)
- container filled with about 1 L water

A "pop-beaker" made from a cut-off plastic 2-L soft-drink bottle works well.

- plastic tub or bucket
- (optional) toothpicks thin enough (trimmed if necessary) to fit through screen

For the "Variation"
Per group
All materials listed for the "Procedure" plus the following:
- different types of cloth, including cheesecloth
- rubber band

For the "Extensions"
❶ All materials listed for the "Procedure" plus the following:
Per class
- soap

❷ All materials listed for the "Procedure" plus the following:
Per group
- screen with different mesh sizes

❸ Per class
- 1 or more cloth umbrellas

❺ Per class
- "The Liquid Show" video

This video is available to Ohio teachers from Southwestern Ohio Instructional Television Association (S.O.I.T.A.), Miami University, Oxford, OH 45056; (513) 529-7584. Teachers outside Ohio can order the video from Landmark Films, 3450 Slade Run Drive, Falls Church, VA 22042; (703) 241-2030.

Safety and Disposal

The screen can cause small scratches. If using glass containers, caution students to handle them carefully. No special disposal procedures are required.

Getting Ready

Prepare a jar for each group:

1. Use a marker to outline the lid on the screen.

2. Carefully cut the screen so it is neither too small (and not held by ring) nor too large (causing the screen to buckle once put into the ring.)

 If using plastic jars/lids, cut (or melt) out the top of the lid, leaving enough lip around the edge to grip the screen.

3. Place the screen over the mouth of the jar and screw on the ring or cut-out lid.

Introducing the Activity

As a demonstration for the class, do Steps 1–8 of the "Procedure" without the screen. Be sure to include Steps 2 and 6, which allow for class predictions. This demonstration provides students with a point of reference to the activity and allows them to see it as a discrepant event.

Procedure

1. Give each group a One-Way Screen apparatus and a plastic tub or bucket.

2. Ask students to predict what will happen if water is poured onto the screen.

3. Holding the apparatus over the tub, have a student from each group pour water through the screen until the jar is completely full.

4. Tell a student from each group to put the card on top of the screen and hold it down tightly with one hand.

5. Instruct the students to use the other hand to invert the jar while keeping it over the tub.

 *The jar must be in a vertical position, not tilted at an angle.*

6. Ask students to predict what will happen if they remove the card from the screen.

7. Tell students to carefully slide the card from the screen.

8. Ask students to describe what happens to the water. Be sure that they look closely at the bottom of the screen.

9. (optional) Suggest that each group push a toothpick through a hole in the screen. "What happens?" *The toothpick passes through the hole and floats to the top of the jar, yet little, if any, water comes out.* "What does this reveal?" *No unseen barrier is covering the screen and preventing water from running out.* "If the screen is permeable to large objects like toothpicks, how can it hold back the water?"

10. Ask students to tap the screen with a finger. "What happens?"

If water does not gush out of the jar, have the student slowly tilt the jar to one side until the water flows out.

11. Have groups discuss their observations and formulate plausible explanations.

Explanation

The following explanation is intended for the teacher's information. Modify the explanation for students as required.

As illustrated in the introduction, when an open jar of water is inverted, the water falls out (as expected) because of the downward pull of gravity on the water; however, with the screen on the jar, the water seemingly defies gravity by staying in the jar.

Of course, the conditions are not identical in these two cases. A close examination of the inverted apparatus (Step 8) shows that little half-dome drops project from the small holes in the screen. (See Figure 1.) This shows that while the water can come through the screen, its further movement is somehow hindered and the pull of gravity is overcome. This "antigravity" effect can be explained in terms of the nature of water and of air pressure.

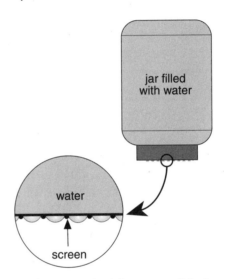

Figure 1: Half-dome drops project from small holes in the screen.

All matter is made up of tiny particles. An important feature of the particles of a liquid is that they are close enough to one another for the attractive forces to hold the particles together. These forces are called intermolecular forces of attraction. ("Inter" means "between.") Water particles have an especially strong attraction for one another. The attraction between particles of the same substance is called cohesion. Water particles also have a strong attraction for particles of some other substances, such as glass. The attraction between particles of different substances is called adhesion.

Another property of water is that its surface behaves as if it were an elastic film because of cohesion between its particles. The measure of this elastic-like force existing at the surface of liquids is called surface tension. The surface tension of a liquid is the amount of energy required to stretch or increase its surface area; the surface tension of water is very high.

A final factor affecting the system results from the air acting as a fluid. Atmospheric pressure exerts its force in all directions, helping support the water inside the jar. But in spite of the forces of cohesion, adhesion, and air pressure, water still falls out of an open inverted jar. If the size of the opening decreases

Teaching Chemistry with TOYS

sufficiently, the strength of the forces can be larger than the gravitational force and the water does not fall out. With the One-Way Screen apparatus, the screen provides lots of surface to which the water particles can adhere. Similarly, in the "Variation" and in Extension 3, the "holding" materials provide enough surface for the water particles to adhere and not pass through.

Although the surface of water behaves like an elastic film, the initial pouring of water through the screen and putting the toothpick through the hole in the screen provide evidence that no separate invisible film holds the water in the jar. Pulling a finger away from the outside of the screen (when tapping on it) adds an adhesive force in the direction of gravity and the water falls out of the jar.

When soap (a surfactant) is added to the water as in Extension 1, the soap particles come between the water particles and disrupt the strong cohesive forces; thus, soapy water will not be held back when the container is inverted because the surface tension is reduced.

Variation

Have each group fill a jar with water and wet a small cloth. Have each group place the wet cloth over the top of a jar of water and attach with a rubber band. Have them turn the jars upside down. "Is the cloth waterproof?" Try this with different types of cloth including cheesecloth.

Extensions

1. Have students redo the "Procedure" with a little soap added to the water. "Is the One-Way Screen still effective?"

    The soapy screen will not work subsequently as a One-Way Screen without being rinsed numerous times.

2. Have the students use screens of different mesh size to find how large the holes can be and still function as a One-Way Screen.

3. The next time a gentle rain is falling, take your students outside with one or more cloth umbrella(s). Ask students, "What keeps the rain from coming through the cloth? Can you blow air through the cloth? What kind of "skin" does an umbrella have? How does a cloth tarp on a truck work? How does a cloth tent keep the rain off the campers?"

4. Have students do one or more of the activities included in the Teaching Science with TOYS activity "A Collection of Surface Tension Activities."

5. As a class, watch the video "The Liquid Show." After viewing the video, students should be able to demonstrate the concept of displacement and how it affects floating objects, define density and explain its relationship to floating objects, explain with example how buoyancy is affected by water pressure, and demonstrate surface tension.

Cross-Curricular Integration

Language arts:
- Pretend you are a drop of water. Write a story describing the activity from that point of view.
- Read aloud or suggest that students read the following book:
  - *Magic School Bus at the Waterworks*, by Joanna Cole (Scholastic, ISBN 0590403613)
    Ms. Frizzle's class gets to see the waterworks from the inside.

Life science:
- Study how surface tension allows water-striders to stay on top of the water.

References

Herbert, D.; Ruchlis, H. *Mr. Wizard's 400 Experiments in Science;* Prism: Book Lab, New Jersey, 1983; rev. by D. Goldbert.

Mandell, M. *Physics Experiments for Children;* Dover: New York, 1968.

Stangl, J. *H₂O Science, Science Lessons and Experiments Using Water* (blackline masters); Simon & Schuster Supplementary Education Group: Carthage, IL, 1990.

Walpole, B. *175 Science Experiments to Amuse and Amaze Your Friends;* Random House: New York, 1988.

Watson, P. *Liquid Magic;* Lothrop, Lee, Shepard: New York, 1982.

Watson, P. *Science Club;* Lothrop, Lee, Shepard: New York, 1982.

Contributor

Jo Parkey, Smith Middle School, Vandalia, OH; Teaching Science with TOYS peer writer.

MYSTERIOUS SAND

Explore the behavior of sand coated with a waterproof material.

Commercial Magic Sand™

GRADE LEVELS

Science activity appropriate for grades 2–9
Cross-Curricular Integration intended for grades 4–6

KEY SCIENCE TOPICS

- attraction and repulsion
- hydrophobic properties

STUDENT BACKGROUND

Students should have had experience with the idea that some substances or objects attract one another and others repel.

KEY PROCESS SKILLS

• observing	Students observe the look, smell, and feel of different types of sand.
• comparing/contrasting	Students compare and contrast the properties of different types of sand.

TIME REQUIRED

Setup	15	minutes on two consecutive days first time;
	10	minutes thereafter
Performance	20–40	minutes
Cleanup	15	minutes

Materials

For "Getting Ready" only

These materials, intended for teacher use only, are needed if making a homemade version of Magic Sand™ the first time the activity is done.

- 1–2 cups of clean fine sand
- silicone spray (such as Scotchguard®, Wynn's Silicone Lubricant, etc.)
- shallow box
- newspaper

For the "Procedure"

Per station (2 or 3 stations per class, 1 for each type of sand used)

- 1 of the following types of sand:
  - ○ regular sand
  - ○ commercial Magic Sand™
  - ○ a homemade version of Magic Sand™

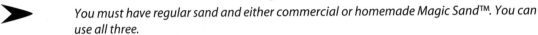 *You must have regular sand and either commercial or homemade Magic Sand™. You can use all three.*

- container filled with about 0.5 L water

A "pop-beaker" made from a cut-off plastic 2-L soft-drink bottle works well.

- closable container to hold sand (such as a zipper-type plastic bag or a jar with lid)
- dropper
- small dish
- 6 layers of newspaper
- spoons and/or other utensils

For storage

Per class

- pan
- paper towels or coffee filters
- rubber bands

For the "Extensions"

❶ Per class
- newspaper or cloth
- silicon spray
- water
- waxed paper
- plastic wrap
- glossy paper

❸ Per class
- hydrophobic powder (See the "Explanation") such as lycopodium
- container of water

❹ Per class
- various paints and/or dyes
- silicon spray
- sand

Safety and Disposal

If you are making the homemade version of Magic Sand™, prepare it in a well-ventilated area or outside. Avoid inhaling the silicone spray fumes and follow the directions on the can. Because the colorful commercial Magic Sand™ could be mistaken for candy or gelatin, caution students not to taste it or the homemade product.

Lycopodium powder (for possible use in Extension 3), as a dust, is very flammable. Keep it away from open flames. Avoid inhaling the dust, as its effects on the respiratory tract are unknown. Some people are allergic to airborne lycopodium.

Sands should be saved for reuse. (See the "Procedure," Step 6.) Homemade or commercial Magic Sand™ should not be used in fish tanks as it may kill the fish. Spills must be disposed of in a solid waste trash container, not in the sink. Wash lycopodium residue down the drain, or if you wish, filter it and save it for reuse.

Getting Ready

To make the homemade version of Magic Sand™:

1. Place newspaper in a box so that the paper lines the box with no gaps or cracks.

2. Sprinkle 1–2 cups of fine, clean sand in a thin layer on the newspaper.

3. Thoroughly and evenly spray the sand with the silicone spray.

4. Shake the box to expose all surfaces of the sand. Make sure the sand is evenly distributed and repeat Step 3.

5. Allow the sand to dry overnight.

6. Test a small amount of the treated sand by placing it in water. It should stick together and remain dry even when submerged in water. If the sand is actually wetted by the water, repeat Steps 1–5.

7. Store the treated sand in a marked container.

Introducing the Activity

Options:

- Encourage team observation, comparison, investigation, and data recording of each type of sand. Emphasize the scientific method. (Wait until the wrap-up discussion to explain the lesson concepts.)

- Encourage students to bring different materials to class, test their ability to soak up water, and classify them based on this ability.

- With a plastic glove on one hand, put both hands in water, showing how the glove "coats" the skin, keeping it dry.

Procedure

Have the students move from station to station, and do Steps 1–4 at each. Instruct the students to fill out the Data Sheet (provided) as they make observations:

Caution students not to taste any of the materials!
1. Observe how the sand flows while pouring some into the small dish. Everyone should see, touch, and smell.

2. Collect some sand on a spoon, then use the dropper to put a drop of water onto the sand.

3. Pour some sand into the container of water.

Allow time for all students to move the sand with spoons and/or other utensils.

4. Spoon some of the sand out of the water, put it on newspaper, then feel it.

5. Label areas on the chalkboard for students to record their observations about each station. Make sure students compare each type of sand, both dry and in water.

6. To save each type of sand, place a coffee filter or paper towel over the container opening and secure it with a rubber band. Carefully pour off as much water as possible from the sand. Pour each type of sand onto a sheet of paper, spread the sand into a thin layer, and allow it to dry. Store each type of dry sand in its container.

Explanation

The following explanation is intended for the teacher's information. Modify the explanation for students as required.

In this activity, students observe the behavior of different types of sand in water. Regular (untreated) sand becomes wet when placed in water; commercial or homemade Magic Sand™ stays dry. Such behavior is an example of a general phenomenon involving water. A substance attracted to water is hydrophilic. ("Hydro" means "water" and "philic" means "loving.") A substance repelled by water is hydrophobic. ("Phobic" means "fearing.") Grains of regular sand become wet because they have hydrophilic portions on their surface and thus are attracted to water. In contrast, the surfaces of grains of Magic Sand™ (either commercial or homemade) have been coated with a hydrophobic substance and so they are not "wetted" by water; that is, they tend to stay in contact with each other. When the water is removed, the grains are observed to be dry.

More Advanced Levels

A compositional classification scheme of matter categorizes compounds as either covalent or ionic. Covalent compounds (generally those comprised of nonmetal elements) are further categorized as either polar (different atoms bonded to one another) or nonpolar (same atoms or carbon and hydrogen bonded to one another). These distinctions allow us to predict how various substances will interact with one another when mixed together: covalent compounds of the same type (polar or nonpolar) generally have an affinity for another while those of the opposite type do not. This generalization is the source of the expression "Like dissolves like." Since water is polar and silicone is nonpolar, they are repelled by one another.

The same classification scheme categorizes two or more substances combined together as a mixture, either homogeneous (properties are uniform throughout) or heterogeneous (properties are nonuniform). Which type of mixture results depends upon the nature of the particles of the substances. A heterogeneous mixture occurs when the simplest particles of one substance are large (visible to the eye) *or* when repulsion occurs between particles of the different substances. A homogeneous mixture occurs when the particles of one substance are smaller *and* attraction occurs between particles of the different substances. Regular (untreated), commercial, or homemade Magic Sand™ in water comprises a heterogeneous mixture.

Extensions

1. Tear a sheet of newspaper or cloth in half. Spray both sides of one half with silicone and allow it to dry. Have students compare the behavior of drops of water on treated and untreated halves. Have them compare this behavior to water drops on waxed paper, plastic wrap, and glossy paper.

2. Have students do a long-term study of water-repellent materials in water to investigate whether or not the items remain hydrophobic. Try commercial and homemade Magic Sand™, the cloth or paper from Extension 1, or other water-repellent materials.

3. Spread a hydrophobic powder on the surface of water. Push your hand through the powder, and then pull it out. The hand remains dry. (See Sarquis reference.)

4. Have students investigate methods for coloring the sand, both before and after silicone spraying.

Cross-Curricular Integration

Language arts:
- Have students describe possible uses for a hydrophobic substance.
- Have students write about hydrophobia.
- Have students investigate other words containing "hydro," "phobic," or "philic" (such as "Philadelphia").

References

"Powder Glove;" *Fun with Chemistry: A Guidebook of K–12 Activities;* Sarquis, M., Sarquis, J., Eds.; Institute for Chemical Education: Madison, WI, 1993; Vol. 2, pp 177–180.

Robson, D.P. "Magic Sand™," *ChemMatters.* April 1994, 8–9.

Contributors

Sue Ehrlich, Tri-County North Elementary School, Lewisburg, OH; Teaching Science with TOYS, 1988–89.
Jo Parkey, Smith Middle School, Vandalia, OH; Teaching Science with TOYS peer writer.

Handout Master

A master for the following handout is provided:
- Mysterious Sand—Data Sheet

Copy as needed for classroom use.

Names _____

MYSTERIOUS SAND

Data Sheet

Procedure	Station 1	Station 2	Station 3
Pour some sand into the dish. Describe how it pours and looks.			
Smell the sand. Describe any odor.			
Rub the sand between your fingers. How does it feel?			
Use a dropper to put a drop of water on a spoonful of sand. Describe what you see.			
Place a spoonful of sand into the container of water. What happens?			
Spoon some of the sand out of the water, put it on some newspaper, and feel it again. How does it feel?			

Teaching Chemistry with TOYS

SUMI NAGASHI

By creating Sumi Nagashi (a traditional Japanese art, pronounced sue-me na-ga-she), students discover that some materials "dislike" water.

Sumi Nagashi

GRADE LEVELS

Science activity appropriate for grades 3–12
Cross-Curricular Integration intended for grades 4–6

KEY SCIENCE TOPICS

- nonpolar/polar (hydrophobic/hydrophilic) properties

STUDENT BACKGROUND

Before doing the activity, students should be familiar with the concepts of mixtures and attractive and repulsive forces between particles of various substances and water (hydrophilic versus hydrophobic).

KEY PROCESS SKILLS

- observing | Students observe the behavior of two hydrophobic materials, ink and oil, on water.
- hypothesizing | Students form hypotheses to explain how Sumi Nagashi works.

TIME REQUIRED

Setup	10	minutes
Performance	10–25	minutes
Cleanup	10	minutes

Materials

For the "Procedure"
Per class
- sink or tub for disposal of inky water
- newspaper or paper towels

> *If desired, each group could have a small tub for disposal.*

Per student
- at least 1 sheet of art-quality drawing paper
- 2 cotton swabs or 1 double-ended swab cut in half

Per group of 3–4 students
- permanent-type india ink
- shallow pan such as a pie pan
- stirring stick
- a small amount of oil (olive, peanut, baby, corn) if students' skin is not oily enough
- container filled with about 1 L water

 A beaker made from a cut-off plastic 2-L soft-drink bottle works well.

For the "Variations"

❶ All materials listed for the "Procedure" plus the following:
Per class
- assorted papers, such as oak tag, construction, newsprint, tissue
- inks such as printers, permanent or water-based fountain pen, stamp pad
- (optional) a variety of oils, such as olive, peanut, baby, corn

❷ Per class
- a dark powdered substance, such as cinnamon or pepper
- a small amount of liquid dish detergent
- small plastic cups
- inexpensive white paper

For the "Extensions"

❶ All materials listed for the "Procedure" plus the following:
Per class
- larger sheets of paper
- pans larger than the paper used

❷ Per class
- a commercial kit for marbling paper or fabric (See Extension 2) or the following:
  ○ paint (oil- or water-based)
  ○ turpentine (if using oil-based paint) or Marble Thix® powder (See Extension 2) or similar product (if using water-based acrylic paint)

Safety and Disposal

Spilled ink will cause permanent or difficult-to-remove stains on clothing; wearing aprons or smocks is advisable. Doing Extension 3 with turpentine and oil-based paints is not recommended due to the extensive safety and disposal procedures required for turpentine. If you decide to use turpentine, check a science education supply company (such as Flinn) catalog for safety and disposal or read the turpentine container.

Getting Ready

To avoid disappointment, test the activity with your paper and ink to make sure that the ink transfers onto the drawing paper without too much smearing. If smearing occurs, try different paper.

If you are using double-ended swabs, cut them in half with scissors. Cut paper into a size that fits flat inside the shallow pan.

Introducing the Activity

Options:

- Discuss the artistic aspects of this activity. Sumi Nagashi is similar to marbling, a process in which paint is floated on a gel, then transferred to paper. Marbled paper is sometimes used as end pages in a book. The advantage of this option is that it better enables students to visualize what they will be doing; the disadvantage is that it spoils the surprise.

- Introduce or review the scientific topics to be studied. (See "Key Science Topics.")

- Present the introduction in a problem-solving format by relating what they know about oil and water to oil spills and their cleanup.

Procedure

One student from each group should complete Steps 1–9 on the Student Instructions and Observations Sheet (provided), recording observations after each step. Then another student from each group should complete the steps. Groups should continue in this way until all students have had at least one turn. Then do the following:

1. Have students compare their observations and discuss possible explanations for how Sumi Nagashi works. By asking students guided questions, lead them to observe the ink spreading, rings forming, and ink transferring to paper if they have not already made these observations.

2. Through a class discussion, lead students to an understanding of the scientific concepts behind Sumi Nagashi.

Explanation

The following explanation is intended for the teacher's information. Modify the explanation for students as required.

India ink (similar to the sumi used in Japanese art) is a special mixture of a black pigment (either carbon black or lampblack) in water. Both pigments are forms of carbon. When a small amount of ink is placed on the surface of the water, the black pigment tries to spread in a thin layer over the entire surface. Similarly, oil placed on the surface of water also tries to spread in a thin layer over the entire surface. This behavior occurs because both the black pigment and the oil are hydrophobic. ("Hydro" means "water" and "phobic" means "fearing.") Hydrophobic substances do not mix with water. Conversely, a substance that is attracted to water is hydrophilic. ("Philic" means "loving.")

In this activity, the presence of both ink and oil prevents either material from completely spreading out; thus, as the process of alternately putting down drops of ink and oil is repeated, a series of concentric circles of ink and oil results. Gentle swirling of the water surface disturbs the symmetrical pattern of the circles but does not allow the separated oil and ink to join up, and a swirled pattern results. The pattern can be transferred to paper because the black pigment is attracted to the paper. So, when the paper is laid upon the surface, the ink adheres to the paper, maintaining the swirled pattern. Another familiar form of carbon, the graphite used in "lead" pencils, has a similar affinity for paper.

More Advanced Levels

To explore the explanation in greater detail, consider a compositional classification scheme for matter that categorizes covalent compounds (generally those comprised of nonmetal elements) as either polar (different atoms bonded to one another) or nonpolar (same atoms or carbon (C) and hydrogen (H) bonded to one another). These distinctions allow us to predict how various substances will interact with one another when mixed together. Covalent compounds of the same type generally have an affinity for one another while those of the opposite type do not; thus, the rule of thumb that "Like dissolves like."

Because oils consist mostly of carbon and hydrogen, they are nonpolar and will not dissolve in water, which is polar. Oil molecules with no polar regions form oil beads on the surface of the water to minimize contact just like polar water beads on the surface of a car coated with nonpolar wax; however, some oil molecules have small polar regions that affect their behavior with water. A small amount of an oil with a few polar regions will spread into a very thin layer (possibly only one molecule thick, a monolayer) upon the surface of the water so that all polar regions can contact the polar water. This is what happens in this activity.

Because the pigments used in Sumi Nagashi (either carbon black or lampblack) are mostly carbon, they are nonpolar and do not dissolve in water. Rather, the particles of the pigments are small enough to constitute a sol, a type of colloid in which solid particles are dispersed in a liquid phase.

Variations

1. Have students investigate the specific properties of the india ink and drawing paper by doing the activity with several different materials: Have student groups rotate among alternate stations set up with different papers and inks (and oils, if desired) and then compare results. Because the india ink-drawing paper combination gives the sharpest pattern, students may be disappointed if they don't get to do at least one of this type. Before doing with students, test the various papers and inks so a range of qualities is obtained.

2. Younger students can make a simpler "surface tension print" as follows: Fill a cup with water so that the water surface curves above the top of the cup. Have students sprinkle a small amount of a powdered substance such as cinnamon or pepper on the surface of the water, dip a swab in liquid dish detergent, and touch the swab to the water. Then, have students gently place a piece of paper on the water and remove the print.

Extensions

1. Have students decorate larger sheets of paper using larger pans or tubs.

 Doing Extension 2 with turpentine and oil-based paints is not recommended. See Safety and Disposal.

2. Have students try marbling with paints. Oil-based paints must be floated on turpentine or paint thinners. For oil-based methods, see Barbara Taylor, *Step into Science™; Sink or Swim! The Science of Water* (Random House, pp 34–35; ISBN 0679808159) or Linda Allison, *Trash Artists Workshop* (Fearon Teacher

Aids, a division of Pittman Learning, pp 42–43, ISBN 0822497808). Water-based acrylics can be used if floated on water thickened with Marble Thix® powder from Delta Technical Coatings, 2550 Pellissier Place, Whittier, CA 90601, (800) 423-4135. Marbling kits are also available. One brand is EZ2 Do Twist and Swirl® from Kenner® Toys. Another marbling kit is available from Educational Innovations (# ED1 #PM-1), 151 River Road, Cos Cob, CT 06807; (203) 629-6049.

Cross-Curricular Integration

Art:
- Have students study Japanese origami and/or calligraphy.
- Bring in a sample book of washi (handmade Japanese paper). Washi is usually made of mulberry fibers and often is translucent with tiny flowers or other items imbedded in it. You can order a book with 150 3½-inch x 6¾-inch samples from Aiko's Art Materials, 3347 North Clark Street, Chicago, IL 60657; (312) 404-5600.

Language arts:
- Read aloud or suggest that students read the following book:
  - *Sadako and the Thousand Paper Cranes,* by Eleanor Coerr (Dell, ISBN 0-440-77465-9)
    This book provides a look at another Japanese art form that uses paper—origami. In the story, a young girl struggling with leukemia makes origami cranes.

Life science:
- Have students study cell membranes and/or lipids, solutions, and suspensions.
- Discuss oil in feathers of birds and ducks.
- Discuss the effects of oil on skin, including repulsion of water.

Social studies:
- Have the students research the history of paper. Where and when was it first developed? What types of fibers are used to make paper? Paper companies will provide free swatch books that contain many interesting paper samples.
- Have the students study oil spills in large bodies of water and cleanup procedures.

References

Shakhashiri, B.Z. *Chemical Demonstrations, A Handbook for Teachers of Chemistry;* University of Wisconsin, Madison, WI: 1989; Vol. 3, pp 301–304, 358–359.

Suzuki, C., Dept. of Education, Shiga University, Hiratsu, Ohtsu, Shiga, Japan. Abstract P3.35; 11th International Conference on Chemical Education, York, England, August 1991.

Contributor

Jo Parkey, Smith Middle School, Vandalia, OH; Teaching Science with TOYS peer writer.

Handout Master

A master for the following handout is provided:
- Sumi Nagashi—Student Instructions and Observations Sheet

Copy as needed for classroom use.

SUMI NAGASHI
Student Instructions and Observations Sheet

Perform the following steps and use another sheet of paper to record responses when indicated. This experiment requires observations in most steps. Take care—india ink will stain clothing and skin.

1. Pour enough fresh water into the shallow pan to cover the bottom.

2. Put a small amount of india ink on the tip of one swab, either by dipping or by using a dropper. Barely touch the ink swab tip to the center of the water surface and quickly remove. (Very little ink is needed—the more noticeable the ink, the darker the resulting picture. Use your own judgment to determine desired darkness.) Record your observations.

3. Put a very small amount of oil on the tip of another swab (either by lightly rubbing it on your nose or forehead, or by touching it into the oil container). Touch the oil swab tip to the center of the spreading ink. Record your observations.

4. Again, barely touch the ink swab tip to the center of the water and quickly remove; then touch the center of the ink with the oil swab tip.

5. Repeat Steps 3 and 4 several times. Record your observations.

6. VERY GENTLY swirl the surface with a stick to make a complex pattern of the ink. (Do not stir vigorously because this spoils the effect.) Record your observations.

7. Place paper on the water, press down any corners that curl up, then remove it. Let the paper drip for a moment, and lay the resulting Sumi Nagashi artwork flat (ink side up) on newspaper or paper towels. (If some ink still appears on the surface of the water, you may try to collect it on another piece of paper. However, you generally have to begin again with fresh water to prepare another design.) Record your observations.

8. Discard inky water into a sink or tub.

9. Explain your observations.

CHROMATOGRAPHY COLOR BURST

Separate ink pigments into flower-like color bursts.

Chromatography color bursts

Materials

For the "Procedure"
Per student
- 2 plastic cups
- water

- 2 water-soluble, fine- or medium-point felt-tipped pens of different brands or colors

➤ *Black ink is preferable; Crayola® and Vis-a-Vis® brands work well.*

- paper circles, 9–15 cm in diameter (made from filter paper or coffee filters)

➤ *Chromatography on filter paper produces a much clearer color separation than chromatography on coffee filters, but coffee filters are much less expensive. You may wish to let each student do several color bursts on coffee filters and then do one design on the more expensive filter paper.*

- piece of a pipe cleaner (about 4 inches in length)

➤ *The large, fluffy pipe cleaners, available at craft and discount stores, work best. The cost is minimal—about $1 for 25.*

Per class
- sharpened pencil, nail, or similar tool to poke a 2–3-mm hole in the paper
- scissors

For the "Variations"

❶ All materials listed for the "Procedure" plus the following:
- 1 stick of porous (not dustless) chalk

❷ Per student
- white cloth (cotton or cotton blend), such as a T-shirt or fabric square
- rubbing alcohol
- dropper
- 2 different permanent felt-tipped pens

➤ *Black ink does not work well.*

- a wide-mouth container such as a plastic margarine or ice cream tub
- plastic lid for the wide-mouth container or a rubber band

➤ *The lid or rubber band is used to hold the fabric in place over the container. If you use a lid, cut the middle out of it.*

- paintbrush
- (optional) latex

➤ *Latex is available from Flinn Scientific, (800) 452-1261, catalog # L0004 for 500 mL. Latex is also available from other science education suppliers.*

Safety and Disposal

No special safety or disposal procedures are required.

Getting Ready

1. Test each type of pen to make sure that the ink will migrate and/or separate on the paper. All water-soluble pens do not work equally well.

2. If using latex to set the design in Variation 2, prepare a 50/50 latex/water solution by mixing equal parts of latex and water.

Introducing the Activity

Have each student do the following to observe capillary action before making color bursts:

1. Poke a small hole (2–3 mm in diameter) through the center of the paper circle with a sharpened pencil or similar tool.

2. Wet the piece of pipe cleaner completely, then push it through the hole in the paper circle (from the bottom).

3. Put enough water into a cup so that the bottom of the pipe cleaner will dip into the water. Dry the rim.

4. Place the paper circle on the rim of the cup with the pipe cleaner dipped into the water. Observe as the water moves toward the edge of the paper.

5. Have students suggest reasons why the water moved toward the edge of the paper. Through a facilitated discussion, lead them to the topic of capillary action.

Procedure

Have each student follow the steps listed on the Student Instructions and Data Sheet (provided).

Explanation

The following explanation is intended for the teacher's information. Modify the explanation for students as required.

Although the ink in a marking pen appears to be just one color, it often consists of more than one color. That is, the ink is a mixture, comprised of two or more substances, each of which retains its own properties within the mixture. One characteristic of a mixture is that the component substances can be separated from one another by physical processes. In this activity, the water-soluble property of the inks is used to separate the component substances.

When the paper circle and pipe cleaner are put into contact with water, the water travels up the pipe cleaner and outward through the paper circle by capillary action. The leading edge of the water moves because of the attraction of water particles to particles in paper (adhesion); the trailing water follows along because of strong attraction between water particles themselves (cohesion). When the water (which is called the mobile phase) contacts a water-soluble ink, the ink dissolves in the water. As the water continues to move, the component substances in the ink are carried along. The different substances spread outward at different rates on the paper circle (which is called the stationary phase).

The rate of travel for a substance depends on two factors: the magnitude of the attraction between the particles of the substance and the particles of water and the attraction between the particles of the substance and the paper. Because the attractions for each of the component substances is different, the pigments separate from one another as the water moves. Those substances with greatest attraction for the water move across the paper the most; those with greatest attraction for the paper move the least.

The process of separating the components of a mixture of compounds in this way is called paper chromatography. The resulting "separation picture" or "color burst" produced on the paper circle is called a chromatogram. There are types of chromatography other than paper chromatography, but all separate a mixture by using a stationary phase and a mobile phase. For example, in Variation 2 the cloth is the stationary phase and the alcohol is the mobile phase. Chromatography is used to separate and identify the components of mixtures.

Variations

1. Separate the component substances of the ink of a single pen on a stick of porous chalk. Use the pen to make a circle around the chalk about 1 cm from one end, then stand the chalk up on that end in a small amount of water (with the level of water below the circle). Remove the chalk when the leading edge of color approaches the top.

2. Students can use the chromatography color burst technique to decorate white clothing such as T-shirts by following these steps:

    a. Stretch the cloth over a container with a wider opening than the desired design and hold in place with a cut-out lid or rubber band.

    b. Make the circle-of-dots pattern (as described in the Student Instructions and Data Sheet, Step 3) on the cloth using brightly colored permanent markers.

    c. Using a dropper, gradually drop rubbing alcohol into the center of the dots until the desired design size is reached.

    d. After drying, iron to help set the design. In addition, you may wish to set the design by painting over it with a 50/50 latex/water solution and allowing the design to dry thoroughly.

 Use cold water when washing the cloth to minimize fading.

Extension

Have students compare the color patterns of different designs to determine which ones used the same brand of pen.

Cross-Curricular Integration

Art:
*   Bend a piece of flower wire or a green pipe cleaner in half and push both ends through a small piece of foam (that is to be the flower center). Push both ends of the wire or pipe cleaner through the top of the color burst design (beside and around the hole) until the foam is against the paper. Use transparent tape to secure the back side of the paper to the wire or pipe cleaner. If using the flower wire, use green floral tape to wrap the wire (making a stem). A plastic or paper leaf or two can be wrapped in if desired.

Math:

- Use linear measurement to compare the distance traveled by each pigment (from the center of the spots) to the distance traveled by the water. (Stop the water before it reaches the edge of the paper.) What percent of the water distance is each of the pigment distances?

References

Becker, R.; Ihde, J.; Cox, K.; Sarquis, J.L. "Making Radial Chromatography Creative Chromatography," *Journal of Chemical Education.* 1992, 69, 979–986.

"Separating Colors," "Chromatography Flowers," "Chromatography T-shirt Designs;" *Fun with Chemistry: A Guidebook of K–12 Activities;* Sarquis, M., Sarquis, J., Eds.; Institute for Chemical Education: Madison, WI, 1993; Vol. 2, pp 3–8, 23–28, 29–35.

Handout Master

A master for the following handout is provided:

- Student Instructions and Data Sheet

Copy as needed for classroom use.

CHROMATOGRAPHY COLOR BURST
Student Instructions and Data Sheet

Perform these steps and use another sheet of paper to record responses when indicated.

1. Poke a small hole (2–3 mm in diameter) through the center of the paper circle with a sharpened pencil or similar tool.

2. Write your name lightly in pencil on one side of the paper circle.

3. Prepare a coin-sized ring of small dots around the hole in the paper circle: use one pen to make five or six equally-spaced dots, then use a second pen of a different color or brand to equally space dots in between the first ones.

4. Draw a picture of the color pattern.

5. Put enough water into a cup so that the bottom of the pipe cleaner will dip into the water. Dry the rim.

6. Predict what will happen to the dots and/or to the pattern when the paper becomes wet.

7. Wet the pipe cleaner completely, then push it from the bottom through the hole in the paper circle. (See Figure 1.)

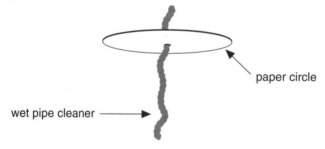

Figure 1: Insert the wet pipe cleaner through the hole in the paper circle.

8. Place the paper circle on the rim of the cup with the pipe cleaner dipped into the water. Record your observations of changes until any color comes near the edge of the paper circle.

9. Lift the paper off of the cup, remove the pipe cleaner, and set the paper on the rim of another cup to dry.

10. Compare the observed results to your predictions.

11. Do the inks appear to be a single substance or a mixture of two or more substances? How can you tell?

Activities for Grades 7–9

Properties of Silly Putty®

Marshmallow in a Syringe

Liquid to Gas in a "Flick"

Salt Solutions and Grow Creatures

The Liquid Timer Race

Density Bottles

Frustration Bottles

Expanding, Floating Bubbles

Hats Off to the Drinking Bird

Heat Solution™

Color-Changing Cars

Investigating the Effect of Temperature on Lightsticks

Experimenting with Light-Sensitive Paper

The Diving Whale

PROPERTIES OF SILLY PUTTY®

Why does Silly Putty® adsorb ink from comics? Explore the solubility properties of Silly Putty® and inks as well as some of the mechanical properties of Silly Putty®.

Silly Putty® and newspaper

GRADE LEVELS

Science activity appropriate for grades 4–9
Cross-Curricular Integration intended for grades 7–9

KEY SCIENCE TOPICS

- polymers
- properties of solids and liquids
- solubility (like dissolves like)

KEY PROCESS SKILLS

- communicating — Students discuss their observations and experimental results of working with Silly Putty®.

- investigating — Students investigate the transfer of various inks from paper to the surface of Silly Putty® and relate it to solubility.

TIME REQUIRED

Setup	10	minutes
Performance	20–40	minutes
Cleanup	5	minutes

Materials

For the "Procedure"
Part A, per group
- 1 package of Silly Putty®
- 1 pen with water-soluble ink
- 1 pen with water-insoluble ink
- newsprint
- comic books
- variety of other printed materials as desired:
  - photocopies
  - magazine pages
  - computer print
  - typewriter print

- variety of other ink pens as desired:
    ○ permanent markers
    ○ ball-point pens
    ○ felt-tip markers
    ○ water-soluble overhead projector markers
  - scrap paper

For "Variations and Extensions"

❶ Per group
  - 3 different colors of paper clips (or pop beads)

❷ Per group
  - materials for students to make their own inks

Safety and Disposal

No special safety or disposal procedures are required.

Introducing the Activity

Discuss the idea of two liquids mixing with each other. Challenge students to think of two liquids that form a solution when mixed and two liquids that don't form a solution when mixed. For example, a solution results when rubbing alcohol and water are mixed but doesn't occur when vegetable oil and vinegar are mixed, as in salad dressing. In this activity, students investigate the polar or nonpolar nature of Silly Putty®.

Procedure

Part A: Silly Putty® Pick-up Test

1. Allow student groups 10–20 minutes to examine the ability of Silly Putty® to pick up different inks from a variety of printed materials.

2. Ask groups to make summary statements on their findings.

3. Ask students to rub their own fingers across the newsprint

   - after having handled the Silly Putty® in the steps above;

   - after washing hands with soap and drying; and

   - after rubbing their fingers across their noses.

4. Challenge students to suggest explanations for their observations.

Part B: Investigation of the Mechanical Properties of Silly Putty®

1. Allow student groups 10–20 minutes to examine the mechanical properties of Silly Putty®. For example, students could roll it, bounce it, stretch it, and roll it into a ball and let it sit several minutes.

2. Ask groups to summarize and discuss their observations.

3. Ask what happens when Silly Putty® is pulled slowly (it stretches) versus pulled rapidly (it snaps).

4. Challenge students to suggest explanations for their observations.

Variations and Extensions

1. Have each group build a model of the silicon-oxygen polymer chain using two different colors of paper clips (or pop beads). Have one member from each group bring his or her chain to the front of the classroom and join the two chains somewhere in the middle by using a third color paper clip to represent the link between chains. Tell students that the cross-links are weak and can be easily broken by a stress. Bouncing causes some cross-links to break but those remaining intact cause the Silly Putty® to regain its original shape. Stretching applies stress for a longer time and will break more of the cross-links so the original shape is not regained when the stress is removed.

2. Challenge students to design their own ink for Silly Putty® "Pick-Up" pictures.

3. Study the properties of polyvinyl alcohol polymer gels such as Slime®. (See "Make-It-Yourself Slime" reference.) The observations of the two different polymer systems can then be compared and contrasted.

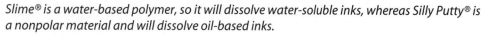

Slime® is a water-based polymer, so it will dissolve water-soluble inks, whereas Silly Putty® is a nonpolar material and will dissolve oil-based inks.

Explanation

The following explanation is intended for the teacher's information. Modify the explanation for students as required.

Silly Putty® is a polymer that was discovered in 1941 as General Electric Laboratories was attempting to make a synthetic rubber using silicon instead of carbon. A silicone polymer, which contains silicon-oxygen chains instead of the carbon-carbon chains found in many polymers, was heated with boric oxide to a temperature of about 200°C. When the polymer was cooled, the material now known as Silly Putty® was formed.

Silly Putty® is well-known for its ability to pick up ink from the newspaper. But, as your students observe, Silly Putty® does not pick up all the inks tested. The reason it picks up some inks but not others is due to differences in solubility of the inks.

A rule of thumb for solubility of two substances is "Like dissolves like." The "like" refers to the polar or nonpolar nature of the two materials, and the polarity of a substance depends on the elements involved, the type of bonding, and the molecular shape of a substance. Water and isopropyl alcohol (found in rubbing alcohol) are examples of polar substances, and oil and fat are examples of nonpolar substances. Water and isopropyl alcohol (both polar) dissolve in each other in all proportions, but water and oil or water and fat (polar and nonpolar, respectively) do not dissolve in each other.

Newspaper ink is a pigment suspended in oil (a nonpolar material) which is adsorbed by the paper. Adsorption is the binding or attraction of particles to a surface. Different colors of ink are obtained by mixing particular pigments with the oil. (See Table 1.) Since Silly Putty® picks up the ink from a newspaper, it must also be a nonpolar material. The pigment-oil suspension of the oil-based inks is readily adsorbed by Silly Putty®. Our oily skin often picks up newsprint for the same reason.

Table 1: Common Pigments in Ink	
Color	Pigment
white	titanium dioxide/zinc oxide
red	iron(III) oxide (rust)
blue	sodium aluminum silicate
yellow	chromates of lead and zinc
black	carbon black

Silly Putty® has several unusual mechanical properties. It can be rolled into a spherical ball, but, if left to sit for a period of time, it will spread out and flatten. It can be stretched if pulled slowly, but a rapid pull causes the two pieces to break with a snap. Thus, Silly Putty® is a non-Newtonian fluid, a fluid that doesn't behave like most fluids. The viscosity of most fluids only depends on the temperature of the fluid. (See the Teaching Science with TOYS activity "Liquid Timer Race.") In non-Newtonian fluids, the viscosity also depends on the amount of force that is applied. These properties of Silly Putty® can be related to its molecular structure. The basic structure is a silicon-oxygen chain with boron atoms in place of some of the silicon atoms. Because each boron atom in the Silly Putty® polymer is attached to a hydroxyl (–OH) group, there are many opportunities for hydrogen bonding. However, water-soluble inks, such as those in washable overhead projector pens, are not significantly adsorbed by nonpolar Silly Putty®. In this case, the hydrogen bond is the attraction between a hydrogen atom that is bonded to an oxygen atom and an oxygen atom on an adjacent molecule. (See Figures 1 and 2.) The hydrogen bonds are much weaker than the covalent cross-linking bonds and as a result can be easily broken. If pulled slowly, not as many bonds are broken and Silly Putty® tends to flow instead of snap.

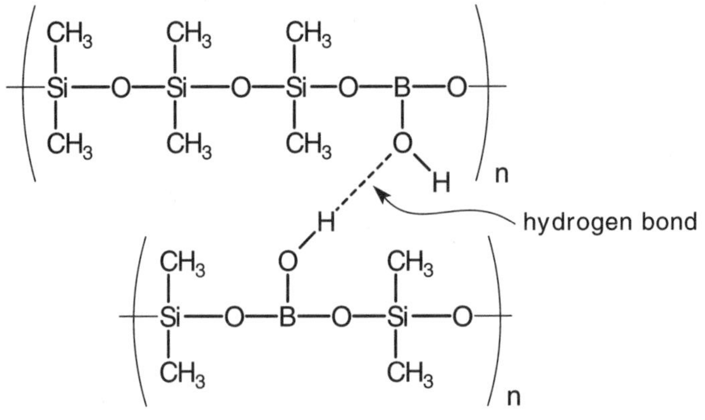

Figure 1: Hydrogen bonding in Silly Putty®

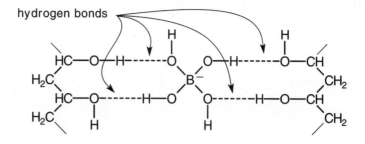

Figure 2: Hydrogen bonding in polyvinyl alcohol gel Slime®

Cross-Curricular Integration

Home, safety, and career:
- Have students research the history of other cases where a product produced by "accident" turned out to be important. Examples include Teflon®, Ivory® soap, and DuPont Stainmaster stain guard.

References

Armitage, D.A. et al. "The Preparation of Bouncing Putty: An Undergraduate Experiment in Silicone Chemistry," *Journal of Chemical Education.* 1973, 50(6), 434.

Casassa, E.Z.; Sarquis, A.M.; Van Dyke, C.H. "The Gelation of Polyvinyl Alcohol with Borax," *Journal of Chemical Education.* 1986, 63(1), 57.

"Make-It-Yourself Slime;" *Fun with Chemistry: A Guidebook of K–12 Activities;* Sarquis; M.; Sarquis, J., Eds.; Institute for Chemical Education: Madison, WI, 1993; Vol. 2, pp 67–76.

Marsella, G. "Silly Putty®," *ChemMatters.* 1986, 4(2), 15.

Walker, J. "The Amateur Scientist—Serious Fun with Polyok, Silly Putty, Slime and Other Non-Newtonian Fluids," *Scientific American.* November 1978, 239, 186–196.

Contributor

Alison Dowd, Talawanda Middle School, Oxford, OH; Teaching Science with TOYS peer writer.

MARSHMALLOW IN A SYRINGE

Students use marshmallows to study the effect that changing pressure has upon the volume of a gas.

Marshmallows in syringes

GRADE LEVELS

Science activity appropriate for grades 3–12
Cross-Curricular Integration intended for grades 7–9

KEY SCIENCE TOPICS

- colloids
- gases
- compressibility of gases
- incompressibility of liquids
- pressure-volume relationship of a gas (Boyle's law)

STUDENT BACKGROUND

This activity works best after students have studied the states of matter, particularly gases. It may be used either to introduce and stimulate discussion of the gas laws or as an opportunity for students to apply their knowledge of Boyle's law (pressure-volume relationship) to explain the phenomenon of the expanding marshmallow. The activity may also be used to illustrate a common colloid.

KEY PROCESS SKILLS

• inferring	Students develop ideas concerning the relationship of gas volume and pressure by observing a marshmallow in a syringe.
• controlling variables	Students change the pressure inside the syringe so that the variation of gas volume in the marshmallow may be observed.

TIME REQUIRED

Setup	5	minutes
Performance	15	minutes
Cleanup	5	minutes

Materials

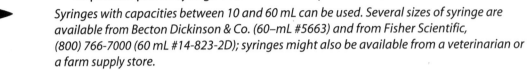

For "Getting Ready" only

These materials, intended for teacher use only, are needed to make the syringe caps the first time the activity is done.

- Bunsen burner, candle, or match
- 2 pairs of tongs, forceps, or tweezers
- small container with water

For the "Procedure"

Per group
- disposable plastic syringe with LEUR-LOK tip

Syringes with capacities between 10 and 60 mL can be used. Several sizes of syringe are available from Becton Dickinson & Co. (60–mL #5663) and from Fisher Scientific, (800) 766-7000 (60 mL #14-823-2D); syringes might also be available from a veterinarian or a farm supply store.

- syringe cap (made from the plastic connector of a disposable syringe needle)

Becton Dickinson & Co. #5167; available from Fisher Scientific, # 14-826-5B. Students will NOT be using the needle in this activity, only the plastic connector.

- water
- several fresh mini-marshmallows of the same size

Safety and Disposal

Prepare the syringe cap (See "Getting Ready") outside of class. Take care not to get melted plastic on your skin. Proper fire safety should be exercised, such as working on a fire-resistant surface and removing unnecessary flammable materials from the area. Long-haired people should tie hair back when working near flame. Dispose of the discarded needle by placing it in the plastic needle cover and wrapping tape over the open end. Place the wrapped needle cover in the trash.

Dispose of the discarded needle by placing it in the plastic needle cover and wrapping tape over the open end. Place the wrapped needle cover in the trash.

Getting Ready

Prepare an inexpensive cap for each syringe as follows: Hold a disposable needle with a pair of tongs, forceps, or tweezers, and heat the needle close to where it enters the plastic connector. As the plastic begins to melt, pull the needle out with the second pair of tongs. (See Figure 1.) A match, candle, or Bunsen burner can be used as a source of heat. Take care not to get melted plastic on your skin. If the plastic catches fire, extinguish the fire by dipping the cap in water. Once prepared, the cap may be saved and used again. Dispose of the discarded needle as specified in "Safety and Disposal."

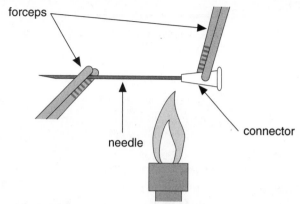

forceps

needle

connector

Figure 1: Remove the syringe needle to make a cap.

Introducing the Activity

Have students discover the effect of pushing and pulling the syringe plunger with the syringe cap off and with the cap on (and some air in the syringe). Then have students expel all the air from the syringe, place the tip under water, pull on the syringe plunger until the syringe is about half-full with water, and replace the tip. Once again have the students pull and push the syringe plunger. Have them contrast the behavior of a liquid and a gas in the syringe.

If students have not yet studied the gas laws, tell them to look for clues to identify how the volume of gas inside the syringe changes when the plunger is pulled and pushed. For students who have already studied the gas laws, challenge them to observe the activity, identify which gas law applies, and explain the phenomenon.

Procedure

Have student groups do the following:

1. With the cap off, remove the plunger from the syringe barrel. Choose two miniature marshmallows. Place one inside the syringe, leaving the cap off, and use the other as the control.

2. Place the plunger in the syringe barrel and push it in to force out as much air as possible without squeezing the marshmallow.

3. Place the cap on the tip of the syringe.

4. Pull on the plunger, hold it, and observe. (The marshmallow expands.)

5. Compare the size of the marshmallow in the syringe with the plunger pulled out with the size of the control marshmallow.

6. Predict what will happen if the plunger is released. Release the plunger and observe.

7. Repeat Steps 4–6 several times, allowing each student within the group an opportunity to manipulate the syringe. Explain what is happening.

8. Remove the marshmallow from the syringe and compare it to the control marshmallow. (The marshmallow from the syringe usually appears shrunken and shriveled when compared to the control marshmallow.)

Variations and Extensions

1. Set up the activity as a learning center.

2. After completing the experiment ask students to predict what would happen to a marshmallow carried by an astronaut on a space walk or carried by a deep sea diver on an ocean dive. (The marshmallow is outside the space suit or a diving suit.)

Explanation

The following explanation is intended for the teacher's information. Modify the explanation for students as required.

In this activity, the compressibility of a gas is illustrated. As the students observe when manipulating the syringe in "Introducing the Activity," the air in the syringe is compressed when the plunger is pushed, and it expands when the plunger is pulled out. This is in contrast to the behavior of water in the sealed syringe when the plunger is pushed and pulled (because liquids are essentially incompressible).

This activity also illustrates the pressure-volume relationship of a gas, known as Boyle's law. Boyle's law states that volume varies inversely with pressure at constant temperature and constant amount of gas; therefore, as volume increases, pressure decreases. Likewise, if volume decreases, pressure increases. In the closed system of the capped syringe, when the plunger is pulled out, volume increases and the pressure inside the syringe decreases.

The marshmallow is a convenient item to illustrate Boyle's law because it is a gas in a solid, one type of colloid. (Similar colloids are whipped cream and shaving lather.) When the pressure inside the syringe is reduced by pulling out the plunger, the volume of trapped air in the marshmallow expands, and the volume of the marshmallow increases. As the plunger is released, volume decreases, pressure increases, and the process is reversed. The marshmallows often appear shrunken afterwards because some of the air initially trapped inside them escapes when the pressure is decreased.

Assessment

Have students prepare data sheets similar to Table 1. Tell students that their data sheet responses should be descriptors such as "same," "less," and "more."

Ask students to imagine a marshmallow sealed on Earth in a steel container at 1 atmosphere pressure. Ask students to predict what change (if any) would occur in the volume, weight, and mass of a marshmallow after the container is opened in each of the following situations (assuming no temperature change):

1. in the space shuttle ("weightless" but pressurized at 1 atmosphere),
2. on a space walk ("weightless" with zero atmospheric pressure), and
3. on a deep-sea dive at a depth of 100 feet. (The pressure is about 4 atmospheres.)

Table 1: Sample Student Data Sheet					
	Before Opening			After Opening		
	Volume	Weight	Mass	Volume	Weight	Mass
Inside a Space Shuttle						
During a Space Walk						
During a Deep-Sea Dive						

Answers:

1. No change in volume or mass before or after opening; weight will be zero.
2. Before opening, mass and volume are the same (but weight is zero because of zero gravity); when opened, the marshmallow will expand, and some trapped gas will escape, thus lowering the mass.
3. Before opening, mass, volume, and weight are the same; when opened, the marshmallow will decrease in volume (due to higher pressure), mass will stay the same, as will weight (since gravity is the same).

Cross-Curricular Integration

Earth science:
Mark a map of the U.S. or the world with one color for high-altitude areas, which would have lower atmospheric pressure. (You decide the cutoff altitude.) Discuss the effects of this lower pressure, such as increased baking time and rapid fatigue during exercise in people who are not accustomed to high altitudes.

Language arts:
- Have students read one or more short stories about space travel by Isaac Asimov. (*I Robot* is a good collection.) Ask them to look for any references to pressure changes (such as use of air locks and space suits, illnesses due to space travel).

Life science:
- Have students investigate the physiological adaptations of Korean pearl divers and of deep sea organisms that live under great pressure.
- Have students investigate the physiological adaptations of people who live at very high altitudes.

Math:
- Have students mathematically determine the volume of the mini marshmallow 1) before it is expanded and 2) after it has been expanded and removed from the syringe. (The volume of a cylinder is $\pi r^2 h$ where r is the radius and h is the height of the cylinder.) Discuss the difference and the reason for the difference.

Contributors

Alison Dowd, Talawanda Middle School, Oxford, OH; Teaching Science with TOYS peer writer.
Gary Duncan, Harvard Elementary School, Toledo, OH; Teaching Science with TOYS, 1992.
Steve Peterson, Burroughs Elementary School, Toledo, OH; Teaching Science with TOYS, 1992.

LIQUID TO GAS IN A "FLICK"

Is butane a liquid or a gas? This activity shows its phase change from a liquid to a gas by changing the pressure.

Butane lighter
with a transparent case

GRADE LEVELS

Science activity appropriate for grades 4–12
Cross-Curricular Integration intended for grades 7–9

KEY SCIENCE TOPICS

- phase change
- temperature

STUDENT BACKGROUND

This demonstration is most effective after students have discussed the three states of matter: solid, liquid, and gas. The demonstration challenges them to question the factors that determine the state in which matter is found. It may also be used to stimulate thinking prior to discussion of the gas laws.

KEY PROCESS SKILLS

- collecting data — Students collect data relating temperature to the rate of bubble release from the butane lighter.

- making graphs — Students construct bar graphs of bubble release data collected from different temperature trials.

TIME REQUIRED

Setup	5	minutes
Performance	20	minutes
Cleanup	5	minutes

Materials

For "Introducing the Activity"
- overhead projector
- (optional) molecular motion simulator made from the following:
  - plastic "clamshell"-shaped food container (used at salad bars) or 2 plastic ready-made pie crust covers
  - tape
  - 1 box of BBs

For the "Procedure"

Per class

- 2 thermometers
- (optional) food color
- hot plate or electric coffee maker for heating water
- ice
- butane lighter with a transparent case
- 3 clear plastic containers (large enough to immerse the butane lighter in; at least 1 that can be heated)
- (optional) 6-inch (15-cm) test tube, transparent pill vial, or 50-mL graduated cylinder
- 2 thermometers
- overhead projector
- timer with a second hand

For "Variations and Extensions"

❸ Per class

- an aerosol product that uses butane (or another hydrocarbon) as a propellant

Safety and Disposal

Butane gas is flammable and should not be used around an open flame. Do not allow younger students to use the butane lighter by themselves. Removing the lighter wheel and the flint will prevent ignition of the gas by the lighter itself; use a screwdriver to push apart the metal tabs in which the flint is mounted. Monitor the lighters carefully to prevent igniting or sniffing abuse.

Because of potential breakage of thermometers, alcohol or metal cooking thermometers should be used. Should mercury thermometers be used and a break occur, the mercury should be cleaned up with a mercury spill kit. Avoid handling mercury or inhaling the vapor. Dispose of according to local ordinances.

Getting Ready

1. Fill the clear, plastic container with room-temperature water, making sure it will not overflow when immersing your hand.

2. (optional) Add a few drops of food color to the water.

3. (optional) If you desire to simulate molecular motion, prepare the simulator as follows: pour enough BBs into the plastic clamshell-shaped container or one of the pie crust covers so that there is a single layer of BBs that covers ⅓–½ of the bottom of the container. If the pie crust cover is used, put a second cover on top. If the clamshell-shaped container is used, close the top. Tape the two halves or the bottom and top together. This will prevent BBs from being spilled.

4. Prepare the warm-water bath for Part B by mixing hot and cold tap water to get a temperature of 40–45°C or heating water to a temperature of 40–45°C.

➤ *The bubbles form too quickly to count if the temperature is greater than about 45°C.*

5. Prepare the cold-water bath by placing ice and water in a container. The temperature should be about 10°C.

➤ *The container of water used in Part A can serve as the room-temperature bath in Part B.*

Use the overhead projector and the dish described in "Getting Ready," Step 3, as a model to simulate the motion of particles in the different states of matter. Tilt the pan slightly so that all the BBs are in one area. Move the dish gently to model the solid state where particles vibrate but do not change positions relative to adjacent particles. Shake gently until the BBs are changing position but still in contact with each other. (This illustrates the liquid phase, in which particles still touch but adjacent particles can move relative to each other.) Finally, shake vigorously so the BBs move throughout the dish. (This illustrates the gas phase where particles occupy the entire volume and are independent of the other particles.) The degree of shaking is analogous to the temperature; little shaking represents a lower temperature (and lower average kinetic energy of the particles), and more vigorous shaking represents a higher temperature (and higher average kinetic energy). Be sure that students observe the arrangement of the particles and the relative distances between them.

Procedure

Part A: The Flick

1. Show students the butane lighter by placing it on its side on the stage of an overhead projector. Gently shake the lighter from side to side so that all the students can observe the movement of fluid.

2. Ask, "Is the butane a solid, liquid, or gas?" *Liquid.*

3. Depress the valve and release some gaseous butane (but don't ignite the butane). Ask students what is happening.

4. Now, lower the lighter into the container of room-temperature water.

5. With the lighter on its side, depress the valve and ask the students to observe.

6. Ask, "Are you observing a solid, liquid, or gas? How can you tell?" *Gas bubbles escape.*

7. Determine the amount of gas escaping from the lighter using the method described in 7a or 7b.

   a. Count the number of bubbles escaping in a 15-second period. Keeping the lighter on its side slows the rate at which the bubbles come out, thus making it easier to count them.

   b. Collect gas bubbles by holding an inverted test tube, transparent pill vial, or graduated cylinder filled with water above the lighter for 15 seconds. (See Figure 1.) After the gas is collected, position the container so the level of water inside is the same as outside. Seal it using a finger, remove it from the water, and measure the volume of water remaining in the container after the gas is collected. When this volume is subtracted from the volume of water in the full container, the volume of gas released is determined. (If a graduated cylinder is used, the volume may be read directly.)

 Depending on the lighter and the size of the test tube or graduated cylinder, you may need to change the length of time from 15 seconds.

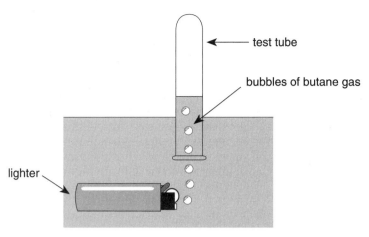

Figure 1: Collect gas bubbles in an inverted test tube.

8. Ask students to hypothesize how just a "flick" can change the state of butane.

9. After students have had a chance to speculate, tell them the freezing point (fp) and boiling point (bp) of butane. (At 1 atmosphere pressure, fp = -138.3°C and bp = -0.5°C.)

10. Ask a student to read a thermometer to determine the room temperature. "How does room temperature compare with the freezing point and boiling point of butane?" *Room temperature is higher.*

11. Challenge students to explain how butane can be found as a liquid at room temperature. Or ask them to explain why butane comes out of the lighter as a gas when the valve is opened.

Part B: The Effect of Temperature on Bubble Rate

1. Measure the temperature of the room-temperature-water bath, the cold-water bath, and the warm-water bath.

2. Lower the butane lighter into the warm- or cold-water bath.

3. Depress the valve on the side of the lighter to release the gas as before (Part A, 7a or 7b) and measure the gas escaping (by counting bubbles or measuring the volume) in the same time period as used before.

4. Repeat steps 1–3 with the other water baths.

5. Challenge students to explain any differences they may observe.

6. Have students record the data from different trials, calculate averages (if duplicate trials were done), and make a bar graph of the data.

Variations and Extensions

1. Have students investigate the following question at home: What household products in aerosol cans use butane or other hydrocarbons as the propellant?

2. Challenge students to speculate as to how they might change a gas to a liquid.

3. Show students an aerosol product that uses butane (or another hydrocarbon) as a propellant. Challenge students to hypothesize how the tube is arranged inside the can.

Explanation

 The following explanation is intended for the teacher's information. Modify the explanation for students as required.

At room temperature (about 25°C) and atmospheric pressure (1 atm or 760 torr), butane is a gas. Butane belongs to a group of organic compounds known as alkanes. All alkanes have the general formula of C_nH_{2n+2}. At room temperature and atmospheric pressure, the low-molecular-weight members of the group (methane, CH_4; ethane, C_2H_6; propane, C_3H_8; and butane, C_4H_{10}) are gases. Members of the group with larger numbers of carbon atoms are liquids or solids. Pentane (C_5H_{12}) is the first liquid in the series of alkanes, and octadecane ($C_{18}H_{38}$) is the first solid.

When a pressure greater than 2.5 atm (as it is in the butane lighter) is applied to gaseous butane at 25°C, the butane condenses into the liquid state. A butane lighter contains liquid and gaseous butane. Pressing down on the lighter valve allows some gaseous butane to escape. Since the butane that comes out of the lighter is at atmospheric pressure (about 1 atm), it is in the gaseous state. Butane in camp stove canisters is also under enough pressure that it exists mostly as a liquid at room temperature. If you move the canisters, you can hear the liquid sloshing inside. Likewise, the canister for a propane torch contains propane mostly as a liquid.

Both pressure and temperature affect the state of matter. Generally, a gas can be liquefied by increasing the pressure. At the molecular level, increasing the pressure forces the gas molecules closer and closer together. When molecules get close enough, their tendency to behave independently is overcome by the strength of the intermolecular attractions, and the gas condenses into the liquid state.

The pressure of a given amount of a gas is directly proportional to the absolute temperature, the Kelvin (K) temperature. When the temperature increases, the pressure of the gas increases; when the temperature decreases, the pressure decreases. Thus changing the temperature of the gas inside the lighter changes the pressure inside the lighter which, in turn, affects the rate at which the butane comes out of the lighter.

Cross-Curricular Integration

Home, safety, and career:
- Have students investigate the safe handling and storage of flammable materials.

References

Marzzacco, C.J.; Speckhard, D. "Simple Demonstrations of the Liquefaction of Gases," *Journal of Chemical Education.* 1986, 63(5), 436.

Shakhashiri, B.Z. *Chemical Demonstrations;* University of Wisconsin: Madison, WI, 1985; Vol. 2, pp 48–50.

Contributor

Alison Dowd, Talawanda Middle School, Oxford, OH; Teaching Science with TOYS peer writer.

SALT SOLUTIONS AND GROW CREATURES

This toy creature grows to many times its original size when placed in water.
This activity explores the effect of salt concentration on the grow creature.

Grow creatures

GRADE LEVELS

Science activity appropriate for grades 1–9
Cross-Curricular Integration intended for grades 7–9

KEY SCIENCE TOPICS

- physical change
- polymers
- solutions

STUDENT BACKGROUND

This activity is most effective as a hands-on cooperative learning activity with each group responsible for gathering data on its creature. Thus, students should be familiar with working in cooperative groups. Students should also be familiar with metric measure, making observations, and recording data.

KEY PROCESS SKILLS

- communicating   Students share information and compile class data.

- measuring   Students measure the changes in length, width, and mass of grow creatures in various salt solutions.

TIME REQUIRED

Setup	15	minutes
Performance	20	minutes (plus sitting overnight)
Cleanup	10	minutes

Materials

For "Getting Ready" only
- (optional) 1 grow creature
- (optional) container of very hot water
- masking tape and pen for labels

For "Introducing the Activity"

- tap water
- superabsorbent diaper

Different manufacturers make diapers containing superabsorbers; the diapers are identified using a variety of terms, such as ultra dry and extra dry.

- scissors
- salt shaker
- 1 grow creature
- (optional) grow creature treated with hot water in "Getting Ready"

For the "Procedure"

Part A, per group

- distilled water
- tap water
- 35 g table salt (sodium chloride, NaCl)
- measuring cup or graduated cylinder
- set of measuring spoons
- 6 plastic containers or large-mouthed jars
- metric ruler
- (optional) balance
- 1 plastic container or large-mouthed jar

A "pop-beaker" made from a cut-off plastic 2-L soft-drink bottle works well.

- 1 grow creature

All groups' creatures should be the same shape if possible. The Allen-Lewis Company, (800) 525-6658, is an inexpensive source for Grow Dinosaurs. There is a minimum order, but special arrangements may be available for classroom teachers for a smaller minimum order. Mention Terrific Science Programs at Miami University when ordering.

Part B, per group

- metric ruler
- grow creature soaked in Part A
- (optional) balance

For "Variations and Extensions"

❶ Per class
- diapers
- salt
- water
- measuring cup or graduated cylinder

❷ All materials listed for the "Procedure" plus the following:
- thermometers

❸ All materials listed for the "Procedure" plus the following:
- sugar
- rubbing alcohol

❹ Per class
- *Anacharis* sp. (also called *Elodea* sp.) (a plant available in aquarium stores)
- microscope

Safety and Disposal

No special safety or disposal procedures are required.

Getting Ready

1. (optional) Prepare a grow creature framework by pouring very hot water over the creature and allowing it to soak for approximately one hour; some of the material dissolves and the rest can be gently peeled off to reveal the small core of the dinosaur.

2. Label containers for the test liquids (See Table 1); four for the salt solutions, one for distilled water, and one for tap water.

3. Prepare four salt solutions by dissolving the indicated amount of table salt (sodium chloride) in tap water. (See Table 1.) Pour into labeled containers. (Alternatively, each group can prepare its own solution—one solution per group.)

Table 1: Salt Solution Recipes		
Solution	Table Salt	Water
0.5%	2.5 grams	500 mL
	0.5 teaspoon	3 cups
1.0%	5.0 grams	500 mL
	1 teaspoon	3 cups
2.0%	10.0 grams	500 mL
	2 teaspoons	3 cups
3.5%	17.5 grams	500 mL
	3.5 teaspoons	3 cups

4. Pour the distilled water and the tap water into their labeled containers.

Introducing the Activity

Show students a diaper containing a superabsorber. Pour a cup of tap water onto the diaper, then hold the diaper up to show that the water has been absorbed. (To maximize the amount of water absorbed, rock the diaper slowly back and forth after pouring the water on it.) Have students guess how many cups of water the diaper will absorb. Several cups of water will be absorbed, depending on the size of the diaper and the mineral content of the water. Cut open the wet diaper to show the students the beads of gel that have formed. Contrast this with a dry diaper; when it is cut open, a fine powder of sodium polyacrylate is observed and can be removed from the diaper. Tell students that the polymer can absorb over 800 times its weight under certain conditions and is known as a "superabsorber." Let students speculate on the most effective conditions for absorbing water. You may wish to add salt from a salt shaker to the saturated diaper; this will cause the gel to break down and some of the water to run out of the diaper.

Next show students a grow creature. Explain how it is made from a superabsorber as well as another polymer that enables the creature to keep its shape as it absorbs water. If a grow creature was treated with hot water to expose its framework (See "Getting Ready," Step 1), show it to the students. Explain to students that they will be using the grow creature to determine the effects of salt on superabsorbers. Students may be asked to predict the results.

Procedure

Part A: Grow the Creatures

1. Set aside one grow creature as a control.

2. Divide the students into cooperative groups and assign jobs. Assign each group one of the six test liquids, and have the students in each group follow Steps 3–12.

    Each group will need at least one Preparer, Measurer, and (optional) Mass Measurer to perform the following tasks:
    *   *Preparer—to prepare the solution;*
    *   *Measurer—to measure the length, width, and thickness; and*
    *   *Mass Measurer (optional)—to measure the mass.*

3. Measure the length, width, and thickness of the creature. Record this information on the Data Sheet (provided).

    This will generate much discussion, and a class decision must be made on the appropriate way to make the measurements so that results from different groups can be compared.

4. (optional) Measure and record the mass.

5. Place the grow creature in the container of liquid.

6. Leave the grow creature in the container undisturbed for a period of at least 24 hours.

7. Remove the grow creature from the container.

8. Measure and record the length, width, and thickness.

9. (optional) Measure and record the mass.

10. Compare the measurements (Steps 8 and 9) with the original measurements (Steps 3 and 4).

11. (optional) Return the grow creature to the container for a longer period of time. Record measurements daily until no further change occurs.

    The creatures may continue to grow for three or more days.

12. Construct a graph from each group's data. Younger students may actually line up their grow creatures on laminated paper to construct a histogram. Older students can graph size or mass measurements versus time, maximum size or mass versus solution concentration, change of size or mass versus time, or change of size or mass versus solution concentration.

Part B: Shrink the Creatures

Challenge students to shrink the grow creatures. Make observations and record the measurements.

Variations and Extensions

1. Have students measure the amount of salt solutions of different concentration that a diaper can absorb when the solutions are poured onto the diaper (as described for water in "Introducing the Activity").

2. Challenge students to test other factors that may affect the absorbancy of superabsorbers, for example, the temperature of the water.

3. Compare the growth of creatures in aqueous solutions of electrolytes, such as sugar or alcohol.

4. Place *Anacharis* sp. (*Elodea* sp.) in 0.5% salt water under a microscope and observe. Then, place it in 3.5% salt water and observe changes.

Explanation

The following explanation is intended for the teacher's information. Modify the explanation for students as required.

Superabsorbers, found in diapers and toys (such as G.U.T.S. and grow creatures), are "water-loving" (hydrophilic) polymers. These polymers can absorb large amounts of water. Grow creatures contain two different polymers; the hydrophilic polymer that is responsible for the absorption of water and a second polymer that is "water-hating" (hydrophobic). The hydrophobic polymer forms the framework of the creature and it is the core material that remains undissolved after soaking the grow creature in hot water for 1 hour. (See "Getting Ready," Step 1.) Since the framework remains intact in water, the creature can grow without losing its original shape. The hydrophilic polymer is polyacrylamide and the hydrophobic polymer is the copolymer poly(vinylacetate:ethylene). (A copolymer is a polymer made up of two alternating monomer units; in this case the monomers are vinylacetate and ethylene.)

When the hydrophilic polymer sodium polyacrylate comes in contact with water, a gel forms that has many times the volume of the dry polymer. Sodium polyacrylate is a polymer with negatively charged carboxylate ions and positively charged sodium ions. When water is added and the polymer starts to dissolve, the negatively charged carboxylate groups orient themselves as far apart as possible. This orientation to maximize the distance between like-charged groups is partially responsible for the swelling as water molecules get trapped within the polymer matrix. Hydrolysis (reaction with water) of the carboxylate groups of the weak acid is also responsible for absorption of water and causes additional swelling. When sodium ions from sodium chloride are also present, the sodium ions are preferentially attracted to the negatively charged carboxylate groups. This decreases the amount of water attracted to the carboxylate groups, releasing water molecules that previously had been within the polymer matrix. As a result, less water is absorbed when positively charged ions from salt are present. Thus, as the concentration of sodium chloride increases, the amount of water absorbed by the hydrophilic polymer is decreased. As a result, the grow creature in 3.5% salt water has the smallest volume increase while the grow creature in distilled water has the greatest.

When the grow creature is removed from water, the water slowly evaporates, and the grow creature shrinks back to its original size.

Assessment

Have students answer the following questions:
1. Tell about the growth of your grow creature.
2. Use the class graph to compare the growth of your creature to the growth of two other creatures.
3. Why do you think the growth is different in different solutions?
4. What did you learn in this experiment that helps you understand the adaptations of aquatic plants and animals to environments with different concentrations of salt?
5. What does the word *hydrophilic* mean?

Cross-Curricular Integration

Life science:
- Discuss how living organisms are adapted for living in different saline environments. The solutions used in the experiment correspond approximately to different biological environments. For example,
  0.5% - freshwater pond or lake;
  1.0% - human body fluids (urine, blood plasma);
  2.0% - brackish water; and
  3.5% - ocean environment.

Math:
- Graph results.
- Have students complete the Math Worksheet.

References

Bonnie Bachman, Empak Co., Colorado Springs, CO, personal communication.

Chem Fax! Publication Number 755.10, Flinn Scientific Company: Batavia, IL.

Polymers: Linking Chemistry and Fun, developed by Marie Sherman, Ursuline Academy, St. Louis, MO.

Contributors

Alison Dowd, Talawanda Middle School, Oxford, OH, Teaching Science with TOYS peer writer.

Marie Renner, Pickerington Middle School, Pickerington, OH; Teaching Science with TOYS, 1993.

Handout Masters

Masters for the following handouts are provided:
- Data Sheet
- Math Worksheet

Copy as needed for classroom use.

SALT SOLUTIONS AND GROW CREATURES

Data Sheet

Name of your grow creature: _____

1. Record the initial measurements of your grow creature (before growing):

Length		Thickness	
Width		Mass	

2. Identify the solution in which you will be soaking your creature:

_____

3. What do you predict will happen to your grow creature?

_____

_____

Record your results

Soaking Time	Length	Width	Thickness	Mass

SALT SOLUTIONS AND GROW CREATURES

Math Worksheet

Soaking Time	Length	Width	Thickness	Mass
1				
2				
Difference between 1 and 2				
% difference between 1 and 2				
3				
Difference between 2 and 3				
% difference between 2 and 3				
4				
Difference between 3 and 4				
% difference between 3 and 4				
5				
Difference between 4 and 5				
% difference between 4 and 5				
% difference between 1 and 5				

THE LIQUID TIMER RACE

Does temperature affect a liquid timer? This activity is an exploration of the possibility of a relationship between the temperature and the drip period.

Spiral liquid timer

GRADE LEVELS

Science activity appropriate for grades 7–9
Cross-Curricular Integration intended for grades 7–9

KEY SCIENCE TOPICS

- density
- gravity
- viscosity

STUDENT BACKGROUND

Students should be familiar with density and immiscible liquids. The Teaching Science with TOYS activity "Density Bottles" explores these concepts.

KEY PROCESS SKILLS

• collecting data	Students time the "drip period" of liquid timers at various temperatures.
• controlling variables	Students identify and control variables that affect the "drip period" of liquid timers.

TIME REQUIRED

Setup	10	minutes
Performance	30	minutes
Cleanup	5	minutes

Materials

For the "Procedure"
Per group if done as a hands-on activity or per class if done as a demonstration
- liquid timer

A spiral liquid timer works best. (See photo.)

- thermometer
- stopwatch or other timer with a second hand
- (optional) zipper-type plastic bag

Per class
- hot plate or electric coffee maker for heating water
- 2 containers (both large enough to immerse a liquid timer in; 1 container that can be heated)
- water
- tape
- ice or access to a refrigerator

For "Variations and Extensions"
❸ All materials listed for the "Procedure" plus the following:
- sand-filled hourglass timer

Safety and Disposal

Because of the potential breakage of thermometers, alcohol or metal cooking thermometers should be used. Should mercury thermometers be used and should a break occur, the mercury should be cleaned up with a mercury spill kit. Avoid handling mercury or inhaling the vapor. Dispose of according to local ordinances.

Getting Ready

1. Prepare a hot-water bath by heating water to a temperature of 60–70°C.
   When heating and cooling the liquid timer, you may want to place it in a plastic bag in case of a leak.

2. If using a cold-water bath rather than a refrigerator to cool the liquid timer, prepare the cold-water bath by placing ice and water in a container. The temperature should be about 10°C.

Introducing the Activity

Options:

- Introduce the concept of viscosity and review the concept of density. Review important strategies in using the scientific method and planning experimental strategies. For example, instrument calibration (checking the liquid timer against an electric clock), control of variables, and consistent measuring techniques may be discussed.

- Show students a liquid timer and ask them to explain how it is made. *It is made of two immiscible liquids with different densities.* (See Figure 1.) Tell students that they will be investigating the factors that affect the drip period of the timer. Ask them to decide what observations they will make and what data they will need to collect in order to determine the effect of temperature on the drip period. In the discussion, you may wish to have the students review the scientific method, the need for establishing a consistent experimental procedure, and the necessity of using the same timer at different temperatures in order to study the effect of temperature on the drip period. To emphasize this, you may wish to have students compare the drip period of one timer, first with one end on top and then the other end on top, or the drip period of two or more different timers at room temperature. (In general, the drip period can vary even though the timers may appear to be identical.) Discuss the importance of making consistent measurements for each trial. Ask students to predict how temperature will affect the drip period.

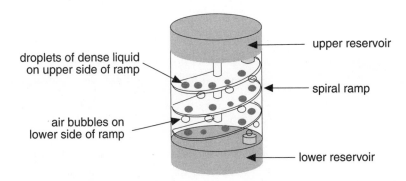

Figure 1: A spiral liquid timer contains two immiscible liquids of different densities. The denser of these liquids flows in drops down a spiral ramp.

Procedure

1. If doing the activity as a demonstration, ask for two student volunteers—one to act as official Timer and one to be the Timer-Turner. If doing the activity in groups, divide the students into groups of three or four and assign jobs.

    Each group will need a Timer, Recorder, Timer-Turner, and a Materials Handler to perform the following jobs:

    *   *Timer—to watch the clock;*
    *   *Recorder—to record results;*
    *   *Timer-Turner—to turn over the liquid timer; and*
    *   *Materials Handler—to get and return materials.*

2. Mark one end of the liquid timer with a piece of tape to designate that end as the "top."

3. Have students practice determining the drip period for the liquid timer at room temperature by doing the following:

    a. Record the temperature.

    b. When the Timer gives a signal (and records the time or starts the stopwatch), the Timer-Turner inverts the liquid timer so that the end marked "top" is on the bottom.

    c. When the last drop of colored liquid drips from the top, the Timer records the time (or stops the stopwatch). The time difference is the drip period of the liquid timer. The drip period is generally about 3 minutes, but the period can vary significantly from one liquid timer to another.

    It takes practice to anticipate when the last drop of liquid comes out of the top, so it is important to agree upon the method of determining the end drop. One way is to record the end time as when the colored liquid stops dripping (from the top) for 3 seconds.

    d. Invert the timer so that the end marked "top" is on top, and wait until the colored liquid stops dripping.

    The drip period for some liquid timers can be quite different depending upon which end is on the top when the liquid timer is inverted. Thus each liquid timer may have two different drip-periods. This is why all trials should be done with the same end on top.

    e. Repeat Steps 3a–d until the results are reasonably consistent.

4. Using the technique practiced in Step 3, have students repeat Steps 3a–d at least three more times and average the times to determine the drip period for the liquid timer at room temperature.

5. Have the students determine the drip period for the liquid timer at a different temperature by doing the following:

   a. Place the timer in a hot- or cold-water bath 5–10 minutes before timing. Make sure that the end marked "top" is on top.

   b. Record the temperature of the hot- or cold-water bath just before the liquid timer is removed.

   c. Remove the liquid timer from the water bath and, as soon as possible after removal from the water bath, invert it so that the end marked "top" is on the bottom, recording the time (or starting the stopwatch).

   d. When the last drop of colored liquid drips from the top, record the time (or stop the stopwatch).

   e. Invert the timer so that the end marked "top" is on top, and wait until the colored liquid stops dripping.

   f. Repeat Steps 5a–e as time allows.

6. Have the students compare the drip period for the timer at different temperatures. Ask students to reevaluate their prediction about the effect of temperature on the drip period.

Variations and Extensions

1. Have students prepare a graph of drip period versus temperature. Have them discuss the question, "Can the liquid timer be used as a room thermometer?"

2. Have students repeat Step 4 of the "Procedure" using the opposite end of the timer as "top." Challenge students to explain why the drip period depends on which end of the liquid timer is on top.

3. Contrast the behavior of a sand-filled hourglass timer at different temperatures with that of the liquid timer.

4. Have students calculate the rate (drops/second) at which the liquid drops fall. For example, count and record the number of drops that fall in a certain time period (for example, 5 or 10 seconds). Does the rate (drops/second) remain constant from beginning to end or does it change?

Explanation

The following explanation is intended for the teacher's information. Modify the explanation for students as required.

Liquid timers contain two immiscible liquids (liquids that do not mix with each other) with different densities. The more-dense liquid will be the liquid that is on the bottom. When the liquid timer is inverted, the more-dense liquid is moved to the top and will drip through the small opening, displacing the lower-density liquid from the bottom of the liquid timer. The drip period, the time it takes for all of the more-dense liquid to flow from the top, is related to the viscosities of the liquids. The viscosity is affected by temperature. As a result, the drip period for the liquid timer will be different at different temperatures.

Viscosity is a measure of the resistance to flow. The more viscous a liquid, the slower it flows. The viscosity is affected by temperature. If viscous solutions such as syrup and honey are stored in a refrigerator, they become more viscous (and pour more slowly) than if they are at room temperature. The Society of Automotive Engineers (SAE) rating on motor oil is a measure of the viscosity of automobile motor oil. Choosing oil of correct viscosity is necessary to ensure proper lubrication. In cold weather, oils with lower SAE ratings (lower viscosity) are used. For example, SAE 10 might be used in winter and SAE 40 in summer. Multiviscosity oils such as 10W-40 are formulated to be effective over a wider temperature range and can be used year-round.

The sizes of the holes that the liquid drips through also affect the rate of the drip. Differences in drip rate from one timer to another or from one end on top compared to the other end (as in Extension 2) are probably due to differences in the hole sizes.

Cross-Curricular Integration

Math:
- Take averages and analyze the results.
- Graph the results.

Social studies:
- Study the development of different timing devices from water clocks through atomic clocks.
- Research the history of time zones, including their relationship to the development of railroads.

Reference

Ebbing, D. *General Chemistry,* 4th ed.; Houghton Mifflin: Boston, MA, 1993.

Contributor

Alison Dowd, Talawanda Middle School, Oxford, OH; Teaching Science with TOYS peer writer.

DENSITY BOTTLES

When a water-soluble dye is added to a bottle with two liquid layers, only one layer becomes colored. Why are two layers present, why does the dye color only one, and why don't the two liquids mix?

Density Bottle

GRADE LEVELS

Science activity appropriate for grades K–12
Cross-Curricular Integration intended for grades 7–9

KEY SCIENCE TOPICS

- density
- mixtures
- polar and nonpolar liquids
- immiscibility

STUDENT BACKGROUND

For young students, this activity can be used to introduce the concepts of density and immiscibility. For students who are familiar with the concept of density, this activity can serve to evaluate their ability to apply the concept of density to explain an unfamiliar system.

KEY PROCESS SKILLS

• observing	Students observe the behavior of two immiscible liquids and the solubility of dyes in the liquids.
• predicting	Students predict the nature of the dye (polar or nonpolar), based on its solubility behavior.

TIME REQUIRED

Setup	10	minutes
Performance	25	minutes
Cleanup	5	minutes

Materials

For "Getting Ready" only
- materials to construct one or more sample Density Bottles

For the "Procedure"

Per group

- materials to construct a Density Bottle:
  - clear plastic 1-L soft-drink bottle*
  - 500 mL water*
  - 500 mL vegetable oil or mineral oil*

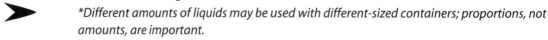

Different amounts of liquids may be used with different-sized containers; proportions, not amounts, are important.

- water-soluble food color or another dye such as oil-soluble Easter-egg dye or Sudan Black B dye

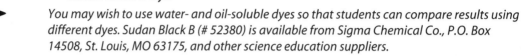

You may wish to use water- and oil-soluble dyes so that students can compare results using different dyes. Sudan Black B (# 52380) is available from Sigma Chemical Co., P.O. Box 14508, St. Louis, MO 63175, and other science education suppliers.

Safety and Disposal

No special safety or disposal procedures are necessary.

Getting Ready

Prepare one or more sample Density Bottles according to the "Procedure."

Introducing the Activity

To introduce the activity to younger students, show them a glass of water and a glass of oil. Ask them what would happen if the two liquids were mixed. Show older students a prepared bottle. Ask, "How many layers do you see?" *Two.* Have students describe why the layers are present and make a hypothesis about the identity of the two substances inside. (The students will probably correctly hypothesize water and oil.)

Procedure

1. Instruct a member of each group to fill the plastic bottle approximately half-full with oil.

2. Ask students to predict what will happen when water is added.

3. Instruct a member of each group to fill the bottle with water; then cap.

4. Have students describe what happens. *Two layers form.* Discuss why. Ask, "What would happen if the water was added first?" *The water would remain on the bottom when the oil was added. The resulting layers would be the same as before.*

5. Give each member of the group a chance to try mixing the two layers by inverting the bottle several times.

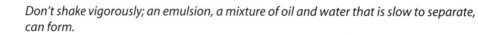

Don't shake vigorously; an emulsion, a mixture of oil and water that is slow to separate, can form.

6. Discuss immiscibility—two liquids that do not mix, but instead form separate layers.

7. Instruct a member of each group to add a few drops of food color or another dye.

8. Be sure that students observe in which layer the food color dissolves. (It will be the bottom water layer with water-soluble dye and the top oil layer with oil-soluble dye.) Have the students determine if the dye is "like" the oil or the water.

You may wish to give different groups different types of dyes and have them compare and explain the results.

9. Discuss the concept of "Like dissolves like."

Variations and Extensions

1. Challenge the students to find other pairs of immiscible liquids at home. (One of the pair will probably be an oil-based substance and the other water-based.) Can students find other liquids that are miscible with vegetable oil? (Probably most will be other types of oil, such as olive oil and mineral oil and alcohol-water solutions that are greater than 91% alcohol, etc.)

2. Have students determine the densities of the two liquids experimentally. Are the calculated values of density consistent with the experimental observations?

Explanation

The following explanation is intended for the teacher's information. Modify the explanation for students as required.

In this activity, two immiscible liquids (liquids that do not dissolve in one another) are combined in one container. Since each liquid has a different density, two layers form. The less-dense layer (oil) is on the top, and the more-dense layer (water) is on the bottom. The relative position of the layers is the same no matter which liquid is added first.

Why don't water and oil dissolve in one another? We can make predictions about solubility if we know something about the attractions between molecules—intermolecular attractions. Water is polar, meaning it behaves like a particle having oppositely charged ends. Because of this, one end of a water molecule has an attraction for the oppositely charged end of an adjacent water molecule. Oil is essentially a nonpolar molecule with no oppositely charged ends. Polar molecules attract other polar molecules, and nonpolar molecules attract other nonpolar molecules. Conversely, attractive forces between polar and nonpolar molecules are very small; thus, water and oil do not dissolve in one another.

In the statement "Like dissolves like," "like" refers to the polar or nonpolar nature of molecules. Substances with similar intermolecular attractions (both polar molecules or both nonpolar molecules) are usually soluble in one another, and those dissimilar (one polar and one nonpolar) are usually not soluble in one another.

By adding dye to the Density Bottle, students study the concept of "Like dissolves like." After observing the solubility behavior of the dye, students can infer the polar or nonpolar nature of the dye molecules. A water-soluble dye is generally a polar compound or ionic compound (one which is composed of two types of ions, one positive and the other negative, like common table salt, sodium chloride). The polar or ionic nature of the water-soluble dye is responsible for its solubility in water and other polar liquids. An oil-soluble dye is nonpolar like oil so it dissolves in oil and other nonpolar liquids.

Cross-Curricular Integration

Earth science:
- Have students study how different layers of the Earth's crust were formed because of different densities.

Reference

"Household Density Columns," "Not on the Level;" *Fun with Chemistry: A Guidebook of K–12 Activities;* Sarquis, M., Sarquis, J., Eds.; Institute for Chemical Education: Madison, WI, 1991; Vol. 1, pp 115–118, 119–122.

Contributor

Alison Dowd, Talawanda Middle School, Oxford, OH; Teaching Science with TOYS peer writer.

FRUSTRATION BOTTLES

Students explore density and solubility as they add liquids to bottles and observe the resulting layers.

Two Frustration Bottles

KEY SCIENCE TOPICS

- density
- discrepant events
- mixtures
- polar and nonpolar liquids

STUDENT BACKGROUND

This demonstration is most effective after students have experimented with density and are familiar with the scientific method. They should have experience with the concept that insoluble liquids form layers based on their relative densities. This demonstration provides discrepant events based on the students' knowledge of density that, in Part B, can be used to introduce mixtures and the concept of "Like dissolves like."

KEY PROCESS SKILLS

- inferring

  Students infer the polar or nonpolar nature of a dye based upon the liquid in which it is soluble.

- hypothesizing

  Students form a hypothesis to explain why the Frustration Bottle contains only two layers instead of three and propose experiments to test their hypothesis.

- investigating

  Students study ways of making a three-liquid layer system and the effect mixing has on the system.

TIME REQUIRED

Setup	10	minutes
Performance	25	minutes
Cleanup	5	minutes

Materials

For the "Procedure"

Part A, per group
- 2 clear containers, such as 15-cm test tubes, baby-food jars, juice bottles, plastic soft-drink bottles, cheese-spread glasses, etc.
- 25 mL baby oil*
- 25 mL 91% isopropyl alcohol solution*
- 25 mL 70% isopropyl alcohol solution* (rubbing alcohol)
- food color

Part B, per group
- 2 clear containers, such as 15-cm test tubes, baby-food jars, juice bottles, plastic soft-drink bottles, cheese-spread glasses, etc.
- 25 mL water*
- 25 mL 70% isopropyl alcohol solution*
- 50 mL vegetable or mineral oil*
- 2 stoppers, corks, or lids to fit the containers
- food color

Different amounts of the liquids may be used with different-sized containers; proportions, not amounts, are important.

For "Variations and Extensions"

❸ All materials listed for the "Procedure" plus the following:
Per group
- oil-soluble Easter egg dye or Sudan Black B dye

Sudan Black B dye is available from Sigma Chemical Co. (#52380), P.O. Box 14508, St. Louis, MO 63175 and other science education suppliers.

Safety and Disposal

Isopropyl alcohol is flammable; keep flames away. Isopropyl alcohol is intended for external use only. Avoid contact with the eyes since damage can result. If contact does occur, rinse eyes with water for 15 minutes and seek medical attention. No special disposal procedures are required.

Getting Ready

Introducing the Activity, Part A:
Prepare two density bottles as described in Part A of the "Procedure."

Introducing the Activity, Part B:
Prepare one Frustration Bottle ahead of time according to Part B of the "Procedure."

Variation 1:
Prepare several Frustration Bottles ahead of time in various sizes and colors for students to observe in groups.

Part A:

Show students the two prepared density bottles. Each contains two layers, but in one bottle the colored layer is on top, and in the other the colored layer is on the bottom. Ask students how many different liquids are in each bottle. (They will probably answer two, not counting the dye.) Tell them that both bottles contain the same liquids: an isopropyl alcohol-water solution and baby oil. Challenge students to discover why the contents in the two containers behave differently.

Part B:

Show students a prepared Frustration Bottle. Ask, "How many layers do you see?" *Two.* Have students describe why the layers are present and hypothesize the identities of the two substances inside. (The students will probably hypothesize correctly water and oil.) Now surprise them with the fact that there are three substances (not counting the dye) inside the Frustration Bottle! Describe your "frustration" in only getting two layers when you know that the third substance, alcohol, is a different density than either the water or the oil. You may want to show them or remind them of the "Household Density Column" from *Fun with Chemistry* (see "References") where rubbing alcohol (which is 70% isopropyl alcohol and 30% water) is layered on top of vegetable oil. Challenge students to find out what is happening to the alcohol layer when you do the demonstration.

Procedure

Part A: What's on Top?

Have students do the following:

1. Fill one container about half-full with baby oil.

2. Pour in 70% isopropyl alcohol (rubbing alcohol) until the container is almost full.

3. Note which solution is on top.

4. Add a drop of food color and observe in which layer it dissolves.

5. Place the lid or stopper on the container and invert it; note what occurs.

6. Fill the other container about half-full with baby oil.

7. Pour in 91% isopropyl alcohol until the container is almost full.

8. Repeat Steps 3–5.

Part B: How Many Liquids in the Bottle?

Have students do Steps 1–6:

1. Fill the bottle approximately ¼-full of water.

2. Add an equal amount of 70% isopropyl alcohol and note if two layers form.

3. Fill the rest of the container with oil.

4. Add a few drops of food color.

5. Observe the food color passing through the oil layer and into the alcohol-water mixture.

6. Suggest different orders of adding the fluids to try to get the three layers.

7. When students are "frustrated" with trying to make three layers, discuss the rule of thumb of "Like dissolves like."

Variations and Extensions

1. Give students time to manipulate prepared frustration bottles in various colors and sizes to observe fluid flow.

2. Allow students working in groups to attempt to meet the challenge of preparing a three-layer frustration bottle using the Part B materials. (If narrow containers such as test tubes are used, three layers can form; with wider containers, the mixing occurring during pouring usually prevents three layers from forming.)

3. Substitute an oil-soluble dye like Sudan Black B for the food color and observe.

Explanation

 The following explanation is intended for the teacher's information. Modify the explanation for students as required.

The behavior of liquids in the bottles in Parts A and B depends on the relative densities of the liquids used and on the solubility of those liquids in one another.

In Part A, three substances, each of different density, are used. They are, in order of increasing density: isopropyl alcohol, baby oil, and water. However, the isopropyl alcohol and water are already mixed in two different isopropyl alcohol solutions; one is 70% isopropyl alcohol, and the other is 91%. These two solutions have different densities because of their different compositions. Relative to the density of the baby oil, the 91% solution is less dense, and the 70% solution is more dense.

The alcohol/water solutions and the baby oil are immiscible; that is, they do not dissolve in one another. Thus, two layers form. Because of the relative densities of the liquids, in one case the baby oil layer is on top, and in the other case it is on the bottom. If a water-soluble dye is added, it will be in the isopropyl alcohol-water layer whether it is on the top or the bottom.

In Part B, students observe that even though water and alcohol have different densities, it is difficult to form layers with them because they readily mix. Students may find this event discrepant based on their experience that liquids with different densities form layers. It is possible to achieve layering of alcohol and water with careful pouring if a narrow container such as a test tube is used. However, when mixed, the two liquids dissolve in one another in all proportions; that is, they are miscible.

Substances with similar intermolecular attractions (for example, both polar molecules or both nonpolar molecules) are usually soluble in one another. Water and isopropyl alcohol are polar, meaning they behave like a particle having oppositely charged ends. Because of this, one end of a water or alcohol molecule has an attraction for the oppositely charged end of an adjacent water or alcohol molecule.

Attractions between molecules are called intermolecular attractions. Polar molecules attract other polar molecules, and nonpolar molecules attract other nonpolar molecules. The rule of thumb "Like dissolves like" refers to the polar or nonpolar nature of the molecules. Oils generally are nonpolar molecules without oppositely charged ends. Thus polar water and alcohol are soluble in each other, but neither is soluble in the nonpolar oil. As a result, two layers are formed, one layer of the polar water-alcohol mixture and the other layer of the nonpolar oil.

By observing the solubility behavior of the dye, one can infer the polar or nonpolar nature of the dye molecules. A water-soluble dye is generally either a polar compound or an ionic compound (made of positive and negative ions) like common table salt, sodium chloride. The polar or ionic nature of the dye is responsible for its solubility in water and other polar liquids. An oil-soluble dye is nonpolar, like oil, so it dissolves in oil and other nonpolar liquids. Since the oil layer has a lower density than water, it will be the top layer, even if it is in the container before the water is added.

Cross-Curricular Integration

Earth science:
- Have students research petroleum, which is a mixture of nonpolar substances.

Home, safety, and career:
- Have students make layered gelatin desserts.
- Have students study the properties of solvent cleaners (such as stain removers and paint thinner).
- Have students research separation techniques used in sewage treatment.
- Discuss oil spills and the technology used to contain and remove oil.

Reference

"Household Density Columns," "Not on the Level;" *Fun with Chemistry: A Guidebook of K–12 Activities;* Sarquis, M., Sarquis, J., Eds.; Institute for Chemical Education: Madison, WI, 1991; Vol. 1, pp 115–118, 119–122.

Contributor

Alison Dowd, Talawanda Middle School, Oxford, OH; Teaching Science with TOYS peer writer.

EXPANDING, FLOATING BUBBLES

Watch a bubble float mysteriously above the bottom of an aquarium.

An expanding, floating bubble

Materials

For the "Procedure"
Per class
- soap solution
- bubble wand

- aquarium or clear plastic box
- cover or piece of cardboard big enough to cover the aquarium or box
- (optional) black poster paper
- 1 of the following as a source of carbon dioxide:
  - slab or chunks of dry ice
  - gloves

  or

  - 1½ cups (400 mL) vinegar
  - ⅓ cup (100 g) baking soda (sodium bicarbonate)
  - plastic 2-L soft-drink bottle or a disposable plastic salad container
  - stirrer
  - clear plastic cup or a zipper-type plastic bag
  - (optional) matches

 If dry ice is used as the source of carbon dioxide, it is much easier to get the soap bubbles to float. However, if dry ice is not available, generating carbon dioxide from baking soda and vinegar is an alternative. The expansion of the bubbles is easily observed, and, with practice, the bubbles can be made to float on the carbon dioxide layer generated.

Safety and Disposal

If using dry ice: Dry ice, solid carbon dioxide, is very cold. (It sublimes at -78°C.) Contact with exposed skin can cause frostbite and blisters. Gloves, mittens, old socks, or a cloth towel must be used when handling dry ice, and it should be used in a well-ventilated area. No special disposal procedures are required.

Getting Ready

(optional) Cover the back of the aquarium or the plastic box with black poster paper.

If using dry ice: Dry ice can be stored for short periods of time in a polystyrene foam (such as Styrofoam™) chest. Big pieces should not be broken until just before use in order to increase the length of time the dry ice will last.

If using baking soda and vinegar: Cut the plastic 2-L soft-drink bottle so it has a height of about 4 inches.

Introducing the Activity

Options:

If using dry ice:
Place a small chunk of dry ice on a table. Ask students if they know what it is and what process is occurring. If they are not familiar with dry ice, explain to them that it is carbon dioxide in the solid state and that it is subliming (changing from a solid to a gas). The sublimation temperature is -78°C, which is why protective gloves must be worn when handling dry ice. Ask them to identify the white cloud observed around the dry ice. *It is condensed water vapor, small droplets of water dispersed in the air/carbon dioxide mixture. The cloud is not carbon dioxide; carbon dioxide is a colorless gas.* If time allows, consider other demonstrations, as students will be quite intrigued. (Be prepared to answer questions like "How much

does it cost?" and "Where can I get some?") Some suggestions are to place a piece of dry ice in a cup of water or to move a lighted match to the vicinity of the dry ice. When your students are familiar with dry ice and know that they are observing the sublimation of solid carbon dioxide, you are ready to challenge them to use their skills of observation to solve the mystery of the expanding, suspended, and then sinking bubbles!

If using baking soda and vinegar:

Place a small amount of baking soda in a clear, plastic cup and add a small amount of vinegar. Ask students to describe the reaction. Alternatively, place 1 tablespoon baking soda in a zipper-type plastic bag. Hold the bag so that the baking soda is in one corner at the bottom of the bag. Then add about ¼ cup (60 mL) vinegar so it runs into the other corner of the bag. (See Figure 1.)

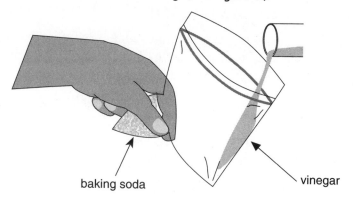

baking soda   vinegar

Figure 1: Students can observe the baking soda-vinegar reaction in a zipper-type plastic bag.

With the baking soda and vinegar still separated, squeeze the bag to force most of the air out of the bag and seal the zipper closure. Then mix the baking soda and vinegar and observe. Rapid foaming and an expansion of the bag are evidence that a gas is being produced. After the reaction stops, a burning match can be placed into the plastic bag just after it is opened; it is extinguished, which shows the gas generated in the bag is nonflammable. This observation is one piece of evidence that the gas is carbon dioxide.

Procedure

You may wish to let students take turns so that they can actively participate in the demonstration.

1. Fill the aquarium or plastic tub with gaseous carbon dioxide using one of the following methods.

   Using dry ice:

   • Spread pieces of dry ice on the bottom of your aquarium or plastic tub.

   • Let the dry ice sublime for several minutes; this allows a layer of carbon dioxide gas to collect in the bottom of the container. You may wish to cover the top of the aquarium or tub loosely to prevent air currents from disturbing the layer of carbon dioxide.

Using baking soda and vinegar:

- Place ⅓ cup (100 grams) of baking soda (sodium bicarbonate) into the salad container or the cut-off 2-L plastic bottle. Place it in the aquarium or tub.

- Slowly add 1½ cups (400 mL) vinegar to the container while the aquarium or tub is partially covered. Adding the vinegar too quickly will cause the reactants to foam up over the edges of the container. Then loosely cover the aquarium or tub completely. Proceed when the froth subsides but while the reaction is still occurring. When the reaction slows, stirring the reaction mixture will allow unreacted material to react to produce more carbon dioxide.

2. With the bubble solution and wand, gently blow and capture a single bubble.

3. Lower the wand with the bubble into the aquarium or tub and encourage students to observe carefully! (They should see color changes as well as size changes.)

4. Remove the wand and bubble from the aquarium or tub to reverse the process. Do changes occur? The bubble can be repeatedly moved into and out of the aquarium until it breaks.

5. Now gently blow several bubbles over the layer of carbon dioxide at the bottom of the aquarium. The bubbles should float on the layer of carbon dioxide at the bottom. Alternatively, you can catch a bubble on the wand and try to flick it off the wand onto the carbon dioxide layer; this technique disturbs the carbon dioxide layer less. If you used baking soda and vinegar, try to place the bubble so that it doesn't go into the soft-drink bottle but instead goes between the bottle and the outside edge of the tub. (See Figure 2.)

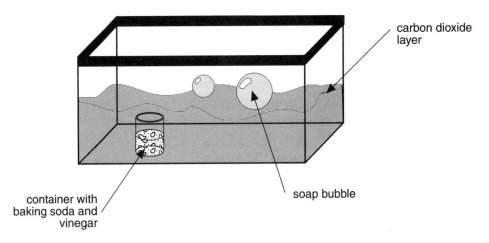

Figure 2: Bubbles float on a layer of carbon dioxide.

6. Encourage students to observe carefully. (They should see color change, size change, and gradual sinking of the bubbles into the aquarium or tub).

Extension

Analyze the color change that occurs when the bubble expands or shrinks.

Explanation

The following explanation is intended for the teacher's information. Modify the explanation for students as required.

At room temperature and atmospheric pressure, solid carbon dioxide (CO_2) sublimes. That means that it goes directly from the solid state to the gaseous state. At normal pressures, carbon dioxide does not exist in the liquid state. It is very useful for shipping products that must be kept frozen because it is colder than ice and it does not leave a liquid residue as "water ice" does when it melts. (This is why solid carbon dioxide is called "dry ice.") Gaseous carbon dioxide can also be prepared chemically by reacting an acid with baking soda (sodium bicarbonate, $NaHCO_3$). In this investigation, the acid is acetic acid ($HC_2H_3O_2$); vinegar is a solution of acetic acid in water. The reaction occurring is:

$$NaHCO_3(s) + HC_2H_3O_2(aq) \rightarrow Na^+(aq) + C_2H_3O_2^-(aq) + CO_2(g) + H_2O(l)$$

Carbon dioxide is more dense than air, which is a mixture of mostly nitrogen and oxygen. As a result, when carbon dioxide is produced in the air, it tends to sink, displacing the air. Thus, in the aquarium, as carbon dioxide is produced, either by sublimation or by a chemical reaction, it sinks and forms a layer at the bottom of the container.

The demonstration shows that carbon dioxide gas moves through the soap bubble film from an area of higher concentration (the carbon dioxide-filled container) to lower concentration (inside the soap bubble). As carbon dioxide moves into the bubble, the bubble expands. When the bubble is lifted out of the container, the process is reversed since there is now a greater concentration of carbon dioxide inside the bubble than outside.

The change of color in the soap bubble is a result of the changing thickness of the bubble film. As the thickness of the soap film changes (due to expansion and contraction of the bubble), the interference pattern resulting from light reflected from the outside and inside surfaces of the bubble also changes. This change in the interference patterns causes the color of the soap film to change.

Many students find the growth of the carbon dioxide bubble counter-intuitive. Students know the carbon dioxide is more dense than air because the soap bubbles are initially suspended on the layer of carbon dioxide in the container. Because carbon dioxide is more dense than air, many students expect that carbon dioxide molecules will diffuse through the soap film more slowly than air (oxygen and nitrogen). If this were the case, the bubble would get smaller. Or, if dry ice is used, students might expect that the size of the bubble will decrease as the air inside the bubble is cooled by contact with the cold carbon dioxide gas formed from the sublimation of the dry ice.

The counter-intuitive behavior of the bubble can be explained by the fact that carbon dioxide is about 50 times more soluble in water than is air (nitrogen and oxygen). The relative solubility of carbon dioxide in water is 0.145 g/100 mL H_2O; the relative solubility of air in water is 0.0029 g/100 mL H_2O. Because carbon dioxide is more soluble in water, it is transported across the soap film faster.

Another, more subtle factor also enhances the solubility of carbon dioxide in this system. The alkaline nature of the soap solution shifts the equilibrium reaction to produce more carbonic acid (H_2CO_3) and therefore dissolves a greater amount of carbon dioxide:

$$CO_2(g) + H_2O(aq) \rightleftharpoons H_2CO_3(aq) \rightleftharpoons HCO_3^-(aq) + H^+(aq)$$

As carbonic acid forms, more carbon dioxide dissolves as the above equilibrium reaction is shifted to the right. Once dissolved in the soap solution that makes up the film, the dissolved carbon dioxide will tend to come out of solution where the carbon dioxide concentration is lower—inside the bubble. These two effects produce an increase in volume which is larger than the decrease that is caused by the lower temperature, so the net effect is an increase in the size of the bubble.

Cross-Curricular Integration

Earth science:
- Students can study the formation of clouds of condensed water vapor.
- Students can study the production of winds (as gravity pulls cooler, denser air beneath less dense, warmer air masses) or ocean currents (produced by density differences in seawater).

Language arts:
- Have students read the novel *20,000 Leagues Under the Sea,* by Jules Verne, and look for situations where density and pressure differences play a part in the story.

Life science:
- Students can study how some animals use air bubbles to survive underwater. Many adult aquatic insects and other arthropods carry pockets of air with them underwater, which they use as an oxygen supply, much like a scuba diver. Good examples of this are diving beetles (families *Hydrophilidae* and *Dytiscidae*), water boatmen (*Corixidae*), and backswimmers (*Notonectidae*), which are common in aquatic habitats throughout North America. The air bubble serves not only as a supply of oxygen but also as a gill that can exchange gases with the surrounding water to extend the length of the dive.
- Students can study gas exchange in respiration. The diffusion of gases through the bubble membrane, as observed in this activity, is very similar to the basic process by which most living organisms exchange gases with their environments.

References

Ross, H.A. *A Textbook of Entomology;* Wiley: New York, NY, 1965.

Shakhashiri, B.Z. *Chemical Demonstrations;* University of Wisconsin: Madison, WI, 1985; Vol. 2, pp 228–231.

Contributors

Alison Dowd, Talawanda Middle School, Oxford, OH; Teaching Science with TOYS peer writer.

Tom Runyan, Garfield Alternative School, Middletown, OH; Teaching Science with TOYS peer mentor.

HATS OFF TO THE DRINKING BIRD

What makes the drinking bird so thirsty? Will it ever stop drinking? Observe the behavior of the drinking bird and use the scientific method to explain the changes occurring as the drinking bird drinks.

Drinking bird

GRADE LEVELS

Science activity appropriate for grades 7–9
Cross-Curricular Integration intended for grades 7–9

KEY SCIENCE TOPICS

- center of gravity
- effect of temperature on gas pressure
- energy and phase changes
- evaporative cooling
- heat engine
- liquid-vapor equilibrium
- rate of evaporation
- work

STUDENT BACKGROUND

This activity is most effective after students have studied the states of matter (solid, liquid, and gas) and have some understanding of changes of state (phase changes). Specifically, students should understand that evaporation has a cooling effect because heat energy is absorbed by the liquid as it is converted into a gas. An understanding of the center of gravity is recommended.

KEY PROCESS SKILLS

- observing — Students observe the movement of the drinking bird.

- predicting — Students predict the effect that changing temperature and humidity will have on the behavior of the drinking bird.

TIME REQUIRED

Setup   5 minutes
Performance   20–30 minutes, if demonstrated*
Cleanup   5 minutes
*Additional time is required if done as a student investigation.

Materials

For "Introducing the Activity"
- cotton balls or swabs

For the "Procedure"
Per demonstration or group
- 1 drinking bird
- 1 cup room-temperature tap water
- (optional) 1 drinking bird with felt removed from the head

For "Variations and Extensions"
❶ All materials listed for the "Procedure" plus the following:
- 1 cup rubbing alcohol
- 1 cup hot tap water
- 1 cup cold water (or ice cubes and tap water)
- masking tape and marker to label cups

❸ All materials listed for the "Procedure" plus the following:
- 1 of the following:
  ○ large jar
  ○ zipper-type plastic bag
  ○ covered aquarium
- cup of rubbing alcohol

❺ All materials listed for the "Procedure" plus the following:
- stopwatch
- graph paper

❻ All the materials listed for Extension 5

❼ All materials listed for the "Procedure" plus the following:
- several coins
- tape

Safety and Disposal

The drinking bird is made of thin glass and is fragile. Care should be taken not to break it because it contains freon or methylene chloride. Freon should not be released into the atmosphere because of its environmental effect on the ozone in the upper atmosphere. Methylene chloride is toxic; if a drinking bird is broken, avoid breathing fumes or allowing contact with skin. Rubbing alcohol is intended for external use only. No special disposal procedures are required.

Getting Ready

It is imperative that the drinking bird be tested before being used in class. Often some adjustment is needed for the bird to bob properly. The pivot point must be correct for the bird to bob, and the tube has a tendency to slide out of adjustment, which prevents proper action. Sometimes the metal supports need to be bent so that the bird sits slightly forward of the support points. Also, the height of the water container must be adjusted so that the liquid in the top chamber flows back into the bottom chamber when the bird bobs. On a humid day, it will be harder to get the bird to bob, so the adjustments just described become even more critical.

Label cups of room-temperature water, hot water, cold water, and rubbing alcohol for the demonstration. If done as a hands-on activity, different student groups can be assigned different temperatures of water to investigate.

(optional) Carefully remove the exterior felt (without removing the beak) from the head of a second drinking bird.

Introducing the Activity

Show students a drinking bird without providing an explanation. You may wish to display the bird for one or more days to arouse curiosity. As a preliminary activity, use a cotton ball or swab to place a small amount of water and/or rubbing alcohol on the back of the students' hands. This will remind them that as a liquid evaporates, cooling occurs. If both water and rubbing alcohol are used, the relative amounts of cooling can be compared. Explain to the students that they will be applying the scientific method to discover how the drinking bird works.

Procedure

1. Allow students time to write down their observations and descriptions of the drinking bird phenomenon. Tell students that they are NOT to make hypotheses or inferences—only to write down observations.

2. List and discuss observations; emphasize the difference between observations and inferences. Make sure that all students have seen the complete cycle of the bird and have noted the flow of the colored liquid in the drinking bird before proceeding further.

3. Ask the class for hypotheses as to why the bird bobs. If suggestions are slow, prompt students by showing them the lack of action in another drinking bird that has a dry head or that has had the felt removed from the head.

4. Experiment with student suggestions or ask them guided questions such as:

   a. "Would the bird bob if the head is soaked in hot water?" *Yes.*

   b. "If the tail is warmed does the liquid rise faster?" *Yes.* (Apply heat by cupping your hand around the lower bulb or placing the lower bulb in warm water.)

    Do not heat with a flame as the thin glass may break.

   c. "If the tail is cooled (by dipping in cold water), what happens to the level of the liquid in the tube?" *It is lowered.*

5. Facilitate the discussion, helping students to conclude that a temperature difference between the head and tail sections is the driving force of the bird's action. (This temperature difference is primarily a result of cooling by evaporation. The rate of bobbing is faster when warm water is used since the rate of evaporation is faster. See Question 4a.)

Variations and Extensions

1. Have different groups test their drinking bird using different temperatures of water or using rubbing alcohol.

2. Have students determine how long the bird will continue to bob once the cup of water is removed.

3. Challenge students to devise ways of increasing or decreasing the rate of bobbing. Lead them to try the following:

    a. To increase the rate of evaporation, fan or gently blow air across the head (CAUTION—the bird is fragile) or use a more volatile liquid, such as alcohol, in place of the water.

    ➤ *If alcohol is used, the beak has a tendency to come unglued and fall off.*

    b. To decrease the rate of bobbing, prevent evaporation by placing the bird in a large jar, a large zipper-type plastic bag, or a covered aquarium; after a while, the bird stops bobbing because once the atmosphere is saturated with water vapor, evaporation (and thus cooling) stops.

4. Challenge students to design a bobbing bird without the use of any exterior liquid. (See the "Explanation" and Plumb, 1975 reference.)

5. Have students count the number of bird bobs per minute under various conditions and graph the results.

6. Have students count the number of bird bobs per minute on a day with high humidity and on a day with low humidity. Is there a difference?

    ➤ *If humidity is very high, the bird may bob slower or not at all unless fanned.*

7. Show the effects of lowering the center of gravity on the stability of the bird. Taping weights such as coins at or near the bottom of the bird makes the bird remain stable instead of tipping as the liquid rises in the neck.

Explanation

➤ *The following explanation is intended for the teacher's information. Modify the explanation for students as required.*

The drinking bird is a toy that, once set into motion, dips its beak into a glass of water (or alcohol), returns to its upright position, then dips its beak into the liquid again. This bobbing pattern is repeated for an extended period of time. Initially, the bird is in an upright position, shown in Figure 1.

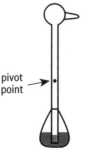

Figure 1: Initially, the drinking bird is in the upright position.

Figure 2: The colored liquid in the lower chamber is pushed up into the neck.

Note the level of liquid in the bottom chamber and in the tube that is the neck of the bird. Initially, the levels are about the same, indicating that the pressure in the upper chamber (the head) and the bottom chamber (the tail) are about the same. When the felt head is placed into the glass of water, the water is absorbed by the felt beak and head as a result of capillary action. As the water evaporates, the upper chamber is cooled. This lowers the pressure of the vapor in the upper chamber. The operation of the bird depends upon the sensitive temperature dependence of the bird's vapor pressure.

Since the lower chamber remains at room temperature, the pressure of vapor in the lower chamber remains the same. Because of the pressure difference, the colored liquid in the lower chamber is pushed up into the neck (moving from higher pressure to lower pressure) as illustrated in Figure 2. As more liquid is pushed from the bottom chamber, it begins to fill the upper chamber. This raises the center of gravity above the pivot point, and the bird becomes unstable and starts to tip toward its "drinking" position. (See Figure 3.)

Figure 3: The bird becomes unbalanced and starts to tip toward its drinking position.

Figure 4: The liquid in the drinking bird is redistributed.

When the bird tips forward until it is almost horizontal, it once again gets its beak wet ("drinks"), replacing the water that has evaporated. At this point the tube opening in the tail is above the surface of the liquid in the tail. This allows gas from the tail to rise into the neck towards the head and liquid to run back into the tail. (See Figure 4.) The redistribution of the liquid causes a shift in the center of gravity, and the bird returns to the upright position, essentially the same configuration as in Figure 1. More evaporation takes place, and the cycle is repeated.

On humid days (See Variation 6) or in an isolated atmosphere such as a covered aquarium (See Variation 3), the action stops as the air becomes saturated with water vapor, and evaporation stops. When the bird "drinks" alcohol, the rate of bobbing generally is faster. This happens because alcohol is more volatile, evaporates at a faster rate, and thus cools the vapor in the head more rapidly.

Without the felt on the bird's upper chamber, water is not absorbed by the glass bulb, and evaporation does not take place; without evaporation and the associated cooling, the bird does not bob. A "waterless" bobbing bird can be made by painting the bottom chamber black and the upper chamber white. With this design, the difference in absorption of radiant heat from the sun or a light bulb causes the temperature difference instead of evaporation.

The bird can be viewed as a heat engine, a device that utilizes a working fluid to exchange heat with two heat reservoirs and perform work. The bird's liquid is the working fluid. It absorbs heat into the lower chamber at room temperature and gives off heat during evaporation at the cooler head. There is a net absorption of heat; therefore, the bird has the capacity to do work, initially in the form of gravitational potential energy of the liquid. In normal operation, this potential energy is converted into the kinetic energy of the observed swinging motion, although some mechanism could be designed to have the bird do work as this motion takes place.

Cross-Curricular Integration

Life science:
- Discuss how the human body cools itself through evaporation (sweating).

References

Frank, D. "The Drinking Bird and the Scientific Method," *Journal of Chemical Education*. 1973, 50, 211.

Juergens, F. University of Wisconsin-Madison, personal communication.

Plumb, R. "Physical Chemistry of the Drinking Duck," *Journal of Chemical Education*. 1973, 50, 212.

Plumb, R. "Footnote to the Drinking Duck Exemplum," *Journal of Chemical Education*. 1975, 52, 728.

Contributors

Alison Dowd, Talawanda Middle School, Oxford, OH; Teaching Science with TOYS peer writer.

Gary Lovely, Edgewood Middle School, Seven Mile, OH; Teaching Science with TOYS peer mentor.

Tom Runyan, Garfield Alternative School, Middletown, OH; Teaching Science with TOYS peer mentor.

HEAT SOLUTION™

Can a small bag containing a solution act as a source of heat at a moment's notice? This activity investigates the Heat Solution™ to discover how it can provide heat and how it can be recycled.

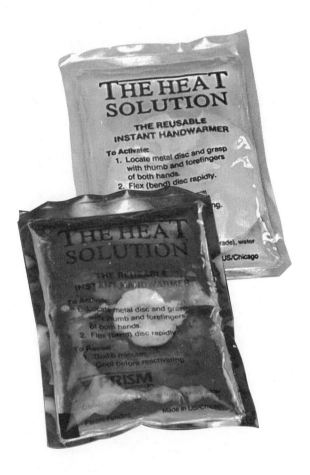

Heat Solution™ packets, crystallized (top) and in aqueous solution against a dark background (bottom)

GRADE LEVELS

Science activity appropriate for grades 4–12
Cross-Curricular Integration intended for grades 7–9

KEY SCIENCE TOPICS

- conservation of energy
- energy changes
- energy sources
- solutions and concentrations

STUDENT BACKGROUND

Students should have studied the types of solutions and changes that produce heat energy.

KEY PROCESS SKILLS

- measuring — Students measure the temperature change as a result of the heat generated from a Heat Solution™ packet.

- defining operationally — Students use their experience with the Heat Solution™ to develop an understanding of a supersaturated solution.

TIME REQUIRED

Setup — 5 minutes (See "Getting Ready.")
Performance — 10 minutes
Cleanup — none (It takes about 10 minutes to get the Heat Solution™ back into solution for storage.)

Materials

For the "Procedure"
Per class
- Heat Solution™ (available from some sporting goods stores and pharmacies)
- water
- (optional) hot plate

- (optional) pan
- (optional) thermometer
- (optional) towel
- (optional) overhead projector
- (optional) Styrofoam™ cup large enough to hold Heat Solution™ bag and about 90 mL water

For "Variations and Extensions"

❶ Per class
- 1 or more Heat Solutions™
- (optional) a "gel" Heat Solution™

❷ Per group
- 175 g (¾ cup) sodium acetate trihydrate ($NaC_2H_3O_2•3H_2O$)
- water
- hot-water bath
- zipper-type plastic bag

❸ Per group or class
- other types of hot packs

Safety and Disposal

Because of potential breakage of thermometers, alcohol or metal cooking thermometers should be used. Should mercury thermometers be used and a break occur, the mercury should be cleaned up with a mercury spill kit. Avoid handling mercury or inhaling the vapor. Dispose of mercury according to local ordinances. If the Heat Solution™ bag breaks, the contents, food-grade sodium acetate and water, can be flushed down the drain with water.

Getting Ready

Make sure the Heat Solution™ is in solution form, not crystalline form.

According to the manufacturer, the Heat Solution™ should always be stored in the solution form, not the crystalline form. If it is crystallized, place the bag in boiling water for about 10 minutes to get it into solution. About 45 minutes are required for it to cool back to room temperature.

Introducing the Activity

Options:

- Ask the students to name several different ways to provide heat. Then find out how many of these are "portable" sources.

- Discuss the terminology of solutions; for example, solute, solvent, unsaturated, saturated, and supersaturated.

Procedure

1. Pass the Heat Solution™ around so that each student can observe the packet. Ask students to make observations. *Observations should include the fact that the bag contains a liquid and a metal disk and a qualitative indication of the temperature, that is, "room temperature." If you will be recording temperatures (see Step 4 below), use a thermometer to measure the temperature before the Heat Solution™ is activated.*

   Caution the students to handle the solution gently as it is passed around so that the disk is not activated until everyone has had a chance to observe the solution.

2. Allow a student to activate the Heat Solution™ by flexing the metal disk gently. Ask the student to hold the bag up so that the rest of the class can see what is happening. Alternatively, place the bag on an overhead projector, and then flex the disk; the resulting crystal formation can be viewed by the whole class. Pass the bag from student to student so that all can observe the increase in temperature.

3. Ask questions such as, "Where does the heat comes from? How can the bag be reused? Have students seen or used other portable sources of heat? How are the other sources similar and how are they different? Are other sources of heat reusable?"

4. If using a thermometer, ask students to determine how high the temperature gets. (Place the thermometer in contact with the Heat Solution™ and wrap a towel around both to monitor the temperature.) Ask, "How long does the Heat Solution™ stay hot?"

   As an alternative to Step 4, place the activated Heat Solution™ bag into a Styrofoam™ cup with about 90 mL water. Monitor the change in temperature of the water.

5. If a hot plate is available, you may wish to have the students get the crystals back into solution. Monitor the recycling closely: the bag MUST be heated in a hot-water bath; it cannot be placed directly on the hot plate.

Variations and Extensions

1. If several Heat Solutions™ are available, several groups can do the experiment. Alternatively, you can have different groups investigate the Heat Solution™ on different days, record their data, and have a full class discussion after each group has done the activity and written a report. If you have a "gel" Heat Solution™, have students determine if there is any difference in the temperature and time data for the two types of Heat Solution™.

2. Have your class make its own supersaturated solution of sodium acetate by combining 175 g (¾ cup) sodium acetate trihydrate ($NaC_2H_3O_2 \cdot 3H_2O$) and 50 mL water (3⅓ tablespoons), then heating in a hot-water bath. Place the solution in a zipper-type plastic bag. Ask, "What is required to initiate crystallization?" *A seed crystal.*

3. Discuss other hot packs. Some other kinds of hot packs used in hospitals and by athletic trainers cannot be reused. In one kind, a breakable inner pouch containing the solution is broken so the solution comes in contact with solid crystals (seed crystals), which initiates the crystallization of the entire solution. In another kind, one pouch contains water and the other a salt that gives off

heat when it is dissolved. Calcium chloride, the salt often used to melt snow and ice, behaves in this manner. You may wish to have students compare the heat given off by one of these types of hot packs with that of the Heat Solution™. Other materials, such as ammonium nitrate, cool when they dissolve. Such substances are used in cold packs.

Explanation

 The following explanation is intended for the teacher's information. Modify the explanation for students as required.

The Heat Solution™ contains a supersaturated solution of the salt sodium acetate in water. A supersaturated solution is one in which there is more solute (sodium acetate) dissolved in the solvent (water) than would normally be possible at a given temperature. Honey is an example of a supersaturated solution of sugar in water. A supersaturated solution is inherently unstable but remains as a solution until something initiates crystallization. You may have seen jars of honey that became crystallized. In the Heat Solution™ the flexing of the metal disk creates a shock wave that is sufficient to initiate crystallization. Once this occurs, the supersaturated solution immediately crystallizes to form the more stable solid. Heat is given off as the solution crystallizes. Supersaturated solutions can also be made to crystallize by adding a "seed" crystal, a crystal of the solid that initiates the crystallization process.

The solution-to-crystals process is reversible. If the crystallized sample is heated, it goes back into solution. The heat absorbed by the crystallized Heat Solution™ to get the salt back into solution is released when the sodium acetate recrystallizes. (When sugar crystallizes in honey, it also can be made to go back into solution by heating).

Cross-Curricular Integration

Earth science:
- Have students research the use of low-melting salts to deliver solar energy. One such salt is sodium thiosulfate pentahydrate ($Na_2S_2O_3 \cdot 5H_2O$), which melts at 48°C. During the day, heat from the sun is absorbed to melt the sodium thiosulfate. When the melted salt crystallizes, the heat released as a result of the crystallization can be used as a source of heat. The melting-crystallization cycle can be repeated any number of times.

Life science:
- Have students investigate the use of heating and cooling in the treatment of injuries.

References

"Crystallization of a Supersaturated Solution;" *Fun with Chemistry: A Guidebook of K–12 Activities;* Sarquis, M., Sarquis, J., Eds.; Institute for Chemical Education: Madison, WI, 1993; Vol. 2, pp 287–291.

Shakhashiri, B.Z.; *Chemical Demonstrations;* University of Wisconsin: Madison, WI, 1983; Vol. 1, pp 27–30.

COLOR-CHANGING CARS

Students investigate the effect of temperature on the color of liquid crystals in color-changing cars or other liquid crystal toys.

Color-changing cars

GRADE LEVELS

Science activity appropriate for grades 4–12
Cross-Curricular Integration intended for grades 7–9

KEY SCIENCE TOPICS

- liquid crystals
- physical changes
- changes of state

STUDENT BACKGROUND

Students should be knowledgeable about the three states of matter, changes of state, and the ordered arrangement of particles that occurs in crystalline solids.

KEY PROCESS SKILLS

- observing — Students observe color changes in toys that contain liquid crystals.

- comparing/contrasting — Students compare and contrast color changes that occur in different cars during temperature changes.

TIME REQUIRED

Setup — 5 minutes
Performance — 2 periods of 40–45 minutes each
Cleanup — 5 minutes

Materials

For "Introducing the Activity"
- liquid crystal color-changing items such as spoons, pencils, Magic Makeup doll, color-changing Barbie™ hair pieces, and Hypercolor clothes

For the "Procedure"

Per group of 3–4 students

- 1 or more color-changing cars of various colors (can be shared with other groups)
- 2 water containers

A "pop-beaker" made from a cut-off plastic 2-L soft-drink bottle works well.

- non-color-changing car
- tongs
- ice
- source of very warm water
- timer with a second hand

For "Variations and Extensions"

❶ Per group

- 4 water containers

A "pop-beaker" made from a cut-off plastic 2-L soft-drink bottle works well.

- 2 color-changing cars
- heat source for boiling water
- timer with a second hand
- (optional) thermometer

❷ Per group

- (optional) hair dryer
- color-changing toys

Safety and Disposal

Be careful not to spill very warm water on skin. The manufacturer cautions against the use of very hot water with color-changing cars.

Because of the potential breakage of thermometers, alcohol or metal cooking thermometers should be used. Should mercury thermometers be used and a break occur, the mercury should be cleaned up with a mercury spill kit. Avoid handling mercury or inhaling the vapor. Dispose of mercury according to local ordinances.

Introducing the Activity

Demonstrate the color change that occurs as a result of a temperature change in several liquid crystal items. Discuss possible reasons for the observed color changes.

Procedure

Have each student group follow the steps listed on the Student Instruction Sheet and then do the following as a class:

Conduct a class discussion of the findings. Look for patterns; for example, do purple cars always change to the same color(s)? Visually compare the paint on a color-changing car to that on a non-color-changing car.

Variations and Extensions

1. See the Student Instruction Sheet.

2. Ask students, "Is water required for a color change to occur? Or is a change in temperature alone the cause?" Suggest that students try to heat the car using a blow hair dryer or by holding the car between the palms of their hands.

Explanation

The following explanation is intended for the teacher's information. Modify the explanation for students as required.

Matter exists in three common states: solid, liquid, and gas. For a typical solid, if the temperature rises to the melting point, it will change to the liquid state. A change of state is also called a phase change. If the liquid is cooled sufficiently, the reverse phase change (freezing) occurs. The three states of matter have characteristic arrangements of the particles (molecules, ions, or atoms) of which they are composed. In crystalline solids, the particles are in a regularly ordered arrangement with each particle occupying a specific position with a specific orientation. Although the particles vibrate, they do not move with respect to one another. In the liquid state, particles are still in contact but are not oriented in the same direction and do not remain in the same position relative to neighboring molecules. Instead, they are free to move past one another. In gases, the particles are independent of each other (no longer in contact with neighboring particles), are constantly moving, and have no regular orientation.

As matter is heated or cooled, it undergoes changes of state; that is, SOLID→LIQUID→GAS and vice versa. Each state has characteristic properties. For example, if ice, the solid state of water, is heated above 0°C, it melts, forming clear liquid water. In 1888, Friedrich Reinitzer, an Austrian botanist, discovered that an organic compound he was studying, called cholesteryl benzoate, melted at 145°C to form a milky liquid. At 179°C, the milky liquid became clear. When the substance was cooled, the reverse processes occurred. The milky white liquid observed by Reinitzer between 145°C and 179°C is what some now call a separate state of matter—the liquid crystal state. Materials that have a liquid crystal state have both interesting and useful properties.

The liquid crystal state is so named because molecules in that state show some of the characteristics of both liquids and solids. At a low temperature, the materials are solids. As they are heated, they change to the liquid crystal state. The molecules in liquid crystals are in a semi-ordered state intermediate between liquid disorder and crystalline order. Liquid-crystalline substances have characteristic molecular shapes and structures. The molecules are long, rigid, and rod-like. The rod-like shape allows for the partial ordering. Liquid crystals are classified as nematic, smectic, and cholesteric. The nematic liquid crystal phase has the least order and is most like a true liquid. The cholesteric phase has the most order since the molecules are confined to layers that give rise to a long-range spiral order. Figure 1 shows the relative orientation of the molecules in three types of liquid crystals and in a regular liquid.

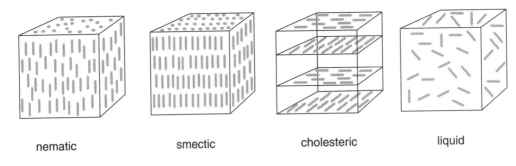

nematic   smectic   cholesteric   liquid

Figure 1: Liquid crystal orientations

Thousands of organic molecules are known to have at least one liquid crystal phase, and the physical properties of this intermediate state have considerable technological importance.

Toys and thermometer strips that change color as a result of temperature change (as in this activity) use cholesteric liquid crystals. These crystals undergo a series of color changes as the layer thickness and the angle of rotation between layers change as the temperature changes. When white light shines upon a liquid crystal, only certain wavelengths of light are reflected. The color of light reflected depends on the thickness of the layer and orientation of adjacent layers of the liquid crystal. A change in temperature causes a change in molecular motion which alters the thickness of the layer and the orientation of the molecules; thus, the color of light reflected changes.

The liquid crystal displays of instruments such as watches, electronic calculators, and computer screens use nematic liquid crystals. An electric field pulls the polar molecules of the nematic phase out of alignment and causes the substance to become opaque. Transparency returns when the electrical signal is removed, and the molecules return to their normal nematic alignment.

Assessment

Collect student charts to evaluate student understanding.

Cross-Curricular Integration

Home, safety, and career:
- Students can research the commercial applications of liquid crystal technology.

Life science:
- Students can use liquid crystal display thermometers to measure their temperatures.

References

Brown, T.L.; LeMay, Jr., H.E.; Bursten, B.E. *Chemistry, The Central Science*, 6th ed.; Prentice Hall: Englewood Cliffs, NJ, 1994; pp 415–421.

Collings, P.J. *Liquid Crystals, Nature's Delicate Phase of Matter;* Princeton University: Princeton, NJ, 1990.

"Liquid Crystals," *ChemMatters.* December 1983, 8–11.

"Liquid Crystal Displays," *ChemMatters*. April 1984, 10.

Radel, S.R.; Navidi, M.H. *Chemistry;* West: New York, 1994; p 563.

Contributor

Lee Ann Ellsworth, Franklin Middle School, Springfield, OH; Teaching Science with TOYS, 1991–92.

Handout Masters

A master for the following handout is provided:

• Student Instruction Sheet

Copy as needed for classroom use.

COLOR-CHANGING CARS

Student Instruction Sheet

Purpose

To observe the color change of toy cars when they are heated or cooled; to observe and time the color-changing process.

Procedure

1. Create a chart on notebook paper with these headings: "Color of Car," "Color in Warm Water," and "Color in Cold Water."

2. Go to the sink and fill one container with very warm water from the hot water tap and the second container with cold tap water. Your teacher will come around to put ice cubes into the cold water.

3. Record the color of your color-changing car in your chart.

4. Use tongs to dip the car into the very warm water. Record the color change. Dip the car into ice water. Record the color change.

5. When instructed by your teacher, pass your car to the group designated by your teacher.

6. Repeat Steps 3–6 until all cars have been tested.

7. Answer Questions 1 and 2 before starting the Extension.

Extension

1. Empty the container with the very warm water into the sink and refill it since the temperature has probably dropped considerably. Your teacher will add more ice to the cold water container if necessary.

2. Fill your third container with lukewarm water and the fourth with cold tap water.

3. Get two identical cars from your teacher.

4. Select someone to be the timer. When the timer says "GO," drop both cars: one into the very warm water and the other into the lukewarm water. When each car has COMPLETELY changed color, tell your timer. Record results (Question 3).

5. Place the cars in ice water to return the color to the room temperature color. Repeat Step 4 two more times.

6. Put cars in very warm water to induce color change. Repeat Step #4 but put cars into cold and ice water and time the color-changing process. Record results (Question 4).

7. Repeat Steps 4 and 5 but DO NOT time. Instead observe the color-changing process and answer Question 5.

8. Compare the paint on the color changing car to the paint on one that does not change color. Answer Question 6.

[Continued.]

Questions and Observations

Answer the following questions on a separate sheet of paper.

1. Does the color change occur immediately when a temperature change occurs, or is it a gradual change?

2. Study the color changes you recorded. Is there an observable pattern, for example, do orange cars always turn red or yellow or do purple cars always turn red or blue? Discuss your results.

3. Record the times and calculate the average time for your three trials for the very warm and lukewarm water.

    Does the temperature of the water affect the color-changing process? Discuss the results.

    Does the same color appear when different water temperatures are used?

4. Record your times and calculate the average time for your three trials for the cold and ice water.

    Does the temperature of the water affect the color-changing process? Discuss the results.

    Does the same color appear when different water temperatures are used?

5. Observe the color-changing process and record and discuss your observations. Does the color-changing process occur on all parts of the car all at once? Does it begin at the front and proceed backwards or vice versa? Does it begin on the roof and proceed downwards or vice versa?

6. Visually compare the paint on a color-changing car to the paint on a non-color-changing car. Discuss your observations. Note any similarities and differences.

INVESTIGATING THE EFFECT OF TEMPERATURE ON LIGHTSTICKS

Watch the light intensity of a lightstick change when placed in a hot- and then a cold-water bath. Students investigate how temperature affects the rate of the chemical reaction occurring.

Three brands of lightsticks

GRADE LEVELS

Science activity appropriate for grades 4–12
Cross-Curricular Integration intended for grades 7–9

KEY SCIENCE TOPICS

- chemical change
- energy
- rate of reaction

STUDENT BACKGROUND

This activity is most effective with students who can differentiate between a physical and a chemical change.

KEY PROCESS SKILLS

• collecting data	Students collect data concerning the effect of temperature on the intensity and duration of the light in a lightstick.
• predicting	Students predict how the intensity and duration of light from a lightstick are related.

TIME REQUIRED

Setup	5	minutes (plus time to heat water)
Performance	15	minutes
Cleanup	5	minutes

Materials

For "Introducing the Activity"
- lightstick
- a variety of other chemiluminescent items, such as
  - glow necklaces
  - glow badges
  - glow fishing bobbers

For the "Procedure"

Per class
- 3 lightsticks of the same color
- ice
- water
- hot plate or electric coffee maker to heat water
- 2 clear containers such as glasses, jars, or beakers to hold about 500 mL (2 cups)
- (optional) alcohol or metal cooking thermometer
- (optional) tongs
- access to a room that can be effectively darkened

The room does not have to be completely dark, but it is easier to judge differences in light intensity if the room is darkened.

For "Variations and Extensions"

 Per class
- access to a freezer
- lightsticks

Safety and Disposal

Read the precautions on the lightstick package. If the lightstick is placed in water that is too hot (more than 70°C), the plastic might melt and the contents run into the water. (Melting doesn't cause a serious problem; the material inside the lightstick is not water-soluble so it remains as a glowing glob in the water.)

Because of the potential breakage of thermometers, alcohol or metal cooking thermometers should be used. Should mercury thermometers be used and a break occur, the mercury should be cleaned up with a mercury spill kit. Avoid handling mercury or inhaling the vapor. Dispose of mercury according to local ordinances.

When finished, the lightstick can be disposed of in a waste basket.

Getting Ready

1. Heat the water no higher than 70°C, about the temperature of a hot cup of coffee. (Above 70°C the plastic lightstick might melt.) Pour the water into a clear container.

2. Make an ice-water bath by placing ice in the water in the second container.

Introducing the Activity

Show students a variety of chemiluminescent items with which they may be familiar, such as glow necklaces, badges, fishing bobbers, and the lightsticks. Or if these items are not available, ask students if they have seen them in an amusement park or at Halloween. Activate one lightstick and have students speculate whether it is a physical or chemical change. Give them an opportunity to explain the reason for their answers. Now challenge students to use their observation skills to determine the effect of temperature on chemical reactions. Alternatively, you may wish to show a lightstick or other chemiluminescent toy one day to arouse interest, then do the temperature investigation another day.

Procedure

1. Ask students to record observations on the Explanation Sheet (provided) about the lightstick *before it is activated.* You may wish to pass it around so each student has a close-up view.

2. Activate one lightstick by bending it (to break the inner glass vial; see the directions on the package) and ask students to observe.

3. You may wish to pass the *activated* lightstick around the class and have students make observations.

➤ *The light is produced without noticeable heat; most sources of light also produce heat.*

4. Activate the other two lightsticks. Compare the intensities of the three lightsticks. (They should be about the same intensity.)

5. Place the second lightstick in the hot water (less than 70°C) and at the same time place the third in the ice-water bath. Keep the first lightstick at room temperature as a control.

6. Allow the lightsticks to sit in the containers for the same period of time. Within a few minutes, students should observe a difference in the intensity of light from the lightsticks in the two containers.

7. Pull the glowing lightsticks out of the containers and compare their intensities with that of the room-temperature lightstick.

8. Ask students to complete the Explanation Sheet (provided).

9. Reverse the lightsticks so that the one that was in hot water is now in the ice water and the one originally in ice water is in the hot water. Have the students observe. Ask, "How long does it take for the intensity of the glow to change?"

Variations and Extensions

1. Challenge students to describe the best way to make a lightstick glow the longest and the best way to make one glow the brightest.

2. Ask students to predict which lightstick will stop glowing first—the one in hot or cold water? Let students design their own experiments to test their hypotheses.

3. Assign students to take the lightsticks with them after class and to report how long the glowing lasted.

4. Challenge students to speculate why the temperature affects the rate of reactions.

5. Ask, "How are lightstick necklaces and bracelets stored, before being sold, in amusement parks?" *On dry ice.*

6. If a freezer is convenient, place an activated lightstick in the freezer and observe if it still glows when first removed from the freezer and when warmed to room temperature. Try this with activated lightsticks that have been stored in the freezer for one week, two weeks, one month, two months, etc. Or have students take them home and report the same information back to the class.

7. Have students think of practical uses for lightsticks.

8. Have students investigate whether the color of the lightstick is related to the length of time it will glow.

Explanation

 The following explanation is intended for the teacher's information. Modify the explanation for students as required.

A lightstick consists of a sealed plastic tube that contains two solutions. One solution is in a thin glass vial within the plastic tube. The lightstick is activated by bending the plastic tube which causes the glass vial to break so the two solutions can interact. When mixed, the two solutions react, producing light.

The glass vial contains dilute hydrogen peroxide, and the other solution contains a fluorescent dye and phenyl oxalate ester. The ester and hydrogen peroxide react first, producing an intermediate compound that transfers energy to the dye molecule. The glow is visible as the excited-state dye molecule loses energy back to the ground state. (An "excited"-state molecule is a molecule that has more energy than normal, and a "ground"-state molecule has the normal amount of energy.) If an excited-state molecule loses energy, the excess energy is liberated. In the case of the excited-state dye molecules in the lightstick, the energy given off is in the form of light in the visible region of the spectrum. The details of the chemical reaction are given in the Shakhashiri reference.

In general, the speed of a chemical reaction increases as the temperature increases. At a higher temperature, a larger fraction of the reacting molecules have sufficient energy to react upon collision; thus, at a higher temperature, the glow is brighter, indicating that the number of molecules reacting is greater. Likewise, at a lower temperature, the lower intensity indicates the reaction rate is less. Since each lightstick contains a fixed amount of material, the lower the temperature, the longer the lightstick will glow (but with less intensity). If an activated lightstick is stored in a freezer, the rate of reaction becomes so slow that there is no perceptible glow; however, when removed from the freezer and warmed, the lightstick will give off light, even after being stored for several months.

For a detailed explanation of luminescence, see the Teaching Science with TOYS activity "Things that Glow in the Dark."

Cross-Curricular Integration

Earth science:
- Discuss phosphorescent minerals and the use of this characteristic in identifying mineral samples.
- Discuss triboluminescence—luminescence in some minerals resulting from stress.

Life science:
- Discuss the bioluminescence of fireflies and bacteria that live on some species of saltwater fish.

References

"Chemiluminescence: Dissecting a Lightstick;" *Fun with Chemistry, A Guidebook of K–12 Activities;* Sarquis, M., Sarquis, J., Eds.; Institute for Chemical Education: Madison, WI, 1991; Vol. 1, pp 163–166.

Shakhashiri, B.Z. *Chemical Demonstrations;* University of Wisconsin: Madison, WI, 1983; Vol. 1, pp 146–152.

Contributors

Alison Dowd, Talawanda Middle School, Oxford, OH, Teaching Science with TOYS peer writer.

Elizabeth McLean, Wilder Junior High School, Piqua, OH; Teaching Science with TOYS, 1991–92.

Mike Warner, Benjamin Rush Middle School, Rushville, IN; Teaching Science with TOYS, 1992–93.

Handout Master

A master for the following handout is provided:

- Explanation Sheet

Copy as needed for classroom use.

INVESTIGATING LIGHTSTICKS

Explanation Sheet

Answer the following questions on a separate sheet of paper.

1. a. Explain why the lightstick in cold water behaved the way it did.
   b. Explain why the lightstick in hot water behaved as it did.

2. Write a conclusion to the experiment. Be sure to relate what you know about the effect of temperature on molecules to what you observed in this experiment. (In other words, explain why the lightsticks behaved as they did.)

Going Further

1. Predict which lightstick will stop glowing first, the one in hot water or the one in cold water. When will the one at room temperature stop glowing—first, second, or third?

2. If you wanted an activated lightstick to glow for a longer period of time than it normally would, what could you do to it?

3. Is there any disadvantage in making the activated lightstick glow for a longer period by making the change you suggested above?

4. Think of a practical use for this toy.

5. What makes a lightstick glow?

EXPERIMENTING WITH LIGHT-SENSITIVE PAPER

Design an experiment to determine the effect various types of light sources have on light-sensitive paper.

Light-sensitive paper

GRADE LEVELS

Science activity appropriate for grades 4–9
Cross-Curricular Integration intended for grades 7–9

KEY SCIENCE TOPICS

- chemical change
- light

STUDENT BACKGROUND

To maximize the usefulness of this activity as a challenge in experimental design, the students should be familiar with:
- the concept of chemical change, and able to compare and contrast a physical change and a chemical change;
- the fact that there are different types of electromagnetic radiation, that white light is a combination of all colors in the visible spectrum, and that color filters can be used to filter out (absorb) light of specific wavelengths; and
- the scientific method.

KEY PROCESS SKILLS

- controlling variables   Students test the reactivity of light-sensitive paper using different light sources.

TIME REQUIRED

Setup	5	minutes
Performance	30–40	minutes*
Cleanup	5	minutes

* Part A is designed as a class demonstration. Part B is a student activity. The time listed assumes that student groups test an assigned light source and then report their findings to the class. As an alternative, have the groups individually conduct all parts of the activity; this will take several class periods.

Materials

For the "Procedure"
Part A, per class
- 1 sheet of Solargraphics® paper (10-cm x 11-cm) or homemade light-sensitive paper

 Solargraphics® paper is available from Solargraphics, P.O. Box 7091, Berkeley, CA 94707; (800) 327-9869, or (415) 525-1776. If you wish to use homemade light-sensitive paper, see "Getting Ready," Step 1.

- sunlight or ultraviolet light
- black paper
- red, blue, yellow, and colorless pieces of cellophane
- scissors
- tape
- container of water
- beaker or other container, 250-mL or larger
- tongs or tweezers
- about 15 mL 3% hydrogen peroxide (from a drug store)

Part B, per class
- several different sources of light such as the following:
  ○ incandescent light bulbs: 100, 60, 40, 25, and 15 watts
  ○ colored lights: red, blue, green, and yellow
  ○ black light or ultraviolet mineral light
  ○ 60-watt yellow bug light
  ○ fluorescent light
  ○ 250-watt infrared heat lamp
- (optional) light hood (to help direct the light onto the light-sensitive paper)

Per group
- 3–5 pieces of Solargraphics® or homemade light-sensitive paper (about 4 cm x 4 cm; the exact size is not critical)
- 2–3 pennies
- small beaker of water
- (optional) diluted solution of hydrogen peroxide made in the proportions noted:
  ○ 1 tablespoon 3% hydrogen peroxide solution per gallon of water
- stopwatch (or other timer with a second hand)
- permanent ink pen that won't run or fade in water (such as a BIC® ballpoint pen)
- (optional) a hard surface (cardboard, glass) to transport the light-sensitive paper and to act as one of the controls in the experiment

For making your own light-sensitive paper
Per class
- 15 g potassium ferricyanide, $K_3Fe(CN)_6$
- 20 g iron(III) ammonium citrate (green) or ferric ammonium citrate (ammonium iron(III) citrate) (brown)

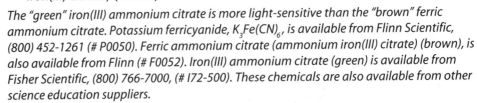

The "green" iron(III) ammonium citrate is more light-sensitive than the "brown" ferric ammonium citrate. Potassium ferricyanide, $K_3Fe(CN)_6$, is available from Flinn Scientific, (800) 452-1261 (# P0050). Ferric ammonium citrate (ammonium iron(III) citrate) (brown), is also available from Flinn (# F0052). Iron(III) ammonium citrate (green) is available from Fisher Scientific, (800) 766-7000, (# I72-500). These chemicals are also available from other science education suppliers.

- water
- 2 flasks or other containers to hold about 125 mL
- pie pan or other shallow container
- plastic or rubber gloves
- sponge, about 2½ inches x 3½ inches

Thin sponges are best because they don't absorb as much of the solution.

For "Variations and Extensions"

❶ All materials listed for the "Procedure" plus the following:
- hair dryer and/or stove or hot plate

❷ All materials listed for the "Procedure" plus the following:
- white cotton muslin

Safety and Disposal

Ultraviolet light can damage the eyes and is the component of sunlight responsible for sunburn. DO NOT look directly at the ultraviolet light and do not expose skin to ultraviolet light for excessive periods of time. Follow the lamp manufacturer's precautions. Keep water away from electrical devices and outlets. Wear gloves if making your own light-sensitive paper; the solution used to make the paper can stain your skin. Excess solutions of potassium ferricyanide and ferric ammonium citrate may be stored for later use or flushed down the drain with water.

Getting Ready

If you are using Solargraphics® paper, start with Step 2.

1. You can make your own light-sensitive paper using potassium ferricyanide (potassium hexacyanoferrate(III)), $K_3Fe(CN)_6$, and ferric ammonium citrate (iron(III) ammonium citrate). Ferric ammonium citrate refers to a compound of ammonia, iron, and citric acid of undetermined structure.

   a. Prepare the following solutions:

      - 15 g potassium ferricyanide (potassium hexacyanoferrate(III)), $K_3Fe(CN)_6$, in 100 mL water

      - 20 g iron(III) ammonium citrate (green) or 20 g ferric ammonium citrate (brown) in 100 mL water

   b. Mix equal volumes of the two solutions and pour them into the pie pan or other shallow container. Saturate the sponge with the mixture; lightly and evenly brush it over the paper. Several pieces of paper can be treated between dips of the sponge. Note that if too much solution is absorbed by the sponge, it is hard to apply an even coating. About 1 mL of the mixture is used for each sheet of 8½-inch x 11-inch paper coated. Allow the coated paper to dry in a dark location, such as a cabinet or drawer. Different types of paper can be used, for example, copier paper, construction paper, or blotter paper. If a more absorbent paper is used, the resulting color is more intense.

The two solutions can be prepared ahead of time and stored as long as they are not mixed together. Once the solutions are mixed, they become sensitive to light and deteriorate; therefore they should be mixed just before the paper is ready for coating.

2. For Part A, prepare a filter cover sheet by cutting a piece of black paper the size of the sheet of light-sensitive paper. In block letters, write a C, R, B, and Y, each in a different quadrant of the black paper. Carefully cut out the letters, keeping the sheet of paper intact. Cut pieces of colorless (C), red (R), blue (B), and yellow (Y) cellophane to fit over the appropriate cut-out area and tape them in place.

3. For Part B, cut the sheets of light-sensitive paper into small (about 4-cm x 4-cm) pieces. These should be large enough for a penny to cover a small portion of the paper and still provide some uncovered area for comparison. To avoid premature exposure to sunlight or ultraviolet light, cut the paper while layered in sandwiches with the light-sensitive sides facing each other.

Helpful Hints for Using Light-Sensitive Paper:

- When transporting the light-sensitive paper, use a piece of cardboard, a book, or a cookie sheet as a tray for moving your assembled sun print in and out of the light.

- Stay in the shade while you arrange objects to be printed on the light-sensitive paper.

- Thin objects used to create the design may not be effective since light may pass through them.

- Place a transparent cover over thin, lightweight objects to prevent them from moving around on the light-sensitive paper.

- When the print is placed in water to develop, the image will disappear. As the paper dries, the print will deepen in color and contrast. When completely dry, the print is permanent.

- Keep the light-sensitive paper inside a black plastic bag or other light-tight container when not in use. If using Solargraphics® paper, always return unused paper to the black plastic bag and store it in its original package.

Procedure

Part A: Introducing the Science (demonstration)

1. If using purchased Solargraphics® paper, read the instructions on the package for use and development. If using homemade light-sensitive paper, go over the instructions with the class. Ask the students to predict what will occur.

 DO NOT expose the light-sensitive paper to sunlight or incandescent light until Step 3. Fluorescent lighting will not affect light-sensitive paper.

2. Position a penny or other coin on the light-sensitive paper.

3. Place in direct sunlight until the light-sensitive paper becomes darker. This generally takes 3–7 minutes; if in doubt, leave longer.

4. Inside or in the shade, place the paper into a container of tap water for about 30 seconds. The exposed area turns blue, and the covered area becomes white.

5. Place the paper on a flat surface to dry.

6. Ask the students what role the water rinse played. As a class, design an experiment to determine the answer. (Possible method: Cut off two small pieces of unused light-sensitive paper; rinse one piece in water [2 minutes is the standard rinse time] before exposure to the light. Place a penny on each piece, expose both as before, and rinse them in water. Compare the results. *The unreacted dye is water-soluble, and is thus removed from the paper when it is rinsed in water. As a result, no reaction occurs on the paper rinsed before it was exposed to light.*)

7. Tell the students that you know a way to develop the blue color much more quickly. Add a small amount of 3% hydrogen peroxide to the rinse water (about 1 tablespoon of 3% hydrogen peroxide per gallon of water). Repeat Steps 2–3, but dip the exposed light-sensitive paper in water that contains the dilute hydrogen peroxide. (The deep blue color of the exposed area will develop immediately.) Rinse the paper briefly in water to remove the unreacted compound and let the paper dry. Compare the results to previous trials. (When developing with hydrogen peroxide solution, the intensity of the color is less than when water is used.)

8. Bring out several pieces of colored cellophane. Ask the students to predict the effect that light passing through these different colored filters will have on the paper.

9. Show the class the filter cover sheet (See "Getting Ready"), and explain that the colorless cellophane will let all of the visible light pass through it. Place the filter cover sheet on an unexposed piece of light-sensitive paper and repeat the standard exposure and rinse procedure. Compare the results.

Part B: Testing Effects of Different Types of Light (hands-on activity)

Divide the class into groups and challenge them to design an experiment to test the effects of light from various light sources. Have them identify the experimental conditions that they will vary and those that will remain the same. One possible procedure might be:

1. Choose one light source from Table 1.

Table 1: Light Sources				
Light Source Key				
A: 100 watt	B: 60 Watt	C: 40 Watt	D: 25 Watt	E: 15 Watt
F: Green	G: Red	H: Blue	I: Yellow	J: Black Light
K: Fluorescent Light	L: Bug Light	M: Infrared Heat Lamp		

2. Choose as many different exposure times from Table 2 as there are pieces of light-sensitive paper in the group.

Table 2: Exposure Times				
Exposure Time Key				
0: Not Exposed	1: 3 Minutes	2: 7 Minutes	3: 15 Minutes	4: 30 Minutes
Optional	5: 45 Minutes	6: 60 Minutes	7: 90 Minutes	8: 120 Minutes

3. With an ink pen, label the blue side of each piece of light-sensitive paper with an identification key that will include the codes for the light source used and the exposure time, as listed in Tables 1 and 2. (For example, if a piece of paper is to be exposed to a 100-watt light source for 60 minutes, the identification key would read, "A6.")

 Use an ink pen that will not run or fade when placed in water.

4. Adjust the chosen light source so it will be 10 cm above the paper.

5. Place the light-sensitive paper labeled "0" directly into the water or hydrogen peroxide/water mixture for development. Rinse and set it aside to dry.

6. Place pennies on two or more remaining pieces of light-sensitive paper and place the paper under the light source being tested. Turn on the light and start the stopwatch.

7. After each piece of light-sensitive paper has been exposed to the light for its designated amount of time (see Table 2 for Exposure Time Key), remove it from the light, and develop, rinse, and let dry as before.

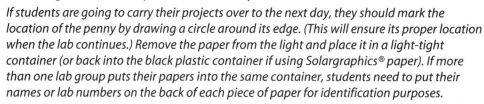

If students are going to carry their projects over to the next day, they should mark the location of the penny by drawing a circle around its edge. (This will ensure its proper location when the lab continues.) Remove the paper from the light and place it in a light-tight container (or back into the black plastic container if using Solargraphics® paper). If more than one lab group puts their papers into the same container, students need to put their names or lab numbers on the back of each piece of paper for identification purposes.

8. Share observations with others in the class. Analyze the results and develop a hypothesis.

Variations and Extensions

1. Compare the effects of dry heat on light-sensitive paper by exposing it to dry heat from a hair dryer and/or from a stove or hot plate.

2. Coat white cotton muslin with the homemade light-sensitive paper coating solution. Expose it to sunlight while still damp, and then allow to dry overnight before rinsing with water.

Explanation

The following explanation is intended for the teacher's information. Modify the explanation for students as required.

While Solargraphics® paper and the homemade light-sensitive paper do not behave in exactly the same way, the overall processes are probably similar. The homemade light-sensitive paper is coated with a water-soluble, bluish-green compound called iron(III) hexacyanoferrate(III), $Fe[Fe(CN)_6]$. The common name for this compound is Berlin green. It is made by reacting potassium ferricyanide, $K_3Fe(CN)_6$, and ferric ammonium citrate (a compound of iron, ammonia and citric acid of undetermined structure).

Berlin green has an unusual property which makes paper coated with it an item of interest to children; it is photosensitive. When exposed to ultraviolet (UV) radiation, Berlin green undergoes a chemical reaction; the water-soluble Berlin green is converted to water-insoluble iron(III) hexacyanoferrate(II), $Fe_4[Fe(CN)_6]_3$. The common name for this product is Prussian blue. Since the homemade light-sensitive paper is coated with Berlin green, it reacts to form Prussian blue when exposed to light which contains some UV radiation, such as sunlight or incandescent light. (Mineral lights also emit UV radiation and will also cause the reaction to occur.) If part of the paper is not exposed to UV light, the Berlin green is not changed. When a piece of exposed light-sensitive paper is rinsed in water, the water-soluble Berlin green is washed out, but the insoluble Prussian blue remains on the paper. This leaves a light silhouette against a deep blue background of Prussian blue. The intensity of the blue color depends upon the nature and intensity of the light source and the exposure time. The longer the exposure time, the darker the blue color. Likewise, the greater the intensity of the light, the darker the color.

Assessment

- Students should be able to identify:
  - the controls and variables of this experiment;
  - the chemical changes occurring in this experiment; and
  - the reactant and product of a chemical change.

- Students should prepare a report for this activity which includes:
  - title of the experiment;
  - identity of the light source;
  - distance the light-sensitive paper was placed from the light source;
  - the mounted test samples and a record of the exposure time for each sample;
  - the controls and variables of this experiment; and
  - the results and conclusion(s) based on the data collected from these experiments.

Cross-Curricular Integration

Art:
- Have a guest speaker such as a photographer or architect talk to the class about photography or blueprinting.

Life science:
- Have the students research reactions from sunlight such as photosynthesis, tanning, or chameleons.

References

Brady, J.E.; Holum, J.R. *Chemistry;* John Wiley & Sons: New York, 1993; p 959.

Coulter, J.C. "Sun Prints," *Science and Children.* 1984, 21(8), 56.

Hurd, D. *Prentice Hall Physical Science;* Prentice Hall: Englewood Cliffs, NJ, 1993.

Marie Sherman, Ursuline Academy, St. Louis, MO, personal communication.

Summerlin, L.R.; Ealy, Jr., J.L. *Chemical Demonstrations;* American Chemical Society: Washington, D.C., 1985; pp 110–111.

Contributors

Bonnie Marx, Miami East Junior High School, Troy, OH; Teaching Science with TOYS, 1991–92.

Susan Briese, Lincoln Junior-Senior High School, Esko, MN.

THE DIVING WHALE

Watch the Diving Killer Whale™ dive and surface. What causes this toy to mimic the diving action of a whale? What chemical reaction is occurring?

Diving Killer Whale™ and
Undersea Explorer™

GRADES LEVELS

Science activity appropriate for grades 4–9
Cross-Curricular Integration intended for grades 7–9

KEY SCIENCE TOPICS

- chemical reactions
- density
- properties of carbon dioxide
- surface tension

STUDENT BACKGROUND

Students should be familiar with the concept of density. You may wish to show some items that float on water and other items that sink in water. A knowledge of surface tension is also helpful but not necessary.

It is also a good idea to review what types of evidence indicate that a chemical reaction is occurring; for example, one sign of a chemical reaction is the formation of a gas.

KEY PROCESS SKILLS

• observing	Students observe the action of the diving whale.
• inferring	Students develop ideas as to why the whale repeatedly dives and resurfaces.

TIME REQUIRED

Setup	10	minutes
Performance	10–20	minutes
Cleanup	5	minutes

For "Introducing the Activity"
- 1 of the following groups of items:
  - small pieces of spaghetti or raisins, clear plastic cup, and light-colored or colorless carbonated beverage
  - needle or metal paper clip, tissue paper, and liquid dish soap, detergent or a bar of soap

For the "Procedure"
Per class (as a demonstration) or per group (as a hands-on activity)
- hot tap water
- (optional) hot plate or electric coffee pot to heat water
- ⅛ teaspoon (approximately) baking powder
- tub (at least 6–12 inches deep) or a cut-off 2-L soft-drink bottle
- Diving Killer Whale™ or Undersea Explorer™

 The Diving Killer Whale™ is available from The Nature Company stores or the manufacturer, DaMert Company, 2476 Verna Court, San Leandro, CA 94577; (800) 231-3722. A toy submarine sold as "Undersea Explorer™" that operates on the same principle is also available from the DaMert Company.

- 5–10 drops of liquid dish soap or detergent or a bar of soap
- (optional) metal or alcohol thermometer

For "Variations and Extensions"
❶ Per class
- ice or access to a refrigerator

❷ All materials listed for the "Procedure" plus the following:
Per class
- timer with a second hand

❸ All materials listed for the "Procedure" plus the following:
Per class
- more baking powder
- timer with a second hand

❹ All materials listed for the "Procedure" plus the following:
Per class
- baking soda
- vinegar
- Alka Seltzer®

❺ All materials listed for the "Procedure" plus the following:
Per class
- flour
- small baking pans
- shortening
- access to a stove

Safety and Disposal

Because of the potential breakage of thermometers, alcohol or metal cooking thermometers should be used. Should mercury thermometers be used and a break occur, the mercury should be cleaned up with a mercury spill kit. Avoid handling mercury or inhaling the vapor. Dispose of mercury according to local ordinances.

Getting Ready

Fill the container to a depth of at least 6 inches. The optimal water temperature for this activity is 60–70°C. If your tap water does not get this hot, or if you do not have facilities to heat water, use the hottest tap water available. Note that although water cooler than 60–70°C can be used, this will often cause a delay of at least 5–10 minutes before the whale starts to dive. Using warmer water speeds up the process significantly.

Introducing the Activity

Options:

- Show spaghetti or raisin pieces rising and sinking in a light-colored or colorless carbonated beverage in a clear plastic cup. Drop small pieces of spaghetti or pieces of raisins into the cup. The spaghetti or raisin pieces will begin to bob.

- Show students a needle or a metal paper clip floating on the surface of the water. To float the needle or paper clip, first place it on a piece of tissue paper. Lower the paper gently onto the water. Carefully poke the paper with a pencil until it sinks. If this procedure is done carefully, the needle or paper clip will remain on the surface. Add a few drops of soap. After a few minutes, the object will sink. The surface tension of water is responsible for holding the object on the surface of the water and the addition of soap lowers the surface tension of water and causes the object to sink.

Procedure

1. Add 5–10 drops of liquid soap or detergent to the water (or dip a bar of soap in the water for a few seconds).

2. Remove the clear plastic bubble chamber from the whale. (See Figure 1.) Make sure the bubble chamber is clear and dry. Fill the chamber with baking powder and wipe off any powder adhering to the outer surfaces. Don't pack the baking powder in the chamber.

Figure 1: Fill bubble chamber and insert.

3. Submerge the whale body in water without the bubble chamber, remove it, and shake off the excess water. Then insert the bubble chamber into the whale.

4. Hold the whale upside down and tap it gently on the table. (This prevents the baking powder from plugging the holes in the bubble chamber.)

5. Holding the whale upside down, submerge it just below the surface of the water for 10 seconds and then let it go. The whale should right itself and gradually start to dive. After diving, it will surface in about 1 minute. The diving and surfacing cycle is repeated and can continue for 15–20 minutes.

   ➤ *If the whale does not dive from the surface or if it is tilting over on its side without diving, try adding more soap to the water and/or cool the water by adding some cold tap water. If the whale sits on the bottom, try adding hot water to warm the bath.*

6. Allow students to observe for 5–10 minutes and to record their observations. Ask students to explain why the whale is diving and surfacing.

   ➤ *Students will need to be close enough to see the bubble that is released when the whale tips as it comes to the surface.*

7. To repeat the experiment, remove the baking powder residue from the bubble chamber, and repeat Steps 2–5.

Variations and Extensions

1. Have different groups study the effect of water temperature on the action of the whale. In this case, you can provide one group with water at room temperature, another group with water from the hot water faucet, and a third group with water from the refrigerator or cooled with ice to a temperature of about 10°C. Ask students to decide if the water temperature affects how fast the whale cycles or how long the whale stays active.

2. Have students measure the time that the whale takes to go through one diving cycle (surface to the bottom to the surface).

3. Have different groups of students vary the amount of baking powder used in the bubble chamber (¼, ½, ¾ full, for example). Ask students to decide if this changes how fast the whale cycles or how long the whale stays active.

4. Challenge students to answer these questions: Will the whale work if baking soda is used instead of baking powder in the bubble chamber? Will it work with baking soda if some vinegar is added to the water? Will it work if a piece of Alka Seltzer® is placed in the bubble chamber in place of the baking powder?

5. Relate the basic activity to a "real-life" scenario.

   a. Make two small cakes. Make the first cake by mixing flour and warm water together until the dough is smooth. Prepare a second cake by mixing three parts flour with one part baking powder. Then add warm water to make the dough smooth.

   b. Put both cakes in small greased pans and heat them on the top burner of a kitchen stove. When the cakes are done, turn off the heat and let them cool.

   c. Compare the two cakes. Ask the students which dough produced carbon dioxide and how can they tell. Ask the students where they think the carbon dioxide came from.

Teaching Chemistry with TOYS

Explanation

The following explanation is intended for the teacher's information. Modify the explanation for students as required.

The Diving Killer Whale™ toy "dives" (sinks) when you first place it in the water because the material of which it is made is more dense than water. As the substances in the baking powder in the bubble chamber react because of the water, bubbles of carbon dioxide gas are slowly produced. These gas bubbles are trapped beneath the bubble chamber. When enough gas is trapped, the whale and carbon dioxide "system" becomes less dense than water, and the whale rises to the surface. At the surface, the whale tips, the gas bubble escapes, and the whale sinks again. This cycle is repeated as long as the substances in the baking powder react.

Why is carbon dioxide produced when baking powder and water are combined? The ingredients of baking powder are corn starch, baking soda (sodium bicarbonate, $NaHCO_3$), sodium aluminum sulfate ($NaAl(SO_4)_2$, an alum), and acid phosphate of calcium (calcium dihydrogen phosphate, $Ca(H_2PO_4)_2$). Both the sodium aluminum sulfate and the calcium dihydrogen phosphate are acidic salts; this means they provide a source of hydrogen ion, H^+, when dissolved in water. Hydrogen ions react with sodium bicarbonate, producing carbon dioxide gas:

$$NaHCO_3(s) + H^+(aq) \rightarrow Na^+(aq) + CO_2(g) + H_2O(l)$$

If you try Variation 1, you will observe that the diving and surfacing rate can be increased by using warmer water. This is because the rate of the reaction between the acid and sodium bicarbonate is increased when the temperature is increased. In general, the rate of a reaction increases with increased temperature.

Variation 5 involves a practical use for the reaction between baking powder and water. The cake baked with baking powder rises, while the other does not. The carbon dioxide gas (produced by the reaction of baking powder in water) is trapped in the batter and causes the batter to "rise" as baking occurs.

Cross-Curricular Integration

Home, safety, and career:
*   Discuss the use of baking powder in baking.

Language arts:
*   Have students compose stories and poems about whales.
*   Suggest that students read one or more of the following stories:
    ○ *Humphrey, the Wrong Way Whale,* by Kathryn Goldner (Dillon, ISBN 0-875183-6-03)
      Introduces information on the behavior and current situation of humpback whales through the story of an individual whale off the coast of California.
    ○ *Little Whale,* by Ann McGovern (Scholastic, ISBN 0590703544)
      Describes the life of a humpback whale from the time of her birth when she weighs almost a ton to adulthood five years later.
    ○ *Whales: The Gentle Giants,* by Joyce Milton (Random House, ISBN 0394898095)
      Describes how whales live and some different kinds of whales.

○ *Chemical Changes,* by Kathryn Whyman (Gloucester, ISBN 0531170322)
Describes properties and uses of chemicals, phase changes, and how chemicals combine to make substances we use every day.

References

Berman, P.; Wicks, K. *Science in Action, Fun with Chemistry;* Marshall Cavendish: New York, 1988; Vol. 4.

"Bobbing;" *Fun with Chemistry: A Guidebook of K–12 Activities;* Sarquis, M., Sarquis, J., Eds.; Institute for Chemical Education: Madison, WI, 1991; Vol. 1, pp 129–132.

Gardner, R. *Kitchen Chemistry;* Simon & Schuster: New York, 1982.

VanCleave, J. P. *Chemistry For Every Kid;* John Wiley & Sons: New York, 1989.

Walpole, B. *175 Science Experiments to Amuse and Amaze Your Friends;* Random House: New York, 1988; pp 37, 41.

Contributors

Carrie Kuhlmann, Greendale Middle School, Lawrenceburg, IN; Teaching Science with TOYS, 1992–93.

Jean Ann Newmeyer, Indian Lake Middle School, Lewistown, OH; Teaching Science with TOYS, 1992–93.

Activities Indexed by Key Process Skills

Process Skill	Grades K–3 Activities													
	Unfixed and Fixed Shapes	Crystal Pictures	Crayon Prints from a Change of State	Smell-Good Diffusion Ornaments	Smelly Balloons	The Scratch-and-Sniff Challenge	Density Batons	Clay Boats	Are Mittens Warm?	Magic Worms	Fortune-Telling Fish	Paint with Water Books	Weather Bunnies	Twirly Whirly Milk
1. Observing	●	●	●		●	●	●			●			●	●
2. Communicating														
3. Estimating								●						
4. Measuring				●			●			●				
5. Collecting Data					●				●				●	
6. Classifying												●		
7. Inferring											●	●		
8. Predicting	●		●											
9. Making Models						●								
10. Interpreting Data														
11. Comparing/Contrasting		●												
12. Making Graphs														
13. Hypothesizing				●						●	●			
14. Controlling Variables									●					●
15. Defining Operationally														
16. Investigating								●						

Process Skill	Grades 4–6 Activities													
	Temperature Mixing	Under Pressure	Water Fountain in a Jar	The Amazing Balloon Pump	Pencil Hydrometers	Plastics Do Differ!	Shape Shifters	Pop the Hood	Things that Glow in the Dark	A Collection of Surface Tension Activities	One-Way Screen	Mysterious Sand	Sumi Nagashi	Chromatography Color Burst
1. Observing		●						●	●		●	●	●	●
2. Communicating									●	●	●			
3. Estimating														
4. Measuring							●							
5. Collecting Data					●	●	●							
6. Classifying									●					
7. Inferring			●					●						●
8. Predicting	●									●				●
9. Making Models					●									
10. Interpreting Data						●								
11. Comparing/Contrasting				●								●		
12. Making Graphs														
13. Hypothesizing				●									●	
14. Controlling Variables	●													
15. Defining Operationally														
16. Investigating		●				●	●							

Process Skill	Grades 7–9 Activities													
	Properties of Silly Putty®	Marshmallow in a Syringe	Liquid to Gas in a "Flick"	Salt Solutions and Grow Creatures	The Liquid Timer Race	Density Bottles	Frustration Bottles	Expanding, Floating Bubbles	Hats off to the Drinking Bird	Heat Solution™	Color-Changing Cars	Investigating the Effect of Temperature on Lightsticks	Experimenting with Light-Sensitive Paper	The Diving Whale
1. Observing						●		●	●		●			●
2. Communicating	●			●										
3. Estimating														
4. Measuring				●						●				
5. Collecting Data			●		●						●			
6. Classifying														
7. Inferring		●					●	●						●
8. Predicting						●			●		●			
9. Making Models														
10. Interpreting Data														
11. Comparing/Contrasting											●			
12. Making Graphs			●											
13. Hypothesizing								●						
14. Controlling Variables		●			●								●	
15. Defining Operationally										●				
16. Investigating	●						●							

Appendix B:
Activities Indexed by Topics

Alphabetical Listing of Activities